Israeli Institutions at the Crossroads

Israeli Institutions at the Crossroads is a unique collection of essays about Israeli society and its institutions. Leading scholars in the field provide an in-depth account of the current obstacles Israel faces, such as the fight against terror, and tackle the question of how its institutions may be adapted to counter current concerns.

We consider relationships between democracy and bureaucracy, the issue of separation of powers in democracy and more specifically the role of the Supreme Court. This book also provides the reader wqith an in-depth comprehension of the roles of other influential insitutions: the government, the Preseidency, the Knesset, the Legal Advisor to the government, and the State Comptroller. Finally, we are guided througha discussion of the education system as well as the press council and its role in a democratic society.

This volume was previously published as a special issue of the journal *Israel Affairs*.

Israeli Institutions at the Crossroads

Edited by
Raphael Cohen-Almagor

Routledge
Taylor & Francis Group

LONDON AND NEW YORK

First published in paperback 2024

First published 2005 by Routledge
4 Park Square, Milton Park, Abingdon, Oxon, OX14 4RN

and by Routledge
605 Third Avenue, New York, NY 10158

Routledge is an imprint of the Taylor & Francis Group, an informa business

Publisher's Note
The publisher has gone to great lengths to ensure the quality of this reprint but points out that some imperfections in the original copies may be apparent.

British Library Cataloguing in Publication Data
A catalogue record for this book is available from the British Library

Library of Congress Cataloging in Publication Data

ISBN: 978-0-415-36360-0 (hbk)
ISBN: 978-1-138-97344-2 (pbk)
ISBN: 978-0-203-08673-5 (ebk)

DOI: 10.4324/9780203086735

Typeset in Sabon 10/12pt by the Alden Group, Oxford

CONTENTS

For Wilfrid Knapp
Wise and Kind
My Learned Middle East Mentor and Most Devoted Teacher

Introduction

RAPHAEL COHEN-ALMAGOR

This volume supplements the collection, *Israeli Democracy at the Crossroads*.[1] It is aimed to shed light on Israeli democracy and its institutions. The articles are written from different perspectives, employing different methodologies that enrich the discussion and exhibit a multitude of views. The collection brings together contributions of leading scholars and decision makers that reflect on crucial themes and questions. Their careful consideration and insights will undoubtedly enrich public discourse concerning Israeli democracy and its institutions.

For each of the themes a leading scholar or decision maker was selected to write the article. Contributors were given a long period of time to write their essays, and then received comments and critique aiming to improve the quality of their pieces and to sharpen arguments. Sometimes contributors submitted a third and a fourth draft, after digesting the constructive critique.

GENERAL THEMES

David Nachmias and Ori Arbel-Ganz analyze bureaucratic efficiency and the stability of the regime. They argue that government instability coupled with the highly centralized public bureaucracy are the main factors that hinder the capacity to govern. They further assert that the public administration is overly centralized, rife with numerous unqualified political appointments, outdated budgeting procedures and impervious to long-term planning. Policy planning is short-term and improvised, the only programmes implemented being of relatively minor importance. Their critique also indicates that the political system is highly partial in its coalition politics behaviour as well as in parliamentary representation. Governments rarely complete more than two-thirds of their possible term in office. The turnover of prime ministers and of cabinet ministers is quite hasty, and the political culture has no institutionalized norms that uphold accountability and transparency. All this combined results in poor governance ability.

The second article by Orit Ichilov, Gavriel Salomon (laureate of the Israel Prize) and Dan Inbar argues that citizenship education progressed from a highly emotional nationalistic focus, centring on civic obligations,

Raphael Cohen-Almagor is the founder and director of the Center for Democratic Studies, University of Haifa.

to a more cognitive, discipline-oriented civic education with greater awareness of civil liberties, minority rights and human rights. However, despite the great variety of programmes and projects, in addition to the teaching of civic studies and other relevant school subjects, turning Israeli schools into islands of peace and democracy is not a simple undertaking. Citizenship education is still inadequately implemented in the schools. A central problem is that the Ministry of Education seems reluctant to implement its explicitly adopted policies. Citizenship education remains a marginal school subject, and it continues to be an eclectic and fragmented endeavour. Ichilov, Salomon and Inbar conclude that although important strides were made over the years to promote citizenship education, it is naïve to expect that citizenship education in its present form would further the emergence of a shared civic identity that would bridge national, cultural, ethnic and social schisms within Israeli society.

In turn, Yoram Peri describes the political–military complex, which existed in Israel in the 1990s. He presents the theoretical problem, and explains how the IDF (Israel Defence Forces, Zahal) adopted a policy which supported arriving at a peace pact with the Palestinians. Peri further discusses the means used by the military in its political actions and the ways in which it pursued its agenda, even to the point of tension and conflict between the IDF and the political stratum during the Netanyahu government's term in office.

The last article in this section relates to the need for a comprehensive constitution that will secure basic rights. Former President of the Supreme Court, Meir Shamgar, describes the Israeli constitution as partly written and partly unwritten. The constitutional rules of Israel are included in Basic Laws and other constitutional provisions, in abstract legal norms defined in Supreme Court rulings as well as in customs and practices. The constitution is thus evolutionary in character, exhibiting a gradual organic growth and development. Shamgar notes that its composition changes from mainly ordinary laws, norms and customs to constituting Basic Laws.

Shamgar, laureate of the Israel Prize, maintained that presently Israel has a series of Basic Laws but only two Basic Laws defining part of human rights: Basic Law: Human Dignity and Freedom, and Basic Law: Freedom of Occupation. It is still in need of a complete, codified and consolidated constitution, which covers each and every subject normally included in such constitutional code. Among the missing Basic Laws, Shamgar mentions laws on Freedom of Expression, Freedom of Religion, Freedom of Scientific Research and Freedom of Demonstration.

INSTITUTIONS

This section is a bit unusual. By and large collections of essays such as this one, which speak of institutions, include papers by scholars scrutinizing the decision makers and the bodies within which they operate. Here I made every effort to recruit decision makers who write about their own roles, analyzing their own institutions. Their articles supply a fresh and unusual outlook, combining personal experience with critique of their respective roles, their advantages and limitations.

Yitzhak Navon, the President of Israel during 1978–83, argues that the president has quite a lot to do although he does not have any actual powers, and that there is no need to add powers to the very few he possesses. Navon describes the Basic Law: The President (1964) and provides a subjective description of his term in office, the ways he acted and achieved the goals he had set for himself, in spite of the limited presidential powers. In his opinion, all this evolves around one question: how does the president see his ability to function being a symbol and a symbol only. Navon describes the relationships he struck with minorities and different segments of the Israeli population, the tensions he had with the political establishment and his relationships with the Jewish Diaspora. Clearly, Navon enjoyed his term in office. He is considered by many, including myself, as one of the best presidents Israel had known, arguably the best of all.

Gad Yaacobi, who served in several Labour governments, discusses the government institution. He opens with some observations on the modern state and then considers the rule of law in a democratic society, emphasizing that all people, without any exceptions, must accept the rule of law and abide by it. Yaacobi explains the principles of constitutionality and separation of powers and makes a plea for increased public involvement in social affairs. This plea is joined with a warning against excessive centralization, which might transform democracy into mere formal structure. A further warning is made against the almost natural inclination on the part of politicians to seek personal power, often at the expense of public interests. Yaacobi also suggests recommendations as to how to improve the electoral system and the ability to govern effectively.

Naomi Chazan, former Deputy Speaker of the Knesset, critically examines the Knesset's formal and informal structures. She explains its operations and role performance, and takes a close look at its standing in the public eye. Chazan assesses the relative power and influence of the Knesset today, arguing that the parliament has undergone a severe depreciation in human resources, organizational capabilities, performance and public standing. She contends that the Knesset's malfunctioning in its communication and deliberation roles means that it has not been able to adequately perform the tasks of public education and socialization to binding political values. Members of the Knesset in recent years have not acted as role models and are not perceived as such. The Knesset's public image has consequently declined, and with it the faith of many citizens in the regime it symbolizes. In Chazan's grim view, the Knesset is viewed nowadays as the antithesis of the model of desirable behaviour. The Knesset mirrors the multicultural character of the country, but it adds to the society's division and discord. Former member of Knesset Chazan goes as far as saying that the Knesset appears eager to forfeit its authority on ethical and immunity matters, which are the basis for its conduct and the key to its institutional independence, and that it does not constitute an instrument of socialization – except in the negative sense – and its mode of operation provides a major disincentive in efforts to attract potential competent political recruits. Furthermore, the Knesset has failed in its basic democratic function: mobilizing consent for the system of government. The overall confidence of the public in the Knesset had fallen drastically from 41% in 1995 to 14% in 2000. Chazan ends her highly critical essay with some recommendations for improvement, saying *inter alia* that if the Knesset wants to maintain its autonomy and improve its public standing, it has to tighten its rules of procedure, draft a binding code of conduct, and augment its disciplinary sanctions.

Elyakim Rubinstein, Israel's attorney general during the time of writing the article, provides an illuminating account of his roles and responsibilities. The position is complex, as the attorney general heads the criminal prosecution, and is the representative of the state and the government in all litigation, both criminal and civil. The attorney general is called upon to defend the government and public authorities in issues of administrative and constitutional law. Furthermore, the attorney general is the legal counsel to the government, and is also the representative of the public interest.

Rubinstein discusses the duties of the attorney general, the tradition the role carries, as well as the difficulties connected with the discharge of these duties. This includes the modalities of appointment, its main responsibilities, and the principal spheres of public law involved. He speaks of the difficult task of deciding to open, not to open, or to close investigations concerning public officials. During his tenure he opened investigations concerning a president, prime ministers and ministers, Knesset members and mayors. Clearly he is very much concerned about the criticisms voiced against his office as well as against the courts.

Rubinstein then probes the question whether the attorney general should participate in cabinet meetings and voices a positive opinion in favour of participation. He explains why he is opposed to the idea of a separation between the roles of the attorney general in the areas of counsel to the government and those related to criminal prosecution. The Attorney General voices grave concerns regarding the Palestinian Authority legal system and expresses hope that the Palestinian Authority will find the wisdom to create a functioning and viable legal system. Finally, Rubinstein offers some proposals for change.

Eliezer Goldberg, the state comptroller, argues that the achievement of national goals can prompt a disregard of rules that are defined as appropriate operational norms. Such disregard may be conscious and volitional, or incidental and unintended. Where tension exists between the realization of national goals and rules that 'disturb' such realization, it should not necessarily be assumed that the norms should invariably prevail. Quite often they are considered as being of secondary importance, or even an obstacle to the promotion of goals regarded as crucial. The result is explicit or implicit legitimacy for violation of the normative system. Furthermore, the repeated states of crises in which Israel finds itself strengthens that sense of urgency and provides legitimization for 'breaking the rules'. Inevitably, this thwarts the internalization of a consensual commitment to compliance with rules.

Goldberg warns against the negative phenomenon of public servants being guided by sectorial considerations. He reports that quite often persons in positions of power find themselves in a conflict of interests, torn between the broad public interest and their desire to act on behalf of a sectorial interest. Unfortunately, the latter interest often enjoys precedence. This phenomenon receives expression at many levels, including the direct allocation of financial resources, the allocation of land and appointments of designated people. Goldberg proposes that in certain cases, where the temptation to act out of party motives is great, the onus moves to the authority to present the data and the considerations, in order to demonstrate that it acted on the basis of relevant considerations. Should it fail to do so, the questionable decision will be declared null and void.

Another flaw against which Goldberg warns is the absence of a strategic perspective in the execution of governmental actions. The operational mode does not necessarily perceive long term goals as preceding or taking precedence over immediate interests and short term political bonuses; in fact it sees a justification for preferring the latter. The Israeli government has no organized process for determining long term national priorities.

The aim of my own essay is to review the work of the Israel Press Council. The essay considers the history of the Press Council, analyzing the way it has developed, its work, and how it reached its current status. As a former member of the Press Council I am quite disappointed with the work and achievements of this organization. It is argued that the existing situation is far from satisfactory, and that the media should advance more elaborate mechanisms of self-control, empowering the Press Council with greater authority and equipping it with substantive ability to sanction. There is a real danger that if the Press Council remains a weakling body then the legislature might resort to drafting laws that would limit free press and media in Israel.

Some readers may find it strange that this section on institutions does not include discussion on the Supreme Court. I can assure you that this is not because of lack of trying. Two senior members of the court committed themselves to contribute but were unable to submit on time. I will make some reflections on the major bones of contention regarding the work of the court in my Final Word, which further develops some of the themes presented in the articles. I highlight problems and pitfalls and suggest amendments and improvements.

CONCLUSION

This is one of the most comprehensive volumes ever to be written on the Israeli institutions. Its topics and main concerns are timely, politically significant, very controversial and hence intellectually compelling. The collection offers its readers a wealth of information and different perspectives on major themes and institutions. Its originality lies in the combination of scholarly articles, and articles written by public officials who were/are involved in the actual decision making process and the drafting of policies.

The volume offers rich analysis that would be useful to people who are interested in Israel studies: scholars and students, philosophers, political scientists, politicians, historians, sociologists, media educators and professionals, jurists and lawyers, and the public at large. The essays cover timely concerns which democracies confront time and again. They ponder practical problems arising from the tensions involved in democratic processes, and analyze the work of important institutions. The authors share a belief in democracy and seek to promote a better, more workable and sustainable polity amidst a hostile environment.

I thank the Research Authority and the Faculty of Humanities of the University of Haifa for granting valuable assistance throughout the project. Specifically, I am indebted to Dean Moshe Zeidner and to Dean Yossi Ben-Artzi. In addition, gratitude is owed to Grace Yaakob, Tali Yanai, Anat Gelber, Eli Dunker and Yahav Rosen for their dedicated and caring work, their enduring patience as well as their unfailing and kind assistance. This project could never have been completed without them. Finally, I am thankful to Johns Hopkins University for facilitating the last stages of working on this demanding volume.

NOTES

1. A special issue of *Israel Affairs*, Vol. II, No.1; also to be published as *Israeli Democracy at the Crossroads*, London, forthcoming 2005.

The Crisis of Governance: Government Instability and the Civil Service

DAVID NACHMIAS and ORI ARBEL-GANZ

THE PROBLEM

On 15 May 1948, David Ben-Gurion proclaimed Israel's national independence. With the establishment of a new Jewish and democratic state, the newborn government faced a variety of tremendous challenges. Retrospectively the Israeli governments faced most of these challenges quite commendably. Their successes – formation of a modern army, launching of a national water system, construction of an oil refinery, development of harbours, establishment of agricultural and urban settlements, building roads, as well as the absorption of hundreds of thousands of immigrants coming from dozens of countries – were completed in a relatively short period of time, suggesting a high capacity for governance. An instructive illustration in the area of infrastructure is the remarkable construction of the national water carrier (*Ha'movil Ha'artzi*), a huge water pipe that transported water from the Sea of Galilee southwards, along the length of Israel (approximately 85 miles).

David Nachmias is Professor of Public Policy at the Interdisciplinary Centre, Herzliya.
Ori Arbel-Ganz Lectures at Tel Aviv University and Ben-Gurion University.

Although construction took a total of 11 years (1953–64) to complete, the carrier was partially operative after five years.

At present governments find it increasingly difficult to initiate and implement public policies even though the projects are relatively minor in scale when compared to those completed during the first two decades following independence. For example, governments were unable to transfer the Glilot fuel and gas depot from the densely populated northern Tel Aviv to an uninhabited area in the south. Although government first resolved to effect the move in 1992, followed by other decisions made by seven consecutive governments, the depot is still in place despite the grave human and environmental risks. Another example is the decision to construct an express railroad line between Tel Aviv and Jerusalem. Ten years after the original government decision, no line is imminent.

What explains the decline in the capacity to govern? In this article we argue that among the many reasons for this regression, a few are immediate and crucial. To substantiate our arguments, two theoretical constructs are examined over time. The first relates to the institutional and cultural characteristics of Israel's public administration and the second to government instability.

THEORETICAL FRAMEWORK

Effective governance involves the ability to execute projects for the purpose of achieving the government's policy goals. The normative basis for government's capacity to govern is rooted in the authority delegated through legislation. Yet, delegation of authority *per se* does not mean that a government will succeed in implementing its policies. Following Montesquieu's theory of the separation of powers, scholars have distinguished the duties of elected officials from those of appointed administrators. The former are responsible for policy formation through legislation whereas the latter are responsible for policy implementation. Following this approach, the public policy literature has distinguished between three stages of the policy process: design, implementation and evaluation. Empirical research has shown that in the real world these stages are not distinctly separated. The public policy process involves complex, dynamic relationships between policy design and designers on one hand, and policy implementation and implementers on the other.[1] Whether beginning from the analytical or the empirical level, we arrive at the same conclusion: successful implementation of public policies depends on the professional abilities of civil servants and on the interests of elected officials that frame them. In other words, a government's capacity to govern is a function of the effectiveness of both systems and of their relationships.

Bureaucratic efficiency, the first variable to be discussed, is composed of five indicators.[2] The first is the intensity of the agency problem, meaning the gap between the interests of the administrator and his or her superior (the politician). Democratic norms compel both to act on behalf of the public interest. However, each actor tends to interpret 'the public interest' in different ways. Politicians frequently use the bureaucracy as a means to promote personal political goals. In such cases, conflict erupts between street-level bureaucrats and the politicians that supervise the bureaucracies.[3] As these conflicts intensify, government capacity to govern is impaired. In their attempts to minimize conflicts with top civil servants, politicians appoint members of their private circle to critical administrative positions. Political intimates are obligated to politicians, their views and approaches.

Another indicator is the extent of bureaucratic control of the market, that is, whether the private sector or non-governmental agencies produce alternative products and services to those provided by the public sector. The more government ownership, the less flexible is the market. In addition, the very size of the administrative mechanism makes it difficult for the organization to adjust to a changing environment or to recognize the changing needs of consumers. Under these conditions, it often happens that demand for certain public products continues not in response to their indispensability or consumer tastes but because no alternative exist.[4]

The third indicator is the centralization and decentralization of central government power. From the perspective of monopoly and competition, especially given specified technical constraints, as centralization grows, effectiveness and efficiency decrease.[5] The fourth indicator, the budgetary process, is influenced by the balance between centralization and decentralization, but not by that indicator alone. Research on budgeting has increased significantly in response to Wildavsky's pioneering work.[6] Studies have revealed how crucial an effect the budgetary process has on policy planning and implementation. The formal budget represents an official declaration of government goals. Proper budgeting is an essential ingredient of policy making. The literature points to the positive relationship between decision making and budgeting for governance capacity. A cumbersome and highly centralized yet overly extended decision making process directly undermines the budget's utility as a management tool. On the contrary, more simplified and decentralized structures are able to focus on the smallest details and thereby introduce flexibility in management together with more efficient use of resources.[7]

The fifth and final indicator relates to the problematic relations between central and local government comprised of bureaucrats and politicians. Whereas the national government focuses on macro issues, such as national security, foreign affairs and economic developments, local governments are concerned with daily quality of life of their residents. To the extent that

central government controls local government, the governing capacity
of both levels is undermined: The central government allocates resources
to local issues that it has no competence to administer, whereas the
local administration loses its influence over local decision making
and implementation.

The second construct, the stability of the regime, also includes a number
of indicators, the first of which is tenure in office. As pointed out, public
policy is framed by the political echelon. Because the time needed to design
and implement public policy is long, whereas the time available for an
elected official to present results is short, a built-in conflict between the
administrative and the elected level often erupts. When a government's
term is short, politicians will aspire to implement policies promising
fruition in the very short or immediate range. This temporal framework
impedes long-term planning. In other words, for a democratic government
to be capable of resolving the deep conflicts that divide every democratic
society, in addition to achieving general well-being, it requires regimes of
long duration and complexity that short political terms do not allow.[8]

Another aspect of the same concern is the turmoil aroused in a
bureaucracy with every change in government. Not only are new plans
made and new goals defined, but new ministers bring with them new
executives who may introduce a new organizational culture. In private
sector hi-tech firms, for instance, adaptation will probably be relatively
swift and smooth because the organization's structure is relatively flat and
flexible as well as accustomed to a volatile environment. Government
agencies, however, require more time to adjust to innovative organizational and behavioural norms, whether formal or informal.[9] Adjustment
of the public administration is likewise dependent on the degree of staff
professionalism, the political affiliation of senior appointees and the
resulting effect on agency.

An additional indicator affecting government stability is the extent of
divisiveness between the Knesset and the governing coalition. The greater
the number of political parties, the more complex, lengthy and costly will
be the negotiations required to pass legislation.[10] In theory, if there is only
one party in parliament, no negotiation costs whatsoever will occur during
the legislative and the policy making process. Alternatively, if the number
of parties in parliament is equal to the number of elected representatives
(that is, each representative represents a different party), the costs of
negotiations will be maximal. In such an instance, it will be most difficult
to achieve the agreement necessary to pass legislation.

In parliamentary systems, divisiveness among coalition members
intensifies the obstacles to legislation. Because the executive branch is
responsible for implementation of public policy, intense divisiveness
between coalition partners hinders policy making.[11] This situation incurs
costs, expressed in the distribution of additional public jobs and benefits to

a growing number of people, with each beneficiary acquiring less power. Ideological competition among coalition members feeds conflict. Even if the coalition remains intact, the conflicts become more complex, in direct proportion to the intensity of the divisions. When both parliament and the cabinet are ideologically split, the frequency and intensity of conflicts based on ideological competition will escalate and governance capacity will significantly decline. Alternatively, if divisiveness is low in both parliament and the government, governance capacity will be likely to increase. The significance of one dominant party in this context should be noted; such a party can balance the divisions on one or both levels. Only the existence of a core party, larger than the remaining parties and positioned in the heart of the ideological space, can maintain the system's stability as well as improve the capacity to govern.[12]

A third indicator of stability is the balance of power between parliament and the prime minister. In other words, under what conditions can the prime minister dissolve parliament and in what situations can parliament overthrow the prime minister.[13] A variety of relationships characterize democratic regimes. In general, when symmetry between authorities exists, regime stability tends to be long lasting. But when an imbalance of power exists, stability becomes tenuous. Various democracies have granted extra powers to one or both authorities but simultaneously set a price for the exercise of this power. For example, if the members of parliament know that parliamentary removal of the government will be accompanied by dissolution of parliament itself, they may hesitate to introduce such an action.

A fourth indicator in this respect is the value of civic responsibility and accountability. Clearly, this measure strongly influences all the other indicators. Organizations that do not encourage their members to take responsibility and be accountable for their actions induce behaviour that promotes political corruption.[14] Political figures and public administrators who allow themselves to betray the public's confidence by promoting their own interests at the public expense do so because they know that such behaviour entails no punishment unless the perpetrator is caught. Corrupt systems therefore rarely remain democratic. Hence, norms of responsibility and accountability must be firmly inculcated throughout all levels of the regime.

The fifth indicator is the intensity of social cleavages. A government system that incorporates too many profound political conflicts will come under intense pressure when attempting to resolve conflicts. We now turn to an empirical analysis of Israeli governments based on those constructs and their indicators.

EMPIRICAL ANALYSIS

Our investigation of the decline of governance capacity calls for a brief historical introduction. From its beginning, the State of Israel displayed a pervasive 'agency system' in combination with traditional political appointments to its public administration. The relationship between elected and appointed officials evolved with the institutional transition of the *Yeshuv* (the Jewish pre-state community under the British Mandate, 1922–48) to the State of Israel. The basic loyalties of civil servants and politicians to the public were later grounded in various Supreme Court decisions but never formalized in an organized compendium of administrative law. The obligations of senior bureaucrats in Israel[15] differ from their peers in the US as described in the Administrative Services Act (1949), and are certainly more ambiguous. As the ultimate purpose of any civil service is to serve the public interest, the main question becomes: how does one identify the 'public interest'? Is the bureaucrat occupying a professional position required to serve the public according to his own interpretation of its interest or according to guidelines set by his superiors? As top bureaucrats are appointed by cabinet ministers, a ministerial committee or the entire cabinet, they tend to follow the agenda advocated by their patrons. As a consequence, top civil servants tend not to contradict their political superiors' directives, irrespective of whether they are of political character or contrary to the public interest. A well known case is the report issued by the state commission of inquiry into Israeli bank share adjustments (these shares were manipulated by bank executives during the period 1978–83). The commission condemned the behaviour of numerous senior officials – the governor of the Bank of Israel, the banks commissioner, the commissioner of insurance and capital markets at the Ministry of Finance, the general manager of the Ministry of Finance, the chairman of the Stock Market Authority – all of whom were well aware of the illegalities performed but preferred to remain silent. When explaining their behaviour, they claimed that the elected political ranks had decided to remain silent as well. In this specific case, the commission stated that the officials' professional duty and civic obligation – not personal or political loyalties – obliged them to use their legal authority in order to end the fraud and reduce its damages.

Israel's elected officials activated the practice of political appointments. Israeli politicians are apparently divided about the legitimacy of this practice. Some are convinced that such appointments are necessary for an efficient, effective public administration; others view the system as a springboard for the promotion of their own personal and political objectives.[16] In fact, most Israeli politicians assign devoted supporters to top positions in the public administration.

Political appointments were very common during Israel's early years. In 1959, new legislation required that nominees for civil service positions must respond to a mandatory public tender.[17] Two years later, an internal civil service commission formulated the tender regulations, which stated that no candidate for a post in the public administration could be asked about his or her political affiliation.[18] Despite these regulations, political appointments remain common in central as well as local governments. For instance, the post of cabinet secretary has traditionally been determined by the candidate's political identity. Among the 14 individuals who have held that office since 1948, eight were purely political appointments. The law dictating the qualifications of cabinet secretary nominees stipulates that the individual must be appointed by the government but recommended by the prime minister. This fact binds the nominee not only to the political coalition that approved the nomination but especially to the coalition leader. Another example is the director general of a cabinet ministry. The position has been filled primarily by individuals sharing either the political outlook or having close personal ties with the respective minister. Whereas appointments of directors general, cabinet secretaries or personal advisers may be acceptable and probably understood by at least a portion of the public, the appointment of political associates to professional positions, especially those requiring partisan neutrality when making decisions, is considered completely unacceptable.

Although public awareness has been growing and the courts have become increasingly critical of political appointments, politicians make more use of this practice. One of the first actions taken by Benjamin Netanyahu upon entering the Prime Minister's Office in 1996 was to ask for the resignation of Yitzhak Galnoor, the civil service commissioner, who had been appointed by the former minister of finance. Galnoor's removal was meant to pave the way for one of Netanyahu's supporters. The Supreme Court prevented this move on the grounds that the civil service commissioner is a senior professional post; hence, removal of a commissioner should be based on professional grounds, not changes in government.[19]

Another, more glaring, example is the attempt to appoint a lawyer, Ronnie Bar-On, to the position of attorney general. Bar-On's chief qualification was membership in the ruling Likud Party. On 10 December 1996, the minister of justice, Tzachi Hanegbi, listed his criteria for nominating a candidate for this office. Among the criteria mentioned was 'a basic orientation toward the ideology of the ruling party'.[20] A month later the cabinet appointed Bar-On to the post. In response to massive public protests and the apprehension that the Supreme Court would overturn the appointment, Bar-On resigned two days later. The subsequent attorney general, Elyakim Rubinstein, who was requested to investigate suspicions of the involvement of senior politicians in the far-fetched nomination, later wrote: 'the use of political power to try to promote personal interests ... is a disastrous trend'.[21] Hanegbi, as minister of environmental protection in Ariel Sharon's first cabinet, later became known in the media as the 'king' of political appointments after it was discovered that during his first two years in that office he appointed more than 80 of his supporters to various public positions.

Bureaucratic Control of the Market

Israel was initially established as a welfare state. The socialist Labour Party, which ruled the country continuously for three decades, promoted nationalization. In fact, up to the mid-1980s, including the Likud's reign, no real competition existed between the market and the public sector. Control over the economy was divided among three institutions: The Jewish Agency, the Histadrut (the General Federation of Labour) and the government. These institutions were, in effect, run by Labour Party politicians. David Ben-Gurion, for example, served as prime minister and, at the same time, chairman of the Jewish Agency. Moshe Sharet was the minister of foreign affairs and also headed the Jewish Agency's political department. The public administration was involved in every arena: commercial banks (Bank Hapoalim), defence production (Israel Military Industries) and infrastructure. Mekorot (water resources development), Solel Boneh (highway construction), Shikun Ovdim (housing construction), the education system, heavy industry (Koor) and the health system (Kupat Holim hospitals, community health centres and medical insurance) were owned by the Histadrut that also controlled the major pension funds, textile and other manufacturing firms. This centralized and personalized system of control has contributed to the dominance of Labour in all spheres of public life but at the same time has impaired the values of accountability and responsiveness to non-partisans.

Up to 1977 (the political upheaval when Labour lost the election to the Likud), Israel's prime ministers not only headed the legislature and executive agencies, they were also the economy's *de facto* leaders. Privatization and deregulation were adopted as official policies only in the late 1980s and early 1990s. A well-publicized example of deregulation is in the field of communication- the Israel Broadcasting Association. Following the introduction of deregulation in the 1990s, another commercial channel went on the air in addition to cable and satellite channels, which have proliferated. In 2002, a second commercial channel was approved.[22] The telephone and telegraph systems underwent a similar change. Previously, Bezeq, a government-owned company, had the sole concession for operating the entire internal as well as international telephone network. Three private communication companies acquired licences to operate international telephony and another three began to operate cellular networks, also in the 1990s. Another important example is higher education: during Israel's first 40 years, only public universities were authorized to grant academic degrees. This monopoly ended in the 1990s, when several private colleges were established following accreditation by the Council for Higher Education. Overall, these processes have created more competition and greater variety of options to the Israeli public.

Despite the accelerating trend of deregulation, the public adminis-tration continues to control sizeable segments of the economy. Private organizations are regulated by at least three different authorities.[23] Foreign entrepreneurs refrain from investing in the local economy because of the over-regulated system. Generally speaking, the privatization of publicly owned firms and services has improved the state of the economy. However, massive regulation still enables government agencies to intervene in the market as they see fit.

Centralization and Decentralization of Central Government Power

Since the establishment of the state government power has been highly centralized. Two institutions fuse this power: the Prime Minister's Office and the Ministry of Finance. The prime minister is the most powerful elected official in government.[24] Irrespective of internal party competitors, prime ministers usually impose their political perspective and policy agenda. Structurally, the prime minister serves as chief of the executive branch, leader of the ruling party and head of the governing coalition concurrently. However, coalition politics with its high price has diminished the power of prime ministers. Subsequent to public demonstrations (with hundreds of thousands participating) demanding reform of the electoral system in order to grant additional authority to the office of prime minister, the Knesset approved direct election of the prime minister in 1992. This change was applied in the 1996, 1999 and 2001 elections. In fact, the electoral reform weakened the prime minister as the electoral strength of big parties declined and his dependency on small parties increased.[25] The direct elections led to an imbalance between Knesset representation and participants in the governing coalition. Despite the formation of a majority coalition the prime minister was unable to promote his own policies, losing the capacity to lead the government. The governance crisis convinced the Knesset to abolish the reform and re-adapt the former single-ballot method in 2001.

The Budgetary Process

The strength of the bureaucracy is most salient with respect the Ministry of Finance. For many years the ministry housed the Civil Service Commission. This enabled it to control the civil service. Moreover, control over the budget of every government ministry and agency rests in the ministry hands, giving its staff enormous power. The characteristics of the budgetary process are not unique to Israel but in amalgamation with other centralizing attributes they create an anachronistic system that most countries have discarded due to its extreme complexity, rigidity and inefficiency.[26] Two major laws determine the constituents of the budget,[27] yet without stipulating its final composition. Budgets are based on inputs rather than on outcomes. No information is available on plans, outputs or results. Such a budgetary system makes it extremely difficult to trace effectiveness and efficiency. Moreover, the budget is composed of highly detailed line items, an approach that prevents macro-level review and reduces managerial flexibility. This effectively thwarts systematic programme evaluation.

Another barrier to effective budgeting is the inappropriate procedural framework. The budget is prepared annually, is effective for one year only and is incremental in character. This means that planning does not extend beyond the observable horizon. Instead, the budget is constructed by weighting sunk costs and adding sums actually required to complete the coming year – a system that cripples attempts at rational planning. In contrast, the budgetary system now operating in the US and most European countries demands allocation of resources according to the planned programmes, goals and targets.[28] The main constituents of Israel's 2003 budget are identical to those that appeared five decades ago, although it is now prepared in its entirety by the Ministry of Finance and its Budget Department.

The budget approval process went through few and insignificant changes. Preliminary cabinet discussions about the coming year's budget are held at the beginning of August, a month after the draft's delivery to the minister of finance. The budget is officially introduced to the public in October, when it is presented to Knesset in all its thousands of clauses.[29] During November-December, after initial approval of the draft at the first round of voting in the Knesset, the budget's details are reviewed in the Knesset Finance Committee. At this time, amendments are introduced and the law is prepared for its second and third round of voting, usually at year's end. Legislators are rarely able to systematically examine the bulky law or know what they are approving or disapproving in any depth. For the same reason, the attentive public is unable to follow its details. This allows the Budget Department officials to strongly influence its composition at both the macro and the agency levels. Improvements of the budgetary process are at least to include greater measures of transparency, delegation of decision making authority to the top civil servants of government ministries and systematic evaluations of government programmes.

Centralization versus Decentralization: Central–Local Government Relations

The relationships between the two levels of government are crucial for the ensuing effective governance. In the US, for instance, residual authority is deliberately allocated to local governments, with the central government taking on only the authority essential for managing national, macro-level policy. The European Pact for Local Self-Government asserts the same.[30] In Israel, the central government monopolizes the distribution of power. Local government authority is framed in the Order of Local Governments enacted by British government during the Mandate. The original logic guiding the order – central control over resources, financing and public order – continues to keep mayors and other local government officials dependent on the Ministry of the Interior and the Finance Ministry. There is no local domain where a mayor must not approach these ministries: local taxes, local development, loans and credit, contracting with suppliers and contractors, planning the local budget and even installing signposts. The centralization of the colonial regime was retained when Israel achieved sovereignty.

Israeli politicians are dealing with various conflicts arising from reciprocation between central and local authorities. Publicly, they continue to declare the need to transfer power to the local authorities. Those were the same conclusions reached by three ministers of the interior: Israel Rokach in 1959, Joseph Burg in 1971 and Aryeh Deri in 1993. Guidelines issued by Rabin's government (July 1992) stated: 'The central government will persevere in its efforts to expand the autonomy of local authorities and limit their dependence.'[31] Almost 20 years earlier (1976), the government appointed a public commission (the Zanbar Commission) to investigate central-local policy problems. The commission's recommendations were submitted to the cabinet in 1981. Essentially, the committee recommended transferring authority, functions and responsibilities from the central to the local government and strengthening local autonomy. Shimon Peres' government accepted these recommendations 'in principle' in June 1985, but they were never implemented because of the strong opposition of the Ministry of Finance and Ministry of the Interior, which fiercely resisted the loss of power.

We now turn to the second construct, government stability, and examine five indicators.

Government's Term of Office

A government's term of office is officially limited to four years. At the end of this period, general elections are held to elect members of the Knesset. Following the Knesset elections, the government is presented to the legislators; its power to rule is based on passing a vote of confidence. Knesset approval of the government remained in effect even during the period of the direct election of the prime minister.

When considering the tenure of Israel's various governments, we refer to four measures: (1) duration – the number of months passed from the Knesset's confirmation of one government to the confirmation of the subsequent government; (2) the actual tenure of a specific government as a percentage of the remaining term stipulated by law for the Knesset; (3) the number of prime ministers replaced during a Knesset term (continuity of an incumbent prime minister indicates stability; for instance, Ben-Gurion resigned several times and each time formed a new government after reorganizing his coalition, as opposed to the last decade, when both the prime minister and the governing coalitions were replaced); (4) ministerial turnover (this measure contributes to government stability not because it indicates differences in government policy but because it captures changes in a ministry programmes and turnover of its senior administrators).

Table 1 shows the patterns of government instability. It is interesting to examine the results during a specific period. For instance, the first four governments ruled for less than 20 months each and completed about 40% of their legal term (four years); all were led by one prime minister, David Ben-Gurion. Considering Labour dominance at the time, the governance capacity of these governments was minimally affected by the changes. On the other hand, following Menachem Begin's entry into office, the terms in office lasted longer but there were many ministerial changes that delayed the implementation of policies. During the period of 1992–2003 five prime ministers were elected. The last three – Netanyahu, Barak and Sharon – were forced to re-shuffle the composition of their cabinets in order to sustain their governments. Review of the data indicates that only one government – that of Golda Meir – lasted in parallel to the Knesset elected for that same period. Although seven other governments had served 100% of their potential time it was not relative to a full term of the Knesset but to the time remaining until the next elections. For example, the sixth government, led by Prime Minister Sharet, served only five months, which were 100% of the months remaining for the Knesset before the next general election. Another example is Ben-Gurion's eighth coalition that served 23.3 months, which were 100% of its remaining term. The average Israeli government stays in office little more than 22 months, completes about 67% of its legal term[32] and changes five cabinet ministers. This reality strongly influences the capacity to govern effectively.

Fragmentation in the Legislature

Since the establishment of the state divisiveness has been high.[33] According to the Rae index (varying from zero to 1, where increasing scores indicate more divisiveness),[34] the degree of fragmentation is rather consistent, with a trend towards intensification in the last three elections. One explanation for that growth is the temporary adoption of the two-ballot reform. The reform enabled voters to cast their votes for relatively small parties and for a prime minister who appealed to the median voter.[35] Parliamentary

TABLE 1

LONGEVITY OF ISRAEL'S GOVERNMENTS, 1949–2003

Knesset	Government	Prime Minister	Term	Months	% of Possible Tenure	Ministerial Changes
1	1	D. Ben-Gurion	10.3.1949–1.11.1950	19.6	42	0
	2	D. Ben-Gurion	1.11.1950–8.10.1951	11.2	43	0
2	3	D. Ben-Gurion	8.10.1951–24.12.1952	14.5	32	4
	4	D. Ben-Gurion	24.12.1952–26.1.1954	13	42.5	2
	5	M. Sharet	26.1.1954–29.6.1955	17	100	1
	6	M. Sharet	29.6.1955–3.11.1955	5	100	0
3	7	D. Ben-Gurion	3.11.1955–7.1.1958	26	54	2
	8	D. Ben-Gurion	7.1.1958–17.12.1959	23.3	100	3
4	9	D. Ben-Gurion	17.12.1959–2.11.1961	22.5	48	1
5	10	D. Ben-Gurion	2.11.1961–26.6.1963	19.7	41	3
	11	L. Eshkol	26.6.1963–22.12.1964	18	63.5	1
	12	L. Eshkol	22.12.1964–12.1.1966	12.6	100	4
6	13	L. Eshkol	12.1.1966–17.3.1969	38	79	6
	14	G. Meir	17.3.1969–15.12.1969	9	100	0
7	15	G. Meir	15.12.1969–10.3.1974	51	100	8
8	16	G. Meir	10.3.1974–3.6.1974	2.75	0.5	0
	17	Y. Rabin	3.6.1974–20.6.1977	36.5	69	11
9	18	M. Begin	20.6.1977–5.8.1981	49.5	93	15
10	19	M. Begin	5.8.1981–10.10.1983	26	51	7
	20	Y. Shamir	10.10.1983–13.9.1984	11	44	1
11	21	S. Peres	13.9.1984–20.10.1986	25	100	6
	22	Y. Shamir	20.10.1986–22.12.1988	26	100	1
12	23	Y. Shamir	22.12.1988–11.6.1990	17.6	44	12
	24	Y. Shamir	11.6.1990–13.7.1992	25	86	3
13	25	Y. Rabin	13.7.1992–22.11.1995	40.3	77.5	18
	26	S. Peres	22.11.1995–18.6.1996	7	58	0
14	27	B. Netanyahu	18.6.1996–6.7.1999	36.6	69	19
15	28	E. Barak	6.7.1999–7.3.2001	20	38	13
	29	A. Sharon	7.3.2001–27.2.2003	23.2	73	18
16	30	A. Sharon	27.2.2003–present	–	–	–
	Averages		–	22.32	67.17	5.48

TABLE 2

FRAGMENTATION MEASURES, 1949–2003

Year	Knesset	No. of Parties	Divisiveness	Second largest party relative to largest party	Centralization
1949	1	12	0.788	0.41	0.212
1951	2	15	0.792	0.44	0.208
1955	3	12	0.832	0.38	0.168
1959	4	12	0.797	0.36	0.203
1961	5	11	0.814	0.40	0.186
1965	6	13	0.788	0.58	0.212
1969	7	13	0.702	0.46	0.298
1973	8	10	0.701	0.76	0.299
1977	9	13	0.707	0.74	0.293
1981	10	10	0.680	0.98	0.320
1984	11	15	0.740	0.93	0.260
1988	12	15	0.770	0.98	0.230
1992	13	10	0.772	0.73	0.228
1996	14	11	0.820	0.94	0.180
1999	15	15	0.884	0.73	0.116
2003	16	13	0.858	0.50	0.142

Source: Asher Arian, David Nachmias and Ruth Amir, *Executive Governance in Israel*, New York, 2002, pp.88, 91.

divisions continued in the 2003 elections even though the system returned to the single-ballot vote (see Table 2).

From 1949 to 1969, the second largest party in the Knesset obtained an average of 40% of the seats relative to the largest party. In this period the regime can be characterized as a multiparty system strongly affected by a dominant core party: no government coalition could have received a vote of confidence from the Knesset. In 1951, for example, 15 parties were elected and the fragmentation index was 0.792, meaning that each party had less seats and less electoral influence. Comparatively, in the 15th Knesset there were also 15 parties but the fragmentation index was higher – 0.884. The difference between those two examples is explained by the relative difference between the two large parties: in 1951 the second large party had 0.44 seats in parliament compared to the biggest party, while in 1999 the second large party had 0.73 seats compared to the biggest party. In 1951 there was one dominant party and 14 small parties while in 1999 there was one large party which was not dominant.

The third index demonstrates the centralization of power in the parliament. It standardizes the fragmentation index to a value of 1. If the fragmentation index equals 1, this indicates maximal divisiveness in parliament, and the centralization index will be equal to zero, meaning that no party has more power than any other. For instance, in 1969 the Labour Party had 56 seats in the Knesset and the second large party had 0.46 seats relative to Labour. The centralization index shows that the Labour had dominant power in the political arena. Labour's loss of the election in 1977 resulted from a change in the electoral balance between the two largest parties that had occurred four years earlier (the score of the second largest party relative to the largest party increase to 0.76). Interestingly, the fragmentation index did not change drastically during those years, as well as the centralization index, because the two parties (Labour and Likud) just exchanged positions.[36]

The fragmentation indices are incomplete for capturing the complexity of the variables that influence Israel's political stability. Also to be considered is divisiveness within the government coalitions themselves. Table 3 demonstrates that the extent of stability is directly dependent on the dominance of the core party that forms the coalition. For example, in Israel's first two decades, the average number of ministers was 16. Only in Golda Meir's term did that average rise to 20. The broad government coalitions that ruled during the 1980s had an average of 24 ministers in order to maintain the coalition. Such large and ideologically fragmented decision making bodies make it most difficult to reach significant decisions.

By weighing the two divisiveness measures the analysis of patterns of instability becomes more focused. Ehud Barak's coalition, for example, governed with a divided Knesset (15 parties and a Rae index value of 0.858, which means a very highly divisive Knesset), the second largest party captured 73% of the seats from the ruling party, 23 ministers affiliated to six different parties were members of the cabinet, 12 affiliated with the dominant Labour Party, and 13 ministers were replaced (an average of one every six weeks) during its term. Not surprisingly, Barak's government resigned after just 20 months or 38% of its legal tenure. Barak's coalition began its term with a solid majority based on 75 Knesset members and ended a minority government.

Balance of Power between Parliament and the Prime Minister

The power to remove the government was delegated to the Knesset in the Basic Law: The Government. Until 1996, the opposition could bring about such a removal by a vote with a majority of even 2 to 1. Although there were hundreds of such attempts, only once was this power used successfully in Israel's history, dismissing Shamir's government on 15 March 1990 (by a majority of 60:55).[37] These failures of the Knesset point less to the coalition's triumph than to the opposition's incompetence. As stated in the law, a government's removal is accompanied by removal of the Knesset as well reducing the incentive of incumbent ministries to disperse the government.

The 1996 direct election law changed the balance of power by granting the Knesset the authority to vote on no confidence in the prime minister alone and to remove him from office with a majority of 80 votes.

TABLE 3

COALITION FRAGMENTATION MEASURES, 1949–2003

Government	Prime Minister	Coalition size	No. of parties in the coalition	Size of the largest party	No. of ministers	Ministers in the prime minister's party
1	D. Ben-Gurion	73/120	4	46	12	7
2	D. Ben-Gurion	73/120	4	46	13	8
3	D. Ben-Gurion	65/120	5	45	13	9
4	D. Ben-Gurion	87/120	5	54	16	9
5	M. Sharet	87/120	5	45	16	9
6	M. Sharet	64/120	4	40	16	11
7	D. Ben-Gurion	80/120	5	40	16	9
8	D. Ben-Gurion	64/120	4	40	16	11
9	D. Ben-Gurion	86/120	5	47	16	9
10	D. Ben-Gurion	68/120	4	42	16	11
11	L. Eshkol	68/120	4	42	15	10
12	L. Eshkol	68/120	4	42	16	11
13	L. Eshkol	75/120	5	45	18	12
14	G. Meir	107/120	6	56	22	14
15	G. Meir	102/120	4	56	24	14
16	G. Meir	68/120	3	51	22	17
17	Y. Rabin	61/120	3	51	19	16
18	M. Begin	62/120	4	45	17	9
19	M. Begin	61/120	4	46	18	15
20	Y. Shamir	64/120	6	46	18	15
21	S. Peres	97/120	9	41	25	9
22	Y. Shamir	96/120	9	41	25	10
23	Y. Shamir	95/120	5	40	26	11
24	Y. Shamir	62/120	10	40	19	9
25	Y. Rabin	62/120	3	44	17	13
26	S. Peres	58/120	3	44	20	15
27	B. Netanyahu	66/120	7	32	18	9
28	E. Barak	75/120	6	27	23	12
29	A. Sharon	73/120	6	19	26	8
30	A. Sharon	68/120	4	40	24	15

Source: Asher Arian, David Nachmias and Ruth Amir, *Executive Governance in Israel*, New York, 2002, p.95.

More. importantly, Knesset members could bring about the removal of the prime minister without dispersing the Knesset. In addition, the law allowed the Knesset to remove the government and disband itself with a majority of 61 votes. As a result of these changes, cabinet members who disagreed with government policy could join the opposition's no confidence vote without jeopardizing their own status. Since 1996, relatively small parties such as the religious ultra-orthodox parties, the short-lived Centre Party, the New Immigrants' Party and even the religious-Zionist parties have taken advantage of the fact that every new government would have to rely on their support as coalition members due to the level of Knesset fragmentation. The three prime ministers elected during the electoral reform period had to form *ad hoc* coalitions alongside the formal ruling coalition in order to win a Knesset vote. Bargaining would end in political payoffs and compromises on important issues that had already been agreed to as part of the coalition agreement. Coalition policy agreements became little more then recommendations open to renegotiation on a daily basis. Consequently, the capacity to govern effectively was considerably impaired.

It was for this reason that in 2001 the Knesset decided to reinstate the single-ballot method with a significant difference. While reaffirming the Knesset's power to remove the government with a majority of 61 votes, a constructive restriction was added: Before such a vote could be carried out, the opposition had to present an alternative candidate who had consented in writing to govern as the next prime minister. This restriction made successful no confidence votes difficult because a spectrum of ideologically opposed parties could no longer join forces merely to overthrow the government. Yet a lacuna also entered the law, one its authors apparently did not adequately consider. If the opposition's candidate is unable to form a new government within 42 days new elections will be held. Although never used, this principle enables the opposition to present any candidates with the understanding that their inability to form a government will lead to the desired new elections.

The return to the single-ballot system will restore the strength of the major parties and the prime minister's ability to lead the governing coalition through the use of authority rather than political payoffs to coalition partners. However, the fragmentation in the Knesset is still relatively high.

Norms: Civic Responsibility and Accountability

These norms are vital for a properly functioning democracy. Personal and administrative responsibility implies the willingness to face the consequences of government actions and the decisions that preceded those actions. Accountability is another necessary condition for professional, public and institutional oversight. These norms are not clearly defined in

Israeli law nor are they informally practised. Paragraph 4 of Basic Law: The Government does state that 'the government is accountable to the Knesset through collective responsibility; a minister is responsible before the prime minister for the duties that are in his charge'. But the content of this responsibility and the possible sanctions if unfulfilled remain unspecified. Although such legislation is vague in many democracies, the national political culture and administrative subcultures give substance, accountability and responsibility.

Social Cleavages

The weakening of Israel's social fabric is directly related to the loss of the capacity to govern. Five major cleavages predominate: political, religious-secular, social structure, ethnic and non-Jewish minorities.[38] These cleavages have created intense tensions among numerous segments of the Israeli society, between politicians who represent these groups, as well as between the general population and government agencies. Israel has often been described as a society exhibiting unusually deep social rifts in comparison to other Western societies. It is consequently weighed down with conflicts.[39] The first two cleavages – the political and the religious-secular – entered the public policy making agenda early, when parties representing their causes were elected to the first Knesset. The three other cleavages acquired Knesset representation in the last two decades.

The Israel–Arab conflict, smouldering beneath the surface since the conclusion of the 1967 war, exploded in October 2000 with a series of demonstrations and protests staged by Israel's Arab sector against the discriminatory practices applied by all governments. The killing of 12 Israeli Arab citizens during police attempts to disburse the crowds inflamed the conflict's intensity, and made it much more difficult to resolve the intense disagreement between the government and the leadership of the Israeli Arabs. Consequently the government had decided not to decide on the major conflicting issues that put apart the Arab minority from the Jewish majority.

The ethnic schism also festered until it found strong expression in the 1977 elections. Menachem Begin, the right wing's leader, extended political legitimacy to the Sephardim, immigrants from North Africa (as opposed to the Ashkenazi immigrants from Europe and Anglo-Saxon countries) who had arrived in Israel *en masse* primarily during the 1950s. The Sephardic community had previously been denied recognition and equality by the ruling left-wing governments. They were excluded from participation in major public institutions, were housed primarily in the periphery, and allocated resources that were disproportionately small in comparison to their numbers and their needs.[40] Yet the political 'rehabilitation' of second and third generation immigrants did nothing to appease the feelings of humiliation and discrimination experienced by their ancestors.

Socio-economic status discrepancies have intensified during the 1990s. The peace process initiated in the middle of the decade, privatization, expanding globalization and the blossoming of hi-tech industries changed the face of Israel's economy. Many Israelis became wealthy overnight whereas others substantially improved their economic status. Importantly, both groups were from major cities and were highly educated. The population of towns and villages in the periphery gained little of this new wealth. In fact, the Gini Index that measures the extent of inequality rose dramatically, indicating significant regression in Israel's status as a relatively egalitarian society.[41]

The major problem facing Israel is the overlap observed between its cleavages. Many of the Sephardic immigrants who still reside in the periphery and development towns where they settled upon arrival are found among Israel's lower classes, have adopted a relatively traditional, religiously observant lifestyle and support right-wing parties. In contrast, many of the Ashkenazim who live in large cities are better educated, belong to the middle and upper classes, have adopted a pluralistic, secular lifestyle and support centre and left-of-centre parties. The direct election of the prime minister led to a dramatic increase in the number of sectoral parties in the Knesset that in turn intensified these cleavages. The difficulties faced in forming stable coalitions out of such a variety of parties have impaired the ability of governments to govern effectively and accountably.

CONCLUSIONS

The continued decline in the capacity of Israeli governments to govern has become most pronounced in the last decade. Although in the past the civil service could boast impressive successes in policy domains including the economy, infrastructure, public education, immigrant absorption, housing and defence, more recently it has been unable to implement any integrative, long-range programmes. The two major reasons for this state of affairs are the inefficiencies of the public bureaucracy coupled with government instability. The analysis of a set of indicators reveals that the public administration is overly centralized, rife with numerous unqualified political appointments, outdated budgeting procedures and impervious to long-term planning in addition to displaying a local government apparatus almost totally controlled by the central government. Further analysis also indicates that the political system is highly partisan in its coalition forming behaviour as well as in Knesset representation. Governments rarely complete more than two-thirds of their possible term in office. The turnover of prime ministers and especially of cabinet ministers is quite rapid, and the political culture has no institutionalized norms that promote accountability and transparency. Each factor can by itself undermine the executive capacity to govern; acting in concert, as in the Israeli case, the factors have paralyzed the government. Policy planning is short-term and improvised, the only programmes implemented being of relatively minor importance.

The return of Israel's governance capacity to former levels requires comprehensive institutional reforms of the public administration. The main objectives of such reforms would be decentralization of government authority, and the institutionalization of greater congruence between authority and accountability, coupled with revision of the balance of power between the Knesset and the executive branch. Local governance should be significantly expanded along with greater measures of accountability and responsibility.

With respect to the public administration, implementing agencies should be created and given a considerable amount of authority, and the national budgeting process should be modernized through the use of performance-based budgeting techniques. Government ministries should have more input into the making of the national budget. In the constitutional domain, the valuable restriction placed on votes of no confidence should be reinforced. This might be accomplished by requiring the opposition's alternative candidates for the prime minister's position to publicly announce their intended policies. The principle of multiparty representation must be preserved while strengthening larger parties. It would be advisable to raise the threshold of entry to the Knesset to at least 5%. This would induce small parties to align with larger party blocs. Finally, a more formal and precise conception of the essence of political and administrative accountability and responsibility is required.

The implementation of these reforms would inaugurate a complex and politically problematic process. Its success would directly depend on the commitment of the prime minister, the cooperation of cabinet ministers, Knesset members and top civil servants. Only combined efforts on their part will make Israel more governable.

NOTES

1. Paul Sabatier, 'Top-Down and Bottom-Up Approaches in Implementation Research: A Critical Analysis and Suggested Synthesis', *Journal of Public Policy*, Vol.6, No.1 (1986), pp.21–48.
2. Guy B. Peters, *The Politics of Bureaucracy*, London, 5th edn. 2001, pp.1–134, 219–79, 299–338.
3. Michael Lipsky, *Street-Level Bureaucracy: Dilemmas of the Individual in Public Service*, New York, 1980, pp.3–26.
4. Alfred D. Chandler Jr., *The Visible Hand: The American Revolution in American Business*, Boston, MA, 1980, pp.1–15, 484–502.
5. David L. Weimer and Aidan R. Vining, *Policy Analysis: Concept and Practice*, Princeton, NJ, 3rd edn. (1998), pp.159–95.

6. Aaron Wildavsky, Budgeting: *A Comparative Theory of Budgetary Processes*, Princeton, NJ, 1986.

7. A. Schick, 'The Road to PPB: The Stages of Budget Reform', in F.J. Lyden and E.G. Miller (eds.), *Planning Programming Budgeting*, Chicago, 1996, pp.26–52.

8. David Nachmias and Itai Sened, 'Governance and Public Policy', in David Nachmias and Gila Menahem (eds.), *Public Policy in Israel*, London, 2002, pp.3–20. See also Asher Arian, David Nachmias and Ruth Amir, *Executive Governance in Israel*, New York, 2002, pp.35–60.

9. Thomas G. Cummings and Christopher G. Worley, *Organization Development and Change*, Columbus, OH, 6th edn. 1997, pp.32–43.

10. D.W. Rae, *The Political Consequences of Electoral Laws*, New Haven, CT, 1967, pp.47–58.

11. Michael Laver and Norman Schofield, *Multiparty Government*, Minniapolis, MI, 1998, pp.144–63.

12. Norman Schofield, 'Coalition Politics: A Formal Model and Empirical Analysis', *Journal of Theoretical Politics*, Vol.7, No.3 (1995), pp.245–81.

13. See Arian *et al.*, *Executive Governance in Israel*, pp.35–60. See also in J.D. Huber, 'The Vote Confidence in Parliamentary Systems', *American Political Science Review*, Vol.90, No.2 (1996), pp.269–83.

14. Bernard Rosen, Holding Government Bureaucracies Accountable, Oxford, 1998, pp.3–16.

15. Meaning the heads of ministerial agencies, regulatory agencies, the attorney general, the civil service commissioner etc. Only elected figures are superior to these positions.

16. David Dery, *Political Appointments*, Tel Aviv, 1993 (Hebrew). See also in Yitzhak Zamir, 'Political Appointments', *Mishpatim*, Vol.20, No.1 (1990), pp.19–42 (Hebrew).

17. The Civil Service Law (Nominations) 1959, Paras.11, 19.

18. Public Service Regulations (nominations) (tenders, tests and examinations), 1961, para.40.

19. High Court of Justice (HC) 4446/96, *The Movement for Quality Government v. the State of Israel*, PD (*Piskei Din*, Judgments, official publication of the judgments of the Israeli Supreme Court) 705(3).

20. See Arian *et al.*, *Executive Governance in Israel*, p.70.

21. See Arian *et al.*, *Executive Governance in Israel*, pp.70–71.

22. See Dan Caspi's article in R. Cohen-Almagor (ed.), *Israeli Democracy at the Crossroads*, London, 2005.

23. See Ori Arbel-Ganz, *Regulation: The Supervision Branch*, Jerusalem, 2003, pp.66–82 (Hebrew).

24. See Arian *et al.*, *Executive Governance in Israel*, pp.35–7.

25. See David Nachmias and Itai Sened, 'The Bias of Pluralism: The Redistributive Effects of the New Electoral Law', in Asher Arian and Michal Shamir (eds.), *The Elections in Israel 1996*, Albany, NY, 1999, pp.269–94.

26. Haim Kobersky, *The Public and Professional Committee for the Examination of the Civil Service*, Jerusalem, 1989 (Hebrew).

27. Basic Law: The State Economy (1975); Budget Law (1985).

28. I.e. zero-based budgeting system (ZBB), planning, programming, budgeting system (PPBS) and managing by objectives (MBO). Usually there is a synchronization of all systems.

29. The typical Israeli budget contains about 7,500–9,000 clauses. Most European countries present budgets containing only about 700 clauses.

30. European Council, *The European Pact for Local Self-Government*, Brussels, Part I, pa. 4/2.

31. See The Government's Basic Principles (July 1992), sub-para. 12.6.

32. This indicator calculated by the number of months the government actually had served and dividing it to the total potential term that the government could have served equivalent to the Knesset term, according to Basic Law: The Government.

33. See Arian *et al.*, *Executive Governance in Israel*, pp.90–91.

34. Rae's fractionalization index is calculated by taking the percentage of each party, squaring the percentage, adding the results, and subtracting the total from 1. For extended discussion, see Arian *et al.*, *Executive Governance in Israel*, pp.90–91.

35. For an extended discussion see David Nachmias and Itai Sened, 'Governance and Public Policy', in David Nachmias and Gila Menahem (eds.), *Public Policy in Israel*, London, 2002, pp.3–20.

36. We should note that beginning with the 1992 elections, the cut-off point for obtaining a seat in the Knesset was 1.5% of the vote, higher than the 1.0% required in previous elections.

37. The 23rd governmental coalition ruled since 1988 and included the Likud Party (40 seats in the Knesset), Labour (39 seats) and three more religious parties (Shas with 6 seats, Mafdal with 5 seats and Agudat-Israel with 5 seats). After prime minister Yitzhak Shamir refused to adopt the American's draft of the Israeli Arabs peace agreement (known as James Baker paper), the Labour leader, Shimon Peres, threatened to resign from the coalition. Peres' ultimatum was based on his verbal agreement with Shas for their support in dismantling the coalition. Prime Minister Shamir found out this and dismissed all 11 ministers of the Labour Party. The day after, five members of Shas were absent from the Knesset and the opposition had the majority to dismiss the government by a vote of no confidence.

38. See articles by Yossi Yonah, Tamar Horowitz, Majid Al-Haj and Hillel Frisch in Cohen-Almagor (ed.), *Israeli Democracy at the Crossroads.*

39. Sami Smooha, 'Democracy and Class, Ethnic and National Conflicts in Israel', in Uri Ram (ed.), *The Israeli Society: Critical Perspectives,* Tel Aviv, 1993, pp.172–202 (Hebrew).

40. Raphael Cohen-Almagor,' Cultural Pluralism and the Israeli Nation-Building Ideology', *International Journal of Middle East Studies,* Vol.27 (1995), pp.461–84.

41. Yaakov Wershevsky and Mehamad Seid-Ahmed, *Inequality in the Distribution of Income,* Jerusalem, 2001, pp.11–12.

Citizenship Education in Israel – A Jewish-Democratic State

ORIT ICHILOV, GAVRIEL SALOMON and
DAN INBAR

The education of future citizens is a field that is frequently institutionally ill defined and greatly sensitive to the macro-political cultures of nations and the micro-political culture of schools within these nations.[1] Thus, to comprehend the enormity of the task of preparing youngsters to become citizens in Israel the major features of both Israeli society and the schools must be considered. Israel, as stated in its Declaration of Independence, was founded as a Jewish and democratic state. Achieving a balance between the particularistic-Jewish component and the universalistic-democratic pillar is more problematic in Israel than in many other Western democracies, as will be demonstrated and explained in this chapter.

We begin by examining the tenets of citizenship education in democracy. Next, in order to assess the role of Israeli schools in fostering and inculcating democratic citizenship orientations it is necessary to analyze the major milestones of citizenship education from the pre-state period (Yishuv) to the present. The historical account will be followed by

Orit Ichilov is Professor at Tel Aviv University Faculty of Education and was recently a fellow at the Woodrow Wilson International Center for Scholars in Washington DC. Gavriel Salomon is the founder and director of the Centre for Research on Peace Education at the University of Haifa. Dan Inbar is a professor and the former dean of the School of Education at the Hebrew University of Jerusalem.

a discussion of current key challenges and problems facing citizenship education. We argue that although citizenship education progressed significantly over the years to encompass concerns of minority groups, and civil and human rights, citizenship education is still inadequately implemented in the schools.

CITIZENSHIP EDUCATION AND DEMOCRACY

Citizenship orientations are the outcomes of a cumulative process of political learning. Democratic societies assign schools a prominent role in the development of citizenship virtues, values and skills. Niemi and Junn maintain that 'schools, along with their teachers and curricula, have long been identified as the critical link between education and citizenship, as the locus from which democratic citizens emerge'.[2] While Converse characterizes formal education as the 'universal solvent' that explains more aspects of democratic citizenship than any other factor.[3]

The term 'citizenship education' commonly refers to institutionalized forms of political knowledge acquisition that take place within formal educational frameworks (such as schools and universities) and informal frameworks (such as youth movements).[4] A distinction should be made between specific and diffuse citizenship education. Specific citizenship education proceeds through curricular and extracurricular school activities (such as civic classes or service learning programmes) that are specifically designed to prepare youngsters for citizenship, as well as through the 'hidden curriculum' of the school (this includes, for example, instructional styles and patterns of authority relationships), better known as the school climate. Diffuse citizenship education refers to educational attainment in general. It is based on the assumption that 'schooling provides civic education even when its content is not explicitly civic'.[5] Citizenship education in Western democracies aims at inculcating simultaneously particularistic identities and values, such as patriotism and national pride, and universalistic and shared democratic codes such as tolerance and respect for a variety of civil liberties. Achieving a shared concept of citizenship that would bridge over ethnic, national and socio-economic rifts is considered vital for the functioning of democracies because it 'helps to tame the divisive passions of other identities'.[6] It is generally agreed that pluralism must fit within certain kind of overarching unity, and certain ultimate values must be shared if the diversity in a democratic society is to be contained democratically.[7] There has been a growing awareness of the potential tensions between cultural, national and social heterogeneity and the virtues and practices of democratic citizenship and national unity.[8]

Studies have shown that forming an affinity with one's country is often more problematic for national and ethnic minorities than for those who form the dominant group, and developing a common civic identity in

multicultural societies is not a simple matter.⁹ Educating the younger
generation for citizenship in a deeply divided society is an especially
sensitive and difficult task.¹⁰

A major attribute of Israeli society is the wide and deep rifts between
religious and non-religious groups, between Israeli Arabs and Jews,
between the political left and right, and between the rich and the poor. The
multicultural and ever-changing texture of Israeli society can be attributed
mainly to the constant flow and at times the massive waves of immigrants
arriving from all over the globe. These waves of immigrants create a vertical
mosaic, in which ethnic and socio-economic rifts merge, as well as rifts
between veteran Israelis and newly arrived immigrants. These divides, that
often intersect and overlap, represent contesting visions of Israel as
a Jewish-democratic state and profoundly shape Israel's political culture.

Israel's engagement in a long intractable conflict creates an aura of
constant threat.¹¹ The sense of threat is reinforced by the vivid memory
of the Holocaust that is transmitted to students via the teaching of history
and visits to the death camps in Europe. Consequently, Israeli society has
become so radicalized that it is more difficult than ever to arrive at a broad
consensus on political and territorial issues, social issues and issues related
to state and religion.¹² It is not surprising that under these circumstances
society is looking to education to try and solve some of the social and
political implications of these basic rifts. So, can Israeli schools make a
difference? Can schools provide students with learning environments that
would be conducive to the acquisition of democratic orientations and
inculcate a shared civic identity that would bridge existing divides?

HISTORICAL PERSPECTIVE

Zionist Citizenship during the Yishuv Period

'Citizenship' is conventionally defined within an existing state. It is,
therefore, interesting to note that citizenship education preceded the
establishment of the State of Israel in 1948, and was entitled 'education for
Zionist citizenship'. Israel, as stated in its Declaration of Independence,
was established as a Jewish-democratic state, a state that attempts to
promote simultaneously Jewish nationalism and democracy. The debate
that is still relevant today, concerning the emphasis that should be given to
national and universalistic values, and the recognitions that these two sets
of values may be at odds with one another, preceded the founding of the
state. During the Yishuv period, this duality was viewed as an abnormality
caused by Diaspora life. One of the major goals of Zionism was to do away
with this split identity, and educate a person and a Jew as a unified entity.
However, given the emphasis during that period on the revival of national
life, the resurrection of the Hebrew language and the renewal of the use of

the Hebrew calendar, clear precedence was given to national values. The aims of education for Zionist citizenship were to instil in the younger generation a strong loyalty to the ideas of national rebuilding and the redemption of the land. The ideal was to produce 'pioneers' dedicated to the cause of erecting the foundations of the future state, who are willing to postpone the fulfilment of their personal wishes and give priority to collective goals. Zionist education permeated all school subjects, and the entire web of school life became a passing parade of national symbols and an identification rite.[13] Teaching the Bible to youngsters even in non-religious schools was a central pillar of Zionist education. It was aimed at making youngsters aware of the historical roots of the nation, and of the source of modern Hebrew, and was also designed to instil in children universalistic values such as compassion for the weak, social justice, desire for universal peace and respect for other people and their way of life.[14] History, too, was enlisted to highlight periods of Jewish independence and heroism, and to bridge the gap between past periods of statehood and present national revival.[15] Geography books aimed at creating affinity and love for the country, emphasizing that the essence of Zionism is the realization of the right of Jews to return to their ancestral homeland. Even arithmetic was mobilized, and students were asked to calculate the number of trees planted by the pioneers, the age of Zionist settlements, or the sum of donations made to the Jewish National Fund. The inculcation of strong national emotions was considered more important than the cognitive aspects of civic education. Educators were nonetheless aware of the dangers entailed in emotion-based education and attempts were made 'not to bring into the schools the emotionalism of propaganda, but vital national emotions. To stay away from the sensational character of propaganda, and stress instead emotional maturity through education'.[16]

Citizenship Education during the First Years of Statehood

The establishment of the State of Israel in 1948 was a turning point that affected citizenship education as well. One of the major objectives of the leadership of the newly born state was to create a strong central government that would transcend narrow partisan interests and affiliations. The institutional framework that had operated during the pre-state period lacked sovereignty and consequently depended on the voluntary compliance of citizens. In addition, these institutions were affiliated with the various factions within the Zionist movement. The educational system, for example, was divided into so-called 'streams': the religious, the general Zionist, and the socialist labour, which persisted until 1953. The tasks of centralization and de-politicization of various organizations and institutions and the creation of an effective central government dominated the first years of statehood. The first years of statehood were also marked by mass immigration of Jews into Israel.

During the first decade of statehood, the Israeli Jewish population almost tripled. About half of the immigrants came from Europe, having survived the Holocaust and war, and half were refugees from Muslim countries in the Middle East and North Africa. Immigrants arrived mainly from non-democratic countries and from countries in which Jews had at best limited citizenship rights. They therefore lacked the experience of participatory citizenship in a democracy. This situation presented a challenge to Israel as a young democracy: there was a need to re-socialize the immigrants to enable them to function effectively within a democracy, as well as preparing the younger generation for the citizenship role. It became clear that pre-state citizenship education must be adapted to the new reality, that schools must carry the burden of educating citizens to function within Israeli democracy, and that schools cannot rely much on families and emerging communities. Initially, however, much of the ideological fervour of the Yishuv period continued to dominate the first years of statehood.

Educators were debating how to refocus Zionist education following the fulfilment of a central Zionist aim: the establishment of Israel. A teachers' organization (Teachers for the Jewish National Fund) that took charge of Zionist education in the pre-state period, convened in 1950, two years after the establishment of Israel, to deliberate the course that national education should be taking. During the pre-state period, the redemption of the Jewish people and land was the central theme in Zionist education, and the Jewish National Fund, an organization that collected money to purchase land in Palestine and build Jewish settlements, came to symbolize the Zionist enterprise in schools. Educators expressed the idea that following the establishment of Israel, new goals should be set for Zionist education, and it has been suggested that the Israel Defence Forces (IDF) be adopted by the schools as a symbol of the new national mission. It was naively anticipated that Israel would enjoy a period of calm following its victory in the War of Independence and the armistice agreements that were signed with neighbouring Arab countries. During the pre-state era, military service was voluntary. It was feared that a transition to compulsory service could erode youngsters' respect and affection for the military, and their motivation to serve their country during peacetime. It was decided that schools should provide para-military education, that would nevertheless be anti-militaristic: 'from the dawn of childhood youngsters embroider their role as pioneers ... Hebrew youth should never regard the army as an adventurous cult, sharpening its swords ... our army is an army of defense and fulfillment of Zionism'.[17] The third Israeli chief of staff, Igal Yadin, addressed a teachers' meeting, and shared with educators his views concerning the partnership that should develop between the IDF and the schools. He claimed that the War of Independence was won because each soldier had a sense of mission, knowing what he was defending and what he was fighting for. Therefore, the most important educational objective is to raise conscientious Zionist soldiers. It was suggested that students should visit army camps, and soldiers should visit the schools, and that school clubs would familiarize students with aviation and nautical affairs.[18] In later years, pre-military training (GADNA) was offered in high schools. Overall, the schools played a key role in inculcating the view that military service is an integral and central component of Israeli citizenship.

In 1953 the State Education Law was legislated. The goals that should be achieved via the state educational system clearly give primacy to national aims and to the ethos of the pioneers, mentioning also the wish to impart to the younger generation the desire to establish a society based on the foundations of liberty, equality, tolerance, mutual help and love of people. The educational system was administratively centralized and was dissociated from the various political parties. The de-politicization of the school system was accompanied by strict instructions that politics and ideological controversies should not enter the schools. Instead, schools should emphasize consensus and avoid partisanship, and even youth movements were barred from schools. Civic education focused on the structural and legal aspects of state institutions. The emotional emphasis that was dominant during the Yishuv period became marginal and cognitive elements took precedence. Civic education came to rely largely on concepts rooted in the social sciences. Civic education during that period centred on the obligations of citizens, rather than on citizens' rights, expanding the pioneer role from involvement in settlement and defence activities into additional social spheres such as science and industry. The teaching of civics centred on the legal and structural attributes of governmental institutions. These trends remained dominant well into the 1980s.

Democratic Education in the 1980s

During the 1980s the Ministry of Education was alerted to the need to foster democratic education in the schools. A series of studies examining students' knowledge and perceptions of democracy revealed great ignorance and intolerance especially among vocational programme students.[19] A policy directive issued in 1985 by the Ministry of Education, Culture and Sports assigns unprecedented importance to the universalistic aspects of citizenship while allotting national values a much more minor role. The document asserts that there exists an inevitable conflict between national and humanistic-universal values. Educators are instructed to teach students that when faced with dilemmas emanating from the clash between national and universalistic values 'citizenship rights that are derived from fundamental democratic principles and procedures should gain precedence [over national values] and provide behavioural guidance'.[20] This policy represents a total reversal of the pre-eminence of Zionist values during the Yishuv period and first years of statehood. Each year, the Ministry of

Education announces a central theme that should be embodied in and articulated through diverse educational activities in the schools. To enforce the new policy, a unit for democracy and peaceful coexistence became part of the Ministry of Education, and the central theme for the academic years 1986 and 1987 was education for democracy.

Education for Citizenship in a Jewish-Democratic State

Developments from the 1990s on, that inspired a more balanced emphasis on national and democratic values, and a much greater attention to civil and human rights, will be discussed in this section.

Two committees were especially instrumental in setting a new agenda for citizenship education. The committee for the examination of Judaic studies in Hebrew state schools was appointed in 1991, and was given a broad mandate to examine any aspect that could promote Judaic education in schools[21] (the 'Shenhar Committee'). A steering committee appointed in 1995 was commissioned to 'develop a comprehensive program for the inculcation of citizenship as a common value and behavioural framework for all Israeli citizens' (the 'Kremnizer Committee').[22]

The Judaic studies ('Shenhar') committee submitted its recommendations in 1994. The committee acknowledged that the nature of 'secularism' itself had changed over the years. During the pre-state period, most of the secular pioneers were raised in traditional or orthodox families. They were familiar with Jewish traditions but took the liberty of interpreting them from a non-theological perspective, infusing in them national, historical, socialist, humanistic and aesthetic meanings.[23] Secular Jews also resented the claim of religious Jews to have a monopoly over the interpretation, preservation and teaching of Jewish traditions, asserting they have the right to interpret Judaism from a non-theological perspective.

During the pre-state period and first years of statehood, a sizeable share of the curriculum in the non-religious schools was dedicated to Judaic studies (such as the Bible). The interpretation, however, was secular. Over the years the representation of the humanities, social sciences and Judaic studies in the high school curriculum greatly diminished.[24] Consequently, the number of hours dedicated to the teaching of Judaic studies declined considerably. Few students choose these school subjects as part of their high school matriculation certificate, or choose to pursue university degrees and teaching certificates in these subjects. These trends are considered to erode the 'Jewishness' of Israel, and to foster alienation among religious and non-observant Jews.

The committee's point of departure was that the non-religious sector is not alienated or detached from Judaism. Instead, it forms a public which considers Judaism to be 'a national pluralistic culture that is still emerging'.[25] The committee further asserted:

The Jewish component in the identity of the non-religious public is a combination of elements derived from religious traditions; attachment to the land and its past; its historical and natural sites; the Hebrew language, and the variety of works written in Hebrew or translated into Hebrew; the Jewish calendar with its religious and national holidays; forming new patterns for celebrating the holidays by combining religious elements, ethnic traditions and elements that were renewed as part of the Zionist creation especially in connection to the land and workers' settlements; personal and social moral values that derive from Jewish traditions, the Zionist ethos and universalistic moral ideologies.[26]

This approach resembles and revives the secular interpretations of Judaism that were prevalent during the pre-state era and the first years of statehood. The major recommendation of the committee was to intensify the study of Jewish heritage in Hebrew state schools from a pluralistic point of view; 'Hebrew state schools should focus on the development of a plurality of options for Jewish Israeli cultural existence that is independent of Jewish religious law (Halacha), and that builds on attachment to the history and creation of the Jewish people using a critical, pluralistic and innovative perspective.[27] The committee's recommendations were adopted by the Ministry as one of the curricular pillars of the state education system (alongside science education and democratic education). However, they have scarcely been implemented for a variety of reasons, such as lack of resources and the shortage of educators capable of teaching Jewish traditions from a pluralistic and critical perspective.[28] In time, the Shenhar and Kremnizer reports were structurally incorporated into the new Department of Value Education which was established by the religious minister of education, the late Zevulun Hammer, which might be one more explanation for their relatively minor impact on the educational system.[29]

The steering committee on education for democracy (The 'Kremnizer Committee') was commissioned to provide detailed recommendations concerning the contents of civic education such as the values, knowledge and competences that students should acquire at each stage of their educational career, the pedagogical practices that should be employed, and the organizational frameworks and tools for implementing and evaluating the new citizenship education programme. The decision of the committee to restrict its work to the study of regular state schools and leave out religious Hebrew state schools, Arab, Bedouin and Druz schools, not to mention ultra-orthodox schools that are outside the state educational system and do not follow the state curriculum, enabled the committee to avoid many controversial issues.

A report was submitted to the Ministry of Education in February 1996 providing an overview of the major issues and problems concerning citizenship orientations within Israeli society together with recommendations regarding educational objectives and practices.[30] Three major objectives that should be addressed by the schools were identified. First, prevalent civic identities were described as weak and poor in content, and the committee emphasized the need to create a strong universalistic civic identity that would provide a common basis for allegiance, solidarity and consensus. Secondly, the need to develop a 'culture of discussion', or civilized public discourse, based on tolerance, attentiveness to other views and willingness to settle conflicts through negotiation, was stressed. And finally, to combat alienation and passivity, the development of a realistic approach to politics, i.e. neither one that presents a utopian idealization of politics nor one that condemns politics as 'dirty' was recommended. Citizenship education should aim at the acquisition of knowledge, and the inculcation of attitudes, values and motivations, as well as the necessary civic competences. The achievement of these goals must be given high priority.

This report gained great public attention because it was submitted during a most turbulent and traumatic period for Israeli democracy; only three months after the earth-shattering assassination of Prime Minister Rabin.

The committee identified three subject areas that should be taught in schools. First, Israel as a Jewish and a democratic state should promote the understanding of the foundations of Israel as both a Jewish state and a democracy. Secondly, citizenship obligations and civic and human rights must be articulated in schools. The third area was identified as the study of the principles, processes and institutions of democratic regimes. Thus, the first subject area addresses Israeli society, while the other two address the more universalistic aspects of democratic regimes in general, as well as human rights. The competences that students should acquire included: the ability to consider the overall complexity of issues and to assess the merits and drawbacks of various solutions; ability to offer well-founded and constructive criticism; and to have discourse with those who agree with and those who are opposed to one's own views.

It was recommended that a great variety of teaching methods, such as discussion of controversial issues and simulations and role-play would be employed to engage students. The school climate should enable students to experiment with civic competences and to internalize civic values. This includes mutual respect among teachers and students, democratic decision making processes, active student councils, production of school newspapers, discussion clubs and developing a school's code of students' rights and obligations. Thus, the report calls for a comprehensive change concerning the implementation of civics in the curriculum, and concerning the entire school climate. The recommendations were adopted by the Ministry of Education, but so far have not been implemented.

Three significant events inspired the discourse on the place of civic and human rights in education. One of these was the signing (in 1990) and ratification (in 1991) by Israel of the United Nations Convention on the Rights of the Child. The Convention advances the view that children have inherent rights that should be respected and implemented within various social frameworks, including schools. These rights clearly include citizenship rights, such as freedom of thought, conscience and religion (Article 14), freedom of association and freedom of peaceful assembly (Article 15).

The Ministry of Justice appointed a committee to implement the Convention in Israeli legislation pertaining to the various spheres of children's life. A subcommittee on education was subsequently formed to implement the principles of the Convention in educational legislation. The report is about to be submitted to the new minister of justice, hence its effect on the education system cannot as yet be assessed.

These developments prompted the amendment of the State Education Law that was legislated in 1953. In 2000 the section of the law that explicates the aims it seeks to achieve was amended to include individualistic rather than just collectivist goals, as well as new social agendas such as gender equality and environmental concerns. Included are equal opportunities for self-development, acceptance of and support for 'others', inculcating intellectual curiosity and critical thinking, voluntary work and social involvement.[31] Another significant event was the legislation of the Students' Rights Law in 2001, a law that implements many of the principles of the UN Convention on the Rights of the Child within Israeli schools, and advances a democratic school climate.

A second major event was the signing of the Oslo Accords and the initiation of the peace process between Israel and the Palestinian Authority. This process, that lasted until the recent outbreak of violence, inspired the introduction of peace education in schools. The central theme for the school year 1994–95 was dedicated to 'the peace process'; it was aimed at introducing youngsters to the idea that the era of peace has dawned. To help educators implement the message of peace, the Ministry of Education circulated a catalogue containing hundreds of ideas and programmes illustrating the idea of peace to children K-12.[32]

The third, and perhaps most important, event of the 1990s was the shocking assassination of Prime Minister Rabin by a Jewish right-wing radical. 'The assassination of Rabin plunged Israelis into bewilderment, shock, and deep anxiety.'[33] The immediate reaction was the intensification of communal emotions, into a so-called 'epidemic of communicats'.[34] An analysis of the media in the weeks following the assassination reveals the efforts made to construct a collective identity, based on Rabin's legacy, emphasizing mainly the constituting elements of the Israeli Sabra, peace making and Zionism.[35]

The reaction of the Arab population in Israel was complex and multidimensional. The secular-civic character of the peace rally in which Rabin was assassinated gave the Arab population an opportunity to participate in the Israeli civic discourse. But the discourse that has developed around the assassination was claimed to be a Jewish-Israeli one, and not a civic discourse.[36] As an immediate reaction by the education system to the assassination several interesting programmes were developed and adopted. Since no special budget was allocated, the Department of Curriculum Planning in the Ministry of Education took the initiative to adapt the materials of the Shenhar Report and turn them into new and appropriate programmes. 'Choose Life' (Deuteronomy, 30/19) is a programme that discusses the different meanings of the command, 'therefore choose life' through ethical dilemmas around problems of life and death.[37] The programme does not address directly Rabin's assassination, although it was triggered by it, and is taught these days as part of studies of Jewish philosophy.

Another programme, 'Diversity and Controversy',[38] mentions Rabin's assassination directly: 'The assassination of Prime Minister Rabin is a tragic warning sign to what might happen in our society if we don't learn to cope with deep and painful controversies in thoughtful ways'.[39] Unfortunately, this programme did not find its way into mainstream education.

A special memorial day to commemorate Rabin's assassination was announced and is observed in schools. However, it was later 'balanced' by a memorial day for Rechavam Zeevi ('Ghandi'), a member of parliament, and the leader of the 'National Unity' party who was assassinated by Palestinian terrorists. In all, it appears that Rabin's assassination left little direct impact on civic education, echoing the observation that 'the suppression of public discourse after the assassination did not mould the Israel collective memory or foster the reinvention of Israeli collectivity'.[40]

Recent studies convey the impression that knowledge concerning the legal-structural aspects of government is emphasized more than democratic values. Thus, while 80% of junior high school students identified correctly the branch of government to which the Knesset belongs, only 34% provided a correct answer to the question: 'Tyranny of the majority is a situation that...?'[41] Similarly, an international comparative study of citizenship orientations of upper secondary school students in 14 countries revealed that Israeli youngsters were significantly above the international mean concerning 'love for one's country and pride in its achievements'. They were, however, significantly below the international mean in their evaluation that they 'learned in school to understand people with different ideas'.[42]

CITIZENSHIP EDUCATION AND THE TEXTURE OF SCHOOLING:
CHALLENGES AND PROMISES

The New Civics Curriculum for Upper Secondary Schools

Until 1994 there was no common civics curriculum for Arab and Hebrew
state schools and only partial overlap existed. The Ministry of Education
was determined to formulate a common core curriculum for all state high
schools: Arab, regular state schools, and religious state schools.[43] The
supreme goal of the unified curriculum is:

> To inculcate a common Israeli civic identity, together with the
> development of distinct national identities, and to impart to students
> the values of pluralism and tolerance, educate students to accept the
> diversity that exists within Israeli society, and to respect those who are
> different from oneself, and to help students become autonomous and
> conscious citizens, capable of critical thinking, of analyzing, evaluating,
> and forming an independent opinion, playing by the rules of democracy,
> and being 'immune' to demagogical influences.[44]

The core curriculum should thus provide Arab and Jewish students alike
with an opportunity for:

> A thorough examination of the values on which Israel and its
> government are founded, given that Israel is simultaneously a Jewish
> and democratic state. The analysis should reveal, on the one hand, how
> the Jewish and democratic components are connected, and on the other,
> the fact that tensions may arise between them. Examination of the social
> reality in Israel should be related to these two sets of values.[45]

A textbook was developed over the years in collaboration with Arab and
Jewish educators, and the new curriculum was initially implemented on an
experimental basis in some schools, and was nationally implemented in
2001. Civics teachers participated in training programmes that were
specially designed to familiarize them with the new curriculum, textbook
and form of the civics matriculation examination. The new curriculum
clearly addresses the dual nature of Israel as a Jewish and democratic state,
and enables students to familiarize themselves with how 'others' perceive
this duality and are affected by it.

Civics as a School Subject

It is doubtful that the ambitious undertaking of achieving a shared civic
identity via civic instruction can be realized given the time allocated to the
teaching of civics, and the marginal status of civics in the Israeli
curriculum. The recommendation of the Kremnizer Committee to offer
civics classes throughout the entire process of schooling has not been
implemented. At the elementary school level (grades 1 to 6) civics is not

taught. However, some aspects of citizenship are studied in grades 2 to 4 through a school subject entitled 'Homeland and Society'. For the junior high school level (grades 7 to 9) a civics curriculum together with instructional materials have been prepared. Yet, civics is not an obligatory part of the curriculum, and the decision concerning civic instruction is left to school principals. It is estimated that civics is taught in only about one-third of the junior high schools, at the seventh or eighth grades, one hour per week. Consequently, many students reach high school without previously studying it. Civics is a compulsory school subject at the high school level, and a matriculation examination is obligatory for all students at either the eleventh or twelfth grade, Three hours per week are dedicated to the teaching of civics and that is usually increased during the year in which students take the matriculation examination, but more so in regular state schools than in Arab and religious state schools. A recent study revealed the marginality of civics as a school subject, especially within Arab schools.[46]

The neglect of civics as a school subject is manifested in the results of the matriculation examinations. The scores achieved in this area have been in recent years the lowest of all other school subjects in the humanities and social sciences. A recent study revealed that overall students in Hebrew schools did better on a knowledge test about democracy than students in Arab schools, and Hebrew state school students did slightly better than both religious state school and Arab school students.[47] An international comparison of knowledge of democracy scores in 14 countries revealed no statistically significant differences between the mean score of Israeli eleventh graders and the international mean.[48] Thus, on average, Israeli youth did no worse then their counterparts in other countries.

Inequality and Citizenship Education

The idea that citizens *qua* citizens are equal, without any achieved or ascribed qualifications is echoed again and again in modern political thought.[49] Whatever the social or group differences among citizens, whatever their qualities of wealth, status and power in the everyday activities of civil society, citizenship gives everyone the same status as peers in the political public. The first moral obligation of schools in democracy is, therefore, 'to give all children an education adequate to take advantage of their political status as citizens'.[50] Dewey considers 'equal opportunity to receive and to take from others ... [and the exposure to] shared undertakings and experiences' a hallmark of democratic education. 'Otherwise, the influences which educate some into masters, educate others into slaves.'[51] Do Israeli schools meet these societal expectations and equally prepare all students to become citizens?

As was mentioned earlier, citizenship education is related to educational attainment in general, as well as to educational activities specifically designed to inculcate citizenship orientations. The great inequality on both these dimensions within the Israeli school system is one of the greatest obstacles for fostering Israeli democracy and for educating future citizens. Schools stratify both students and knowledge, and high prestige knowledge is available almost exclusively to students in the high level programmes and tracks.[52] Indeed, civic virtues such as critical thinking, problem solving, drawing conclusions, making generalizations, evaluating or synthesizing knowledge and acting deliberatively in a pluralistic world are intimately related to high level knowledge, notably to literacy, and access to such knowledge is unevenly allocated in schools. Literacy, for example, has long been recognized as a basic skill that is vital for democracy.[53] Reading in particular has been recognized as the 'new civil right'.[54]

A recent report on reading revealed great inequality within Israeli society concerning the acquisition of reading skills.[55] About half of the fourth grade students showed relatively poor reading comprehension, a finding that was further supported by an international study of eighth graders. The development of a differentiated civics curriculum for academic and vocational high schools represents another dimension of educational inequality. Until 1990 civics did not exist as a distinct school subject in vocational schools. It only formed a section within the study of history of the Jewish people and the State of Israel, a school subject that was not universally taught. Civics textbooks for vocational schools were non-existent, as were training programmes for civics teachers. Consequently, only few vocational school students had a chance to taste the subject. It is hardly surprising that programme placement – academic or vocational – had a differential effect on students' expressed interest in politics, media use, willingness to become actively involved, discussion of politics with others, support of freedom of speech and sense of political efficacy. Overall, the positive effect of academic programmes, reinforcing a variety of civic orientations, was greater than that of vocational programmes where zero or negative effects more often prevailed.[56]

These results may be partially attributed to the way teachers observe, classify and react to socio-economic and cultural differences in children, which affects the implementation of the curriculum in classrooms, and evidently results in differential learning experiences and opportunities.[57]

Ichilov reports that high school teachers in academic programmes and in schools that cater to better-off students are more open to discussing controversial issues and conflict situations, and to exposing students to criticism and pluralism as compared with teachers in schools with a majority of disadvantaged students.[58]

The Ministry of Education was alarmed by studies that revealed great intolerance and ignorance among vocational school students, and concluded: 'education for citizenship and democracy in the technological tracks must be invigorated'.[59] Thus, the 1990 civics curriculum represents the first (and so far the only) attempt to establish civics as an independent school subject in vocational schools. As was reported earlier, in 1994 the Ministry of Education decided to implement a unified civics curriculum in all academic schools. However, vocational schools were excluded. Consequently, a differentiated curriculum is implemented in academic and vocational high schools. Analysis of curricular materials designed for the teaching of civics in academic and vocational schools reveals that students in vocational and academic tracks are guided into dissimilar citizenship roles.[60]

Academic school students are expected to acquire the capacity to perceive citizenship issues through a broad, interdisciplinary and multi-faceted prism. Students in vocational schools, in contrast, are initiated into an unsophisticated uncritical and submissive pattern of citizenship, fostering what Whitty calls 'quietism' and 'domestication'.[61]

Recent educational policies that were adopted by the Ministry of Education (notably, school choice) may increase inequality. A policy that allows parents to establish democratic magnet schools is especially peculiar given that it is the responsibility of the government to secure democratic schools for all children. Democratic magnet schools, (about 30 of which are already in existence), offer better-off parents an escape from integrated public schools, establishing quasi-private schools that are publicly funded with parents covering only fringe financial costs. These schools often admit students selectively, but are nevertheless operated through democratic institutions and procedures. Officially, they are run by the Ministry of Education and the municipality, but parents play a decisive role in the selection of the school principal and educational staff. The inevitable conclusion is that such schools provide democratic playgrounds for children of better educated and more affluent parents.

Extracurricular Programmes for Citizenship Education

Formal education and instruction in civics are not the only activities related to citizenship education, and attempts to bridge existing gaps and rivalries. There is a wealth of activities, programmes and instructional materials offered through the Youth and Society Division and the Unit for Democracy of the Ministry of Education. In addition, non-profit organizations, such as the Adam Institute, the Israeli Civil Rights Society, the Van Leer Institute, the Jewish-Zionist Institute and the Rabin Centre for Peace, to mention only few of them, since the list contains about 72 different organizations.[62] Most of these organizations produce instructional materials and operate programmes within schools, such as encounters between Jewish and Arab youngsters, and religious and non-religious Jewish students.

High schools offer a service-learning programme entitled: 'personal commitment – community service'. The programme is implemented in the tenth grade, in schools that choose to participate, and all students are required to be engaged. Participation in the programme is noted in students' certificates of high school graduation. The Ministry of Education estimates that about 70,000 students in about 300 schools take part in the programme. Preliminary findings reveal that although participation is compulsory, students expressed the view that involvement in the programme is a worthwhile experience that benefits both themselves and the community.[63] Many students declared that they would be willing to continue their community work on a voluntary basis.

Civic Education in Arab Schools

Citizenship education in a Jewish-democratic state is a highly sensitive issue in Arab schools. The Jewish and the democratic dimensions of citizenship are both problematic.

The Palestinian citizens of Israel, a term that appears to express the self-definition of Israeli Arabs signifies change in their collective identity. There is a wide agreement among scholars that since 1967 Israeli Palestinians have undergone a radicalization process that involves the strengthening of the Palestinian national identity and a concomitant weakening of the Israeli civic identity.[64] The 1987 first Palestinian uprising greatly fostered the Palestinian identity of Israeli Arabs. Arabs of Israel were in full sympathy with the Palestinian insurgents, sent food and drugs into the territories, held protest rallies, contributed to special emergency funds and donated blood.[65] Islamic fundamentalism also gained a strong hold among some segments of the Israeli Arab population, as a form of collective identity

The collective narratives of the Israelis and Palestinians are to a large extent mutually exclusive, based on vastly differing historical interpretations.[66] Thus, it is not surprising that the national symbols of the State of Israel that represent Jewish themes are not an acceptable form of Israeli identity for the Palestinian Arab. They do not participate in the celebration of national holidays and memorial days, and Israel's Independence is commemorated by them as the day of the 'Nakba', i.e. what they consider to be their national catastrophe. The absence of a more general, more diffused Israeli identity makes it difficult to create a shared ideology between Arab and Jewish Israeli citizens.

The civic-democratic dimension of Israeli citizenship is also problematic. Multidimensional inequality is of special significance. Despite the fact that the Israeli Arab population has undergone an intensive process of modernization over the years, their poverty rate is almost double the rate among Jewish families.[67] There are other visible discrepancies between the populations, for example in the levels of educational attainment, position on the employment ladder, occupational opportunities and housing conditions. Allocation of land and water rations for agriculture also reflect great inequality between Arab and Jewish settlements.[68]

Arab educators and scholars argue that Israel has used the educational system as a means of controlling Palestinian Arab citizens. The state-mandated curriculum is characterized by 'the absence of any reference to Palestinian identity in history, literature, and social studies. Instead the curriculum offers a detailed Zionist narrative of history'.[69] However, the present state curriculum, compared to earlier versions, reflects some movement towards the inclusion of Arab identity and Arabs' relationship to the Palestinian people.[70] A recent study revealed that in Hebrew schools more time is dedicated to the study of history than in Arab schools, while the social sciences are taught more intensively in Arab schools. This could mean that Arab schools prefer to teach the more 'neutral' social sciences, and avoid as much as possible the contesting historical narratives of Jews and Arabs.[71] A similar strategy was taken in post-World War II Germany: the study of history was replaced by the social sciences that were considered more neutral, and offered a break from the Nazi past.[72] Arab schools are more conservative than Hebrew non-religious state schools concerning school climate and teaching practices. Student-teacher relationships tend to be more hierarchical and authoritarian.[73] Thus, the school climate is not conducive to education for democracy.

CONCLUSION

Our discussion of the major milestones and characteristics of citizenship education reveals what may be called a process of maturation. Citizenship education progressed from a highly emotional nationalistic focus, centring on civic obligations, to a more cognitive, discipline-oriented civic education with greater awareness of civil liberties and human rights. However, although there exist a great variety of programmes and projects, in addition to the teaching of civics and other relevant school subjects, turning Israeli schools into islands of peace and democracy is not a simple undertaking. A central problem is that the Ministry of Education seems reluctant to implement its explicitly adopted policies. Civics remains a marginal school subject, and citizenship education continues to be an eclectic and fragmented endeavour.

Citizenship and multiculturalism could be forces that are pulling in diverse directions: unity v. division. Israeli society is characterized by great heterogeneity and wide rifts among segments of the population that hold contesting views concerning the very foundations of the State of Israel. This context makes the emergence of a shared civic identity a mission that is hard to accomplish. Research evidence suggests that existing societal rifts invade the schools. Growing up in a divided society, where political issues are salient, Israeli youngsters appear to be more politicized than their counterparts in a variety of other countries.[74] The major rifts between Jews and Arabs are clearly visible in students' perceptions of the parochial dimensions of citizenship, such as support for Israel and pride in its achievements, history and national symbols, and support for the rights of Jewish immigrants.[75] Religious education at both the high school level and in higher education religious institutions ('Yeshivot Leumiot') produce the next generations of religiously and politically radicalized individuals.[76] Ultra-orthodox schools do not abide by the national curriculum and do not provide citizenship education. Textbooks used in ultra-orthodox schools often include expressions of prejudice against and disrespect for Arabs.[77]

Our conclusion is that although important strides were made over the years to promote citizenship and democratic education, it is naive to expect that citizenship education in its present form, and under current circumstances, could foster the emergence of a shared civic identity that would bridge national, cultural, ethnic and social divides within Israeli society.

NOTES

1. H. Mintrop, 'Teachers and Civic Education Instruction in Cross-National Comparisons', in G. Stiner-Khamsi, J. Torney-Purta and J. Schwille (eds.), *New Paradigms and Recurring Paradoxes in Education for Citizenship: An International Comparison*, Amsterdam, 2002, pp.61–85; J. Schwille and J.A. Amadeo, 'The Paradoxical Situation of Civic Education in Schools: Ubiquitous and Yet Elusive', in Stiner-Khamsi *et al.* (eds.), *New Paradigms and Recurring*, pp.105–37.
2. R.G. Niemi and J. Junn, *Civic Education. What Makes Students Learn*, New Haven, CT, 1998, pp.2–3.
3. P.E. Converse, 'Change in the American Electorate', in A. Campbell and P.E. Converse (eds.), *The Human Meaning of Social Change*, New York, 1972, p.324.
4. O. Ichilov, 'Political Education', in T. Husen and T.N. Postlethwaite (eds.), *The International Encyclopedia of Education*, Vol.8, 2nd edn., New York, 1994, pp.4568–70.
5. D.C. Bricker, *Classroom Life as Civic Education*, New York, 198, p 2.
6. D. Heater, *Citizenship: The Civic Ideal in World History*, London, 1990, p.184.
7. A. Etzioni, 'On the Place of Virtues in Pluralistic Democracy', in G. Marks and L. Diamond (eds.), *Reexamining Democracy*, Newbury Park, 1992, pp.70–79; M. Janowitz, *The Reconstruction of Patriotism: Education for Civic Consciousness*, Chicago, 1983.
8. W. Kymlicka and W. Norman (eds.), *Citizenship in Diverse Societies*, New York, 2000; C. Samson, 'The Dispossession of the Inu and the Colonial Magic of Canadian Liberalism', *Citizenship Studies*, Vol.3, No.1 (1999), pp.5–25; B. Parekh, 'Discourses on National Identity', *Political Studies*, Vol.XLII, No.3 (1994), pp.492–504.
9. Kymlicka and Norman (eds.), *Citizenship in Diverse Societies*; R.D. Putnam, *Making Democracy Work: Civic Traditions in Modern Italy*, Princeton, NJ, 1993; T.W. Smith and L. Jakko, *National Pride in Cross-National Perspective* (University of Chicago, National Opinion Research Center: A Research Report, 2001); J. Coakley, 'National Minorities and the Government of Divided Societies: A Comparative Analysis of Some European Evidence', *European Journal of Political Research*, Vol.18, No.4 (1990), pp.437–56.
10. O. Ichilov, 'Citizenship Education in a Divided Society: The Case of Israel', in J. Torney-Putra, J. Schwille and J.A. Amadeo (eds.), *Civic Education Across Countries: Twenty-Four National Case Studies from the IEA Civic Education Project*, Amsterdam, 1999, pp.371–95; S. Byrne, *Growing Up in a Divided Society*, Madison, Teaneck, NJ, 1997.
11. N. Rouhana and D. Bar-Tal, 'Psychological Dynamics of Intractable Ethnonational Conflicts. The Israeli-Palestinian Case', *American Psychologist*, Vol.53 (1998), pp.761–70.

12. S.N Eisenstadt, *The Changing Israeli Society*, Jerusalem, 1989 (Hebrew); A. Arian, *Politics and Regime in Israel*, Tel-Aviv, 1990 (Hebrew); E. Etzioni-Halevy, *The Elite Connection and Israeli Democracy*, Tel-Aviv, 1993 (Hebrew); S. Cohen and E. Don Yehiya (eds.), *Conflict and Consensus in Jewish Political Life*, Ramat-Gan, 1986 (Hebrew); B. Kimmerling, *The Israeli State and Society*, Albany, NY, 1989; Ichilov, 'Citizenship Education in a Divided Society'.

13. B. Ben-Yehuda, *The Teachers' Movement for Zion and its Redemption*, Jerusalem, 1949 (Hebrew); O. Ichilov, *Citizenship Education in Israel*, Tel-Aviv, 1993 (Hebrew).

14. H.A. Zuta, 'Teaching the Bible', *Hed Ha'Chinuch*, Vol.4 (1934), pp.67–77 (Hebrew).

15. B. Lewis, *History: Remembered, Recovered, Invented*, Princeton, 1975.

16. N. Bistritzki, 'Summary of 20 Years to the Teachers' Movement for Zion and its Redemption', *Shorashim*, Vol.3 (1948), pp.25–30 (Hebrew).

17. Ichilov, 'Citizenship Education in Israel', p.83.

18. Ibid.

19. M. Zemach and R. Zin, *Attitudes Concerning Democratic Values Among Israeli Youth*, Jerusalem, 1984 (Hebrew).

20. Ministry of Education, Culture, and Sports, *Special Dispatch No.5: Education for Democracy*, Jerusalem, May 1985, p.4 (Hebrew).

21. Ministry of Education, Culture, and Sports, Curriculum Department, *Nation and World – Jewish Culture in a Changing World*, Recommendations of the Committee for the Examination of Judaic Education in Hebrew State Schools, Jerusalem, 1994 (Hebrew).

22. Ministry of Education and Culture, *To Be Citizens: Education for All Israeli Students*, Interim Report of the Steering Committee on Citizenship Education, Jerusalem, 1996, p.5 (Hebrew).

23. E. Don-Yehiya, 'Hannukkah and the Myth of the Maccabees in Zionist Ideology and Israeli Society', *Jewish Journal of Sociology*, Vol.34, No.1 (1992), pp.5–23; Ichilov, *Citizenship Education in Israel*.

24. H. Ayalon and A. Yogev, 'The Status of Humanities in the Israeli High School Education', in D. Chen (ed.), *Education Toward the 21st Century*, Tel-Aviv, 1995, pp.221–48 (Hebrew).

25. Ministry of Education, Culture, and Sports, Curriculum Department, *Nation and World*, p.6.

26. Ibid., p.5.

27. Ibid.

28. N. Resh and A. Ben-Avot, *Judaic Studies in Hebrew Middle Schools in Israel: Evaluation of the Implementation of the Shenhar Report Recommendations*, Jerusalem, 1998 (Hebrew).

29. D. Inbar, 'The Bureaucratized Value System', in Y. Iram *et al.* (eds.), *Values and Education in the Israeli Society*, Jerusalem, 2001, pp.421–40 (Hebrew).

30. Ministry of Education and Culture, *To Be Citizens*.

31. Ministry of Education. *Directive of the General Director No.61/1*, Jerusalem, 2000 (Hebrew).

32. R. Firer, 'From Peace Making to Tolerance Building', in R. Moses (ed.), *Psychology of Peace and Conflict: The Israeli-Palestinian Experience*, Jerusalem, 1995, pp.79–86.

33. Y. Peri, 'The Media and Rabin Myth: Reconstruction of the Israeli Collective Identity', in Y. Peri (ed.), *The Assassination of Itzhak Rabin*, Stanford, CA, 2000, p.176.

34. Ibid., p.179.

35. Ibid.

36. M. Al-Haj, 'An Illusion of Belonging: Reactions of the Arab Population to Rabin's Assassination', in Peri (ed.), *The Assassination of Itzhak Rabin*, p.173.

37. I. Galili-Shecter and A. Aviv, *Choose Life*, Ministry of Education Culture and Sports, Jerusalem, 1998 (Hebrew).

38. Ministry of Education, Department of Curriculum Planning, *Diversity and Controversy*, Jerusalem, 1998 (Hebrew).

39. Ibid., p.2.

40. Peri, 'The Media and Rabin Myth', p.192.

41. O. Ichilov, *Citizenhip Orientations of 11th Grade Students and Teachers in the Israeli Hebrew and Arab High Schools*, Israel's National Research Report, IEA Civic Education Study, Tel-Aviv, 2000 (Hebrew).

42. J.A. Amadeo, J. Torney-Purta, R. Lehmann, V. Husfeldt and R. Nikolova, *Civic Knowledge and Engagement: An IEA Study of Upper Secondary Students in Sixteen Countries*, Amsterdam, 2002.
43. Ministry of Education, Culture, and Sports, Curriculum Department, *Citizenship: [Academic] High School Curriculum for Jewish (General and Religious), Arab, and Druz Schools*, 1st edn., Jerusalem, 1994 (Hebrew).
44. Ministry of Education, Curriculum Department, Leaflet for Civics Teachers No.16 (Teacher's Guide for Academic High Schools), Jerusalem, 2001, p.10 (Hebrew).
45. Ministry of Education, Culture and Sports, *Citizenship: [Academic] High School Curriculum*, p.6.
46. Ichilov, *Citizenship Orientations of 11th Grade Students and Teachers*.
47. Ibid.
48. Amadeo *et al.*, *Civic Knowledge and Engagement*, p.57.
49. E. Callan, *Creating Citizens*, Oxford, 1997; Heater, *Citizenship: The Civic Ideal in World History*; A. Gutmann, *Democratic Education*, Princeton, NJ, 1987; R. Dahrendorf, 'The Changing Quality of Citizenship', in B. Van Steenberger (ed.), *The Condition of Citizenship*, London, 1994, pp.10–19; T.H. Marshall, *Class, Citizenship and Social Development*, Chicago, 1977.
50. Gutmann, *Democratic Education*, p.288.
51. J. Dewey, *Democracy and Education*, New York, 1916; 1966, p.84.
52. M.F.D. Young, 'An Approach to the Study of Curricula as Socially Organized Knowledge', in M.F.D. Young (ed.), *Knowledge and Control*, London, 1971, pp.19–47; B. Berenstein, 'On the Classification and Framing of Educational Knowledge', in Young (ed.), *Knowledge and Control*, pp.47–70; M.W. Apple, *Ideology and Curriculum*, 2nd edn., New York, 1990.
53. L.S. Pangle and T.L. Pangle, 'What the American Founders Have to Teach Us About Schooling for Democratic Citizenship', in L.M. McDonnell, P.M. Timpane and R. Benjamine (eds.), *Rediscovering the Democratic Purposes of Education*, Lawrence, KS, 2000, pp.21–47.
54. *The Economist*, 24 February 2001, p.91.
55. PISA (Programme for International Student Assessment), *The PISA 2003 Assessment Framework*, 2003, available at www.pisa.oecd.org.
56. O. Ichilov, 'Political Socialization and Schooling Effects among Israeli Adolescents', *Comparative Education Review*, Vol.35, No.3 (1991), pp.430–47.
57. N. Keddie, 'Classroom Knowledge', in M.F.D. Young (ed.), *Knowledge and Control*, New York, 1971; J. Oakes, *Keeping Track: How Schools Structure Inequality*, New Haven, CT, 1985; I. Davies, I. Gregory and S.C. Riley, *Good Citizenship and Educational Provision*, London, 1999.
58. O. Ichilov, 'Perceptions and Attitudes of Israeli High School Civic Education Teachers Concerning Citizenship in Democracy', *Studies in Education*, Vol.48 (1989), pp.69–89 (Hebrew).
59. Ministry of Education, Curriculum Department. *Citizenship: High School Curriculum for the Lower Vocational Tracks in General and Religious Jewish Technological High Schools*, Jerusalem, 1990, p.5 (Hebrew).
60. O. Ichilov, 'Differentiated Civics Curriculum and Patterns of Citizenship Education: Vocational and Academic Programs in Israel', in David Scott and Helen Lawson (eds.), *Citizenship Education and the Curriculum*. Vol.3 in the 'International Perspectives on Curriculum Series', series ed. David Scott, Westport, CT, 2002, pp.81–111.
61. G. Whitty, 'Social Studies and Political Education in England Since 1945', in I. Goodson (ed.), *Social Histories of the Secondary Curriculum: Subjects for Study*, London, 1985, p.279.
62. D. Shriber, *Directory of Organizations for Tolerance Education*, Jerusalem, 2003 (Hebrew).
63. O. Ichilov, 'Service Learning and Citizenship Education in Democracy', *Iyunim Ba'Chinuch*. (Studies in Education) (in press) (Hebrew).
64. J. Landau, *The Arab Minority in Israel, 1967–1991: Political Aspects*, Oxford, 1993; E. Rekhess, 'Israeli Arabs and Arabs of the West Bank and the Gaza Strip: Political Ties and National Identification', *Hamizrah Hehadash* (The New East), Vol.32 (1989), pp.165–91 (Hebrew); E. Rekhess, *The Arabs in Israel After 1967: The Exacerbation of the Orientation of Problem*, Tel-Aviv, 1976 (Hebrew).

65. Z. Schiff and E. Ya'ari, *Intifada: The Palestinian Uprising – Israel's Third Front*, New York, 1990, p.170.
66. G. Salomon, 'A Narrative-Based View of Coexistence Education', *Journal of Social Issues* (in press).
67. Social Security Institute, *Annual Review 1996/97*, Jerusalem, 1997 (Hebrew).
68. I. Jarbi and G. Levi, 'The Socio-Economic Rift in Israel', position paper, No.21, Jerusalem, 2000 (Hebrew).
69. N. Rouhana, *Palestinian Citizens in an Ethnic Jewish State*, New Haven, CT, 1997, p.86.
70. M. Al-Haj, *Education, Empowerment, and Control: The Case of the Arabs in Israel*, Albany, NY, 1995; E. Podeh, *The Arab–Israeli Conflict in Israeli History Textbooks, 1948–2000*, Westport, CT, 2002.
71. Ichilov, 'Differentiated Civics Curriculum and Patterns of Citizenship Education'.
72. Parekh, 'Discourses on National Identity'.
73. M. Al-Haj, 'Education for Democracy in Arab Schools: Problems and Challenges', in O. Ichilov (ed.), *Citizenship Education in Democracy*, Ramat-Gan, 1993, pp.23–43 (Hebrew).
74. Amadeo *et al.*, *Civic Knowledge and Engagement*.
75. Ichilov, *Citizenship Orientations of 11th Grade Students and Teachers*.
76. M. Bar-Lev, 'Graduates of Yeshiva High Schools in Israel: Between Tradition and Modernity', Ph.D. dissertation, Bar-Ilan University. 1977 (Hebrew); E. Don-Yehiya, 'Hannukkah and the Myth of the Maccabees in Zionist Ideology and Israeli Society', *Jewish J. of Sociology*, Vol.34, No.1 (1992), pp.5–23.
77. Center for Monitoring the Impact of Peace, *Arabs and Palestinians in Israeli Textbooks*, September 2000, available at www.edume.org.

The Political–Military Complex: The IDF's Influence Over Policy Towards the Palestinians Since 1987

YORAM PERI

For many years, theoreticians studying civil–military relations held that an 'instrumental military' model obtains – and ought to obtain – in democracies, i.e. that the professional military must be detached from politics and subject to the control of the political echelon. Israel's case calls this assumption into question, and shows that in a democracy facing continuous war, the military is likely to be a significant political force in its own right. This is becoming increasingly common in the new era of warfare, which is characterized by limited conflicts and low intensity wars.

In the present article, I will describe the political–military complex which existed in Israel in the 1990s. After presenting the theoretical problem, I will explain how the Israel Defense Forces (IDF) adopted a policy which supported arriving at a peace agreement with the Palestinians, and then I will discuss the means used by the military in its political activity and the ways in which it pursued its agenda, even to the point of a conflict between the IDF and the political echelon during the Netanyahu government's term in office.

The failure of the summer 2000 peace talks, and the eruption of the second intifada led the IDF to adopt a hard-line policy of war against

Yoram Peri is a professor of political sociology and communication in the Department of Communication at Tel-Aviv University, and head of the Haim Herzog Institute for Media, Politics and Society.

the Palestinian Authority and its leader Arafat. The IDF continued to play an active role in policy making, just as it had done throughout the peace process. On this occasion as well, a political crisis dragged the IDF into political action, and, just as before, this served to underline inadequacies in civilian oversight of the IDF.

In both eras – both in its efforts at attaining peace, and in its war against the Palestinians – the fundamental characteristics of the IDF's structure, the character of the officer corps, and the latter's approach towards power- and policy-related issues were manifest. The paper concludes with an analysis of the fraught topic of civil control over the military and political–military relations in an era of limited warfare.

THE GEO-STRATEGIC CHANGE OF THE 1990s

A series of events in the international arena in the late 1980s brought about a revolutionary change in Israel's geo-strategic position. Locally, these consisted of the intifada of September 1987, and the dramatic change in the PLO's policy in 1988 when it adopted a policy of recognizing Israel's right to exist side-by-side an independent Palestine. The collapse of the Soviet Union and the end of the Cold War resulted in Syria losing the protection of its superpower umbrella, without which it is incapable of waging war against Israel. Consequently, Syria began to change its international orientation, and in 1991 it joined coalition forces in the war against Iraq. The US-led coalition's success in that war, and the severe blow to Iraq, substantially decreased the possibility that a strong northern front against Israel might be formed. Israel's southern border, with Egypt, had of course already been a peaceful border for a dozen years.

An additional change in the geo-strategic situation concerned the perceived threat from Arab states. The peace with Egypt since 1979; the behind-the-scenes cooperation with Jordan's King Hussein; the PLO's acceptance of the 'two states for two peoples' formula; Syria's diminished power along with signs that Syria had changed course in its policy towards the US and Israel; all of these decreased the foreseeable threat to Israel from its immediate, 'first circle' neighbours. At the same time, Israeli intelligence services perceived an increased threat from Iran, Iraq and Libya; a greater capability – as the Iraqi missile strike had shown – of these 'second circle' states to reach Israel's home front; and the accelerated development of weapons of mass destruction in 'second circle' states.

The IDF reached an unambiguous conclusion from this assessment: in order to enhance preparedness for a possible confrontation with 'second circle' states, Israel would need to reach a political accommodation with its 'first circle' neighbours, even at the cost of territorial assets. At IDF headquarters in Tel Aviv, the idea of a ten-year 'window of opportunity' gained currency, referring to the period of time by which the 'second circle's' military build-up would probably be complete, and during which Israel would probably be able to position itself better strategically with respect to the 'first circle'. Further, the failure of the war in Lebanon (notwithstanding Israel having, for the first time in its history, conquered a substantial part of an Arab capital); and the lesson drawn from the intifada – the high price extracted from Israel as a consequence of its holding on to occupied territories – made it clear that 'Israel cannot enforce peace accords it favours [contingent on] the defeat or conquest of the Arab states. This is an unpleasant state of affairs, but it is how things stand'.[1]

Israel's political leadership during this period found it difficult to assimilate the cumulative significance of these changes, and remained trapped in ideological constraints. Under US pressure, Israel's government agreed to join the Madrid peace talks, but Prime Minister Yitzhak Shamir made it clear that Israel's negotiating principles had not changed.[2] The IDF, on the other hand, did understand that Israel's new geo-strategic situation had far-reaching implications for the state's security, and urged that Israel's negotiating position reflect the new circumstances. IDF Intelligence Division Chief Amnon Lipkin-Shahak stated in his 1989 annual assessment, that the PLO was the force directing the intifada. Shahak was accused of straying into politics and there were even calls for his dismissal.

The IDF drew a further conclusion from the intifada. In the face of calls to crush the Palestinian uprising, IDF chief of staff Dan Shomron announced that the military would be unable to do so, since the means required for crushing it would violate both the norms prevailing in Western democracies generally, and in Israeli society specifically. By publicly acknowledging its own limitations with respect to solving the Palestinian problem, the IDF in effect situated itself on the left within the new political discourse that arose in the wake of the intifada.[3]

During the course of the 1980s, the IDF's security doctrine began to change as well. The pounding suffered by the military during the Yom Kippur war brought about the realization that the era of saturated war theatres had ended. The alternative was the adoption of a doctrine which would facilitate a high capacity for hitting enemy targets without direct battlefield engagement. The site of friction, the result of manoeuvring, would be increasingly determined by technological factors. The code name for this new doctrine was 'a small, smart army', the benefits of which the war in Afghanistan (2002) and especially the war in Iraq (2003) demonstrated spectacularly. This revolutionary change was supposed to begin at the end of the 1980s due to the massive budgetary resources that became available as a result of the peace with Egypt. The latter peace was increasingly referred to in IDF documents as a 'strategic asset'.[4]

In the IDF's new assessment of Israel's security policy, a conception gained currency according to which the relative strategic value of the Occupied Territories diminished, while at the same time changes in the external environment made peace more likely. The IDF came to realize that it would be worthwhile ceding territory in order to change the status quo and to attain a political agreement with Syria, Jordan and the Palestinians. An additional consideration, of a different type, figured in the IDF's assessment: the judgement that Israeli civilian society had tired of the continuous war effort; that there had been a decline in the traditional will of Israelis to be mobilized indefinitely in an unceasing war; and that a significant change in attitude towards the military and towards military service had taken hold.[5]

At the beginning of the 1990s, the IDF began marketing its new security doctrine to the political branch, the Likud government headed by Shamir. The man most representative of this process was the head of the IDF's intelligence section, Major General Uri Sagi. In his 1991 annual assessment, Sagi told the government that:

> Syrian tactical flexibility had prepared the ground and had led to the most recent significant change, at the core of which was a willingness to engage in direct negotiations with Israel within the framework of a peace summit ... In 1991, there is a low threat of an Arab-provoked general confrontation ... [On the other hand] freezing the political process is likely to plant the seeds of the next military confrontation, even if the latter will not take place in the foreseeable future.[6]

This was a very courageous act on the part of the incoming head of the intelligence section, who knew very well that Defence Minister Moshe Arens and Prime Minister Shamir were the leading proponents of the inflexible ideological line within the Likud. But Sagi's assessment was not merely his own private analysis: it expressed, in fact, the view held by the IDF's top leadership. Moreover, in acting as he did, Sagi was operating within the distinctive Israeli norm pertaining to political–military relations. Before proceeding with a characterization of the IDF's political activity in the 1990s with respect to the Palestinians, it is worth briefly discussing that norm and the debate surrounding it.[7]

THE POLITICAL-MILITARY COOPERATION NORM

For almost 30 years, researchers of civil–military relations argued that the Israeli case refuted Harold Lasswell's classic thesis, according to which a state existing in a state of constant war will become, inevitably, a Garrison State. The reason for the Israeli case, they claimed, lay in the quality of the country's institutional arrangements.[8] What explained the Israeli case, according to all of these scholars, was the IDF's identity as a citizen army: the IDF reflects the 'mosaic' from which Israeli society is comprised; the early retirement of officers prevents the formation of a closed military caste; the reserve duty requirement has the effect of weaving the military into the civil system, and prevents the military's alienation from that system; and the military way of life is influenced by the civilian way of life and is not different from it. In sum, it is the existence of permeable boundaries between the civilian sector of society and the military sector, which engenders civil–military harmony in Israel. Contrary to the predictions of the Garrison State thesis, Israeli society is not militarized but, on the contrary, the army is civilianized.[9]

In the 1990s, an alternative school of thought arose among scholars of Israeli society. Proponents of this alternative, radical analysis argued that the positivist research method dominant in military sociology, and the Zionist leanings of researchers, had led to flawed conclusions with respect to the Israeli case. What united the radical researchers was their agreement that Israel's existence in a constant state of war was neither an externally imposed given, nor a state of affairs that had been successfully dealt with by Israeli society without damage to the latter's democratic character. The Israeli case, they claimed, was not a case of the military's civilianization, but rather of civil society's militarization at the hands of the political elite and the state's apparatus, as part of the latter's attempt to use the war and the military to bring about, and then to preserve, their ethno-national supremacy. Put simply, Israel had not remained Athens, but had become Sparta.[10]

At the core of cognitive militarism, according to Baruch Kimmerling, was the principle of using force as the sole instrument for solving external problems, 'a conception according to which there are no alternatives in the political and social world to this approach which is presented as "pragmatic", rational and necessary for survival'.[11]

The claim that the IDF's character as a citizen army – and the existence of permeable boundaries between the military sector and the political sector – resulted in a clear chain of command between the highest ranks of the civilian authority on the one hand, and the military authority subordinate to it on the other, warrants extensive analysis. According to that conception, Israel is an instance of the 'instrumental military model', meaning that the military is professional, national and supra-political, acts purely out of professional considerations and is extra-ideological. Most importantly, according to that conception, the IDF serves as an instrument for executing policy formulated and dictated by the political branch. This conception constitutes part of the hegemonic position of the Israeli political–military elite.[12]

I wish to argue here that the Israeli case is distinctive, and should be called a 'political–military partnership'. It is a symbiotic model, in which the heads of the military cooperate closely with top political leaders in several areas, including the 'policy sphere', i.e., the decision making level.[13] While, legally, the instrumental norm remains and the politicians formally make the decisions in actuality, the professional officers' corps is intimately involved in the policy making process as an equal partner.

In the political–military partnership model, the actors participating in the game are not officers subordinate to their political bosses, but rather one coalition of officers and politicians competing against another coalition of officers and politicians. The question facing Israel during the 1991 Gulf War, whether or not to retaliate to the Iraqi missile offensive, serves as an illustrative example of this model. The head of the air force Major General Avihu Bin-Nun, along with the defence minister, Moshe Arens, argued that Israel must retaliate. The head of the IDF's Intelligence Division Major General Amnon Lipkin-Shahak and the chief of staff, Lieutenant General Dan Shomron, as well as the prime minister, for their part believed that Israel should not operate without US consent and potentially jeopardize the progress of coalition forces in their war against Iraq. In the event, the latter view prevailed.

The political–military partnership model arose in Israel due to the constant state of war. It constituted Israel's unique answer to the Garrison State dilemma. Though Israel did not become Sparta, and the military did not seize power, neither can Israel be called Athens, since the constant state of war engenders constraints on its democratic system. Throughout Israel's existence, the power of the military sector, relative to that of the political sector, has varied within this symbiotic model, and the 1990s saw the beginnings of a shift in the balance of power. One of the central factors contributing to the shift was the constant political crisis as a result of the Israeli political system's inability to 'deliver the goods' and to deal effectively with Israel's central problem since 1967, the occupied territories and relations with the Palestinians. Another factor contributing to the military's enhanced status was the change in the nature of modern warfare.[14]

THE IDF'S POLITICAL ARM

From the beginning of the 1990s, the IDF began promoting its political conception within the Israeli policy arena. Yitzhak Rabin's appointment as defence minister created a very strong axis, and expressed to the utmost the political–military partnership model. True, Rabin did not want the IDF to be involved in the secret talks that led to the Oslo Accords in 1993, but from the moment the Accords were signed, the military was a central player in the political process. IDF officers participated in actual diplomatic meetings and in influencing public opinion. In all of these activities, the role played by the civilian branch within public service was marginal. Further, it was not the state's civil servants, but rather the political leadership itself, which served as the military officers' interlocutors.

The main military body that dealt with the peace process during the 1990s was the strategic planning division, which was responsible for consolidating the fieldwork done in discussions with the Palestinians, Jordan and Syria. In its offices at the IDF general staff headquarters in Tel Aviv, the relevant data for the various areas of negotiation were processed; the various position papers – from security and border arrangements to unambiguously civilian matters – were prepared. Specialist officers from this division of the military directed the work done in other government offices.

The strategic planning division's involvement in these matters was so extensive that in September 2001, the state comptroller spoke of a serious obstacle to his work: as a result of the advances it had made with respect to political issues, there existed no other body, outside the IDF, capable of providing the political branch with a comprehensive analysis of the various implications of the political–military situation. The military remained the sole instrument capable of being used by the political branch as a political–military planning body. Further, the strategic planning section's full involvement in the political sphere had led to its non-fulfilment of the primary role for which it had been created: serving the general staff in planning the building and organization of Israel's military forces.[15]

The state comptroller's remarks were directed both at the strategic planning division and at the IDF generally, but those bodies ought not to have borne the brunt of the criticism. The strategic planning division's involvement in the political process was a consequence of one of the weaknesses of the Israeli political system: a coalition government which is, in many respects, a federation of ministries, particularly weak with respect to long-term planning, and lacking efficient staff machinery capable of carrying out systematic integrative strategic work.

In addition to this structural weakness, there is another more profound weakness at the political level: the unwillingness of politicians to make clear, resolute decisions regarding territory, out of a fear that the electoral costs of such decisions would be too great. This has resulted in political stagnation since 1967, which persisted even when the peace process began.

> In the course of the peace talks, we were asked to prepare the strategic plans, but there was no willingness on the part of the political branch to tell us explicitly what its territorial policy was. There was no open and frank dialogue with us. We had to estimate, to guess, to predict the intentions of the principals. We also knew that if a political problem arose, they would absolve themselves of responsibility for the documents we were preparing. Indeed, this happened on more than one occasion.[16]

Prime Minister Yitzhak Rabin's personality and work patterns also played a role in determining the extent of the military's involvement in the peace process in the 1990s. Rabin preferred the fieldwork done by IDF officers, which he judged to be experienced and efficient, to the work done by the government bureaucracy. Similar reasons, such as a suspicious nature and a centralized management style, led Prime Minister Barak to act in a similar fashion. Barak leaned more on the small cadre he built up alongside himself, but the latter was comprised overwhelmingly of former military people he knew and trusted.

A short time after Benjamin Netanyahu succeeded Shimon Peres as prime minister in 1996 it became evident just how dependent the political branch was on military personnel. Netanyahu rose to power as an opponent of the Oslo Accords who sought to stop the process of Israel's withdrawal from its strategic assets, and he was critical of the military from the start. He was unmoved by the fact that high-ranking officers supported the peace process, and judged it detrimental that the IDF's high-ranking elite was involved in political affairs. He deemed it unhealthy for IDF officers to interact, at diplomatic meetings and cocktail parties, with adversaries they might meet on the battlefield. Indeed, just after taking office, Netanyahu announced that henceforth only civilians would engage in peace process negotiations. But few months passed before he realized that without the military he lacked knowledge, tools and the ability to conduct these negotiations, and he was forced to bring the military back into the picture.

The Strategic Planning Division's political weight was formed when Israel entered the era of political negotiations after the Yom Kippur War. It acquired the status of an independent division within the General Staff in 1974, and three years later it became involved in the first peace talks with Egypt. By contrast, the Intelligence Division, and especially its analysis unit, had a much longer tradition – which gained strength especially after the territories were captured in 1967 – of critical influence over Israel's foreign policy. The split between the two political camps made it difficult to obtain a majority in support of an initiative-centred policy. The prevailing conception – the assumption, or the claim, that the root of the conflict was external, and that circumstances would change only once change occurred in the Arab world's policies – served to legitimize the lack of initiative on the part of Israeli governments. All that could be done was to track events in the Arab world, to protect against belligerent intentions, and to hope for a day when a willingness on the part of the Arabs to reconcile could be discerned. The body in charge of this monitoring activity was the Intelligence Division of the IDF's General Staff.

The ramifications of this conception was that the IDF Intelligence Division was becoming not only Israel's main information gathering agency, and the main body analyzing Israel's strategic position as well as the centre of strategic and indeed political thinking in Israel's policy making process.

THE IDF'S *MODUS OPERANDI*

Immediately after the signing of the Oslo Accords, Prime Minister Rabin organized the taskforce responsible for negotiations. He appointed Amnon Shahak, the deputy chief of staff, to head the delegation to the negotiations, and major generals were also appointed to head the two subcommittees: Uzi Dayan, the IDF's head of strategic planning, led the military subcommittee while the IDF's coordinator of activities in the occupied territories, Dani Yatom, led the subcommittee for civilian affairs. The preparatory work was done under the strategic planning section's auspices, and the position papers drafted in that section were submitted to the chief of staff for approval, and became his recommendations, which were, in turn, submitted to the political echelon. This pattern remained in place until the final stage of the peace talks at the end of the 1990s.[17]

Benjamin Netanyahu's rise to power in 1996 altered the relationship between the government – which brought about a 180-degree turn away from the policies of the Rabin government – and the military, which wished to continue the peace process. The sharp division over national security policy resulted in Netanyahu's term causing the widest split the IDF had ever seen, between its senior officers and the political echelon above them. Netanyahu's working relations with the IDF's high-ranking officers deteriorated rapidly, and publicly exchanged accusations were the norm throughout his term in office.

The split was so deep as to have brought about, for the first time in the state's history, involvement on the part of military men in the arena of electoral politics. The entry of high-ranking officers into political life on the eve of elections is not a new phenomenon in Israel, but rather one that has occurred since the elections to the first Knesset in 1949. Moreover, since 1973 the norm whereby (almost) every IDF chief of staff, upon retirement from the military, joins political life and usually attains high office has taken root. Still, the events of 1999 were unique. This wave of reserve officers was the largest ever and included more than 100 high-ranking officers, who joined political parties, got involved in election campaigns, volunteered at political party headquarters, etc. Moreover, the officers who retired from the IDF in recent years signed up in support of their two colleagues – two candidates for prime minister, Lieutenant General Barak and Major General Mordecai – with the intention of bringing down the incumbent prime minister, due to their opposition to his defence policy.

Ehud Barak's ascension to office was perceived by the IDF's top echelon as a correction of Netanyahu's deviation from Rabin's defence policy. Chief of Staff Mofaz announced that he would be the first 'Peace Chief of Staff' and the military aided Barak in pressing ahead with the peace process. A series of events – the first of which, the opening of the Wailing Wall tunnel, took place during Netanyahu's term, and the last of which was the collapse of the peace negotiations at Camp David in the summer of 2000 – brought about a shift in the IDF's policy. It then became clear that just as the military had been active in advancing the peace process, it was equally capable of initiating and accelerating action in the opposite direction. Legitimizing military involvement in foreign and defence policy is potentially a double-edged sword.

THE SECOND TURNING POINT: THE EL-AQSA INTIFADA

Though the IDF's highest echelons backed the peace process from the beginning of the 1990s, there was also a group of high-ranking officers who approached it with great scepticism.[18] They cast doubt regarding the genuineness of the changes within the PLO, and believed that Arafat's ostensible peace policy was merely a tactic used in order to obtain the occupied territories. Arafat, they concluded, would not yield, in any negotiating process, on any of the principles he had adhered to over the years: a full Israeli withdrawal from all of the territories; the establishment of a Palestinian state with East Jerusalem as its capital; and the right of return for Palestinian refugees. The wave of violence begun by the Palestinians in September 1996 after the opening of the Wailing Wall tunnel reinforced this pessimistic assessment. Four years afterwards, on the eve of the summit meeting at Camp David, the military's intelligence submitted an unambiguous analysis to Prime Minister Barak: Arafat would not be signing a peace treaty at Camp David; after the collapse of talks, the Palestinian Authority would commence violent confrontation in order to extract further concessions from Israel.

The collapse of the talks, and especially the eruption of the intifada in 2000, strengthened the group opposed to the Barak government's position within the IDF General Staff. Barak's government, for its part, continued negotiating with the Palestinian Authority, while at the same time Barak directed his deputy in the Ministry of Defence, Ephraim Sneh, to prepare for an alternative scenario: incremental negotiation.[19]

These two policies – both the continued negotiations and the plans for a unilateral withdrawal – were perceived as serious slights by the IDF chief of staff, and led to the deterioration of the working arrangement between the prime minister and his chief of staff.

In the course of the year preceding the fall of the Barak government in February 2001, there were significant disagreements between the government and the military regarding defence policy. The military treated the intifada as a war in every respect. The government, on the other hand, though it agreed with the military's assessment that 'a war ought to be fought like a war', continued, at the same time, to engage in political negotiations. That policy was perceived by the military to be incoherent and inconsistent. deputy chief of staff, Major General Moshe (Bougi)

Ya'alon, who had served in the past as the head of the military's intelligence section, and as the head of the IDF Central Region Command, and who had previously supported the peace process, was, in the late 1990s, the most senior officer leading the militant cohort within the General Staff. He did not hesitate to criticize – publicly and in strong terms – the cabinet ministers and politicians who, in his analysis, were damaging the IDF's ability to win battles.

Just as at the beginning of the 1990s the military had shown a willingness to make far-reaching concessions in order to reach a settlement with the Palestinians, at the end of the 1990s it pressed for severe measures to counter the second intifada. The IDF came to the new confrontation with the Palestinians armed with a firm decision not to repeat mistakes it had previously made, both when it had fought Hezbollah in Lebanon, and when it had fought Palestinian militants in the first intifada. The military sought to firmly suppress the intifada by adopting an aggressive approach, causing large numbers of casualties on the Palestinian side, and aimed for a decisive military outcome, even with the unfortunate price of hitting innocent civilians. For this reason, it even gave commanders in the field a substantial room to manoeuvre. The IDF intends to win in this confrontation and it was unwilling to allow the political branch, with the latter's conflicting directives and its other considerations, to diminish the military's victory.

Arik Sharon's term as prime minister, which began in February 2001, was supposed to have brought about harmony between the military and the government, since Sharon had opposed the Oslo Accords, and since his party proposed to deal forcefully with Palestinian militants and the Palestinian Authority. In fact, though, relations between the political and military branches remained damaged even during Sharon's first year in office, which started with Sharon expressing frustration with the military's inability to substantially decrease the number of casualties in Israel, and criticizing the officers' corps for their lack of professionalism and imagination. As time went on, though, criticisms were levelled by the military against the political branch, similar in kind to those that had been levelled against Barak. Divergent and contradictory tendencies were rampant in the national unity government, which limited the scope for action demanded by the military. The prime minister himself navigated between these various tendencies, between demands for restraint and eruptions of excessive retaliation against the Palestinians.

The divergent attitudes towards Arafat were also at the centre of the dispute. The military sought to terminate Arafat's command – they believed he had total control over Palestinian operations, and that he would never be willing to reach a political agreement – and if not to terminate Arafat himself, to at least exile him. The military's advice that the intifada be dealt with severely was rejected a few times before being adopted by the Sharon government after a particularly devastating terrorist attack. This pattern recurred frequently, and in the end led to Operation Defensive Shield during Passover 2002; an operation which involved recapturing territory which had been ceded to the Palestinian Authority; severely weakening it. Arafat himself remained alive, but the Muqata, his command centre and the Authority's headquarters, was almost entirely destroyed, and was placed under siege, with Arafat effectively imprisoned within it.

During the first Sharon government's term in office, relations between the military and political spheres became particularly entangled, since in addition to disputes regarding dealing with the intifada, there was a split of civilian responsibility for security between the prime minister and defence minister. The defence minister's personal dynamic in relation to the military further complicated matters. Mofaz had already been granted a great deal of autonomy under Barak, but Barak's professional seniority was never questioned. The IDF's attitude towards Defence Minister Ben-Eliezer, on the other hand, was one of considerable disrespect, as he had neither held high command during war nor served in prestigious rank in the IDF. Thus a relatively weak defence minister was situated between a political chief of staff on the one hand and an authoritative prime minister on the other. This was a recipe for very bad working relations.

Foreign Minister Shimon Peres' position within the government complicated the picture still more. Not Defence Minister Ben-Eliezer, but rather Foreign Minister Peres, was Sharon's real partner, and as distinct from Ben-Eliezer, who – pressed as he was between the military and the prime minister – was unable to suggest an alternative policy, Peres himself did try to bring about a course of events opposed to Sharon's plan.

Peres was perceived by the chief of staff, the deputy chief of staff and the highest echelons of the military as the main figure punching holes in Israel's armour and preventing the military from succeeding in the war against the intifada. They had militarily squeezed Arafat and perceived him, as a result of their pressure, to be closer than ever to waving a white flag, 'and just then Peres scrambled to get him a stretcher and rescue him'.[20] The bitter debates between the high echelons of the military and the Foreign Ministry took place publicly.[21]

The distinguishing feature of political–military partnership consists of the fact that despite the military's high level of involvement in formulating policy, in the final analysis it acts according to the directives of the political branch. Indeed there have been no cases in which the military radically altered the decisions made by the political branch, or in which it did not do what was asked of it. There nevertheless exists a large amount of space in which to manoeuvre, short of such extreme actions. In the course of 2001, the IDF allowed itself vast interpretative leeway in the implementation of government policy. The following was among the descriptions of this state of affairs: 'The military is dragging its feet in an instance where it did not like the order it was given.'[22] In the meetings held by the Knesset's committee on foreign and defence affairs, a more explicit charge was made, that 'the tail was wagging the dog'.[23] When, for example, a political decision was made to open the airport in the Palestinian town of Dahania, the military implemented it, but at the same time blocked the roads and prevented people from getting in. In another instance still, a brigade commander decided not to comply with an explicit order by the minister of defence himself to open the Adam Bridge over the Jordan River for public passage. When asked why he did not comply, he answered that he would not have sufficient manpower to implement the order.

On a few occasions the prime minister and defence minister spoke publicly about the possibility of firing the chief of staff, but this did not happen and in one case the defence minister took no further step than censuring the chief of staff. In light of the chief of staff's great popularity, it was evident that he would join the political arena after his retirement, and no one wanted to alienate him. Indeed, Mofaz set a precedent in political–military relations in Israel when he was parachuted into the office of defence minister directly from his position as chief of staff, even before the 'cooling off' period mandated by law for officers entering parliamentary careers.

A DEBATE: PEACE FROM A POWER-ORIENTED PERSPECTIVE

Throughout the last decade of the twentieth century, the IDF went through an interesting transformation in its attitude towards the Palestinians. It began this period with the adoption of a new policy, which supported achieving a political agreement with the Palestinians in exchange for territorial concessions and the establishment of a Palestinian state. By so doing, the military enabled the governments of Rabin, Peres and Barak to advance the peace process and was itself a power base for the Israeli peace camp at the end of the decade. At the beginning of the first decade of the twenty-first century, on the other hand, the military had become the most powerful interest group in the policy arena supporting the adoption of a policy of offensive war against the Palestinian Authority; of militarily ending the intifada; and of terminating Arafat's command. There was, to be sure, a good fit between Prime Minister Sharon's policies and those of the military, but the military was not merely an instrument for the implementation of policy: it was, rather, an active partner in the formulation of policy and in the marketing of policy within the political sphere.

The change in policy did not arise out of a personnel change in the military's highest echelons. As had been the case in the past, so too in the 1990s there were also officers with emphatic ideological views (for example, Brigadier General Effi Eitam, who upon his release from the IDF became the head of the National Religious Party, was an example of a man of rightist religious faith, whereas Major General Ami Ayalon, head of the navy and then of the General Security Service (GSS), expressed dovish positions). In the final analysis, the vast majority of officers were, in the words of a knowledgeable veteran observer of the IDF, 'dawks' or 'hoves'.[24]

What characterized the vast majority of officers was that throughout the 1990s they acted according to the accepted tradition of the IDF, out of an approach that was pragmatic and practical rather than ideological, and which considered the requirements of the reality on the ground; they assessed that reality, of course, using the traditional conceptual frameworks they found congenial. The shift that occurred in the IDF's policy during the course of the 1990s was thus a reaction to what it characterized as a change in the strategic reality. However, beyond the policy shift itself, there is the larger question regarding the IDF's political activity, meaning the activity not of individual officers, but of the military as an organization. Did the IDF as a social institution conceive of the conflict differently than the civilian system? Were its officers fundamentally different, in their political worldview, from civilians, bureaucrats and politicians?

A deep analysis of the IDF's policies throughout the peace process shows that even when it strategically endorsed a political settlement with the Palestinians, the military expressed reservations about particular measures that it judged excessively concessive and likely to endanger security interests. Put differently, the IDF preferred the more stringent alternative, which promised broader margins for security, to taking military risks even when the latter might have yielded some political gains. For that reason, it also preferred concrete, tangible arrangements that could be clearly viewed, over principles, declarations or dealing with societal or symbolic issues.

Notwithstanding the shift that took place in the IDF's security doctrine in the 1980s, the adoption of a peace-oriented conception was not the result of a paradigm shift. The military's support of peace settlements was the product neither of its adopting the ideological left's basic perspective – according to which the Israeli–Palestinian conflict is a struggle between two national movements, both of which are just – nor of a newfound scepticism regarding the legitimacy of continuing the occupation. Officers who underwent a conceptual change in the late 1980s did not begin to think, as the majority of Peace Now's supporters did, that the Jewish settlements in the occupied territories were an intrinsically negative phenomenon, harming chances for peace.

Assessments of the Israeli–Palestinian conflict and the ways it might be solved continued being made by the IDF in terms of a *realpolitik* paradigm, a power-oriented politics. This is a perspective that views peace not as a primary goal in itself, but first and foremost as a means for attaining security. This is almost a reversal of the classic Clausewitzian formulation, as peace is understood to be the continuation of war by other means. For this reason, the officers showed relatively little interest in the economic agreements that were supposed to create, for the Palestinians, an infrastructure and a stake in maintaining peace. For the same reason, they also did not invest their efforts in the area of preventing incitement to violence, or in education to promote coexistence, as compared to their detailed involvement with security arrangements even for the least important hills and valleys. Their explanation for this is usually: 'our responsibility is to deal first and foremost with security arrangements'. But do not economic development, and education for coexistence, contribute substantially to security? The IDF's tendency, as an organization, has been to attach relatively little weight to those areas.[25]

The shift in the IDF's security conception that began at the end of the 1980s was compatible, in this respect, with its military culture, a culture of 'conservative innovation'.[26] In the final analysis, the willingness of Israel's political–military leadership to grant the Palestinian leadership territorial and political benefits arose out of an expectation that in exchange Israel would be more secure – that the Palestinian leadership would have an incentive to protect Israel from potential terrorist activity by militant Palestinian organizations such as Hamas, Islamic Jihad, Hezbollah and radical leftist groups.

Throughout the peace process, the extent to which the Palestinian leadership succeeded in fulfilling that task was the main criterion by which the Israeli negotiators assessed the Palestinian side. The Palestinian Authority's failure to do so – in particular during a few periods characterized by frequent suicide bombings, in 1996 as in 2001 – was, for the Israelis a sign that the Authority was not in fact interested in achieving real peace. The Authority's claim that it was unable to fully confront militant factions was treated as an evasion of responsibility. On the other hand, the fact that since the signing of the Oslo Accords in 1993 the Palestinian population had not attained tangible benefits (such as a settlement freeze or accelerated economic development) was not seen, in Israel's hegemonic military thinking, as relevant.

During the course of the peace negotiations, Israeli army officers were trapped in a vicious circle. Notwithstanding their willingness to make territorial concessions, they sought wide security margins, both in the interim agreements and in the final status negotiations (about such matters as the monitoring of border crossings; control of Palestinian air space; the continued existence of Israeli bases and military deployment areas within the independent Palestinian state, and so on). These demands were seen by the Israelis as essential for guaranteeing security in the event that the peace treaty would not be complied with. But the fact of these demands was perceived by the Palestinians as evidence of Israel's desire to continue ruling them, a state of affairs in which a genuine reconciliation between the Palestinian people and their strong neighbour would be impossible.

One of the negotiators, Abed al-Razek, explained this matter during a meeting of the security committee in 1995:

> You have a narrow understanding of the meaning of security. You must understand that the answer lies in a change of the psychological atmosphere. If you force us to do something, Arafat will not be able to abide it. If you appoint yourselves judges of what's right and what's wrong, you'll destroy the good will that exists between our people and us. The way to bring about a radical change in the atmosphere, which, in the end, will serve both sides' interests, is to create a security partnership.[27]

An alternative strategy to that adopted by the Israeli delegation to the talks would not, of course, have ignored security considerations, but would have made more of an attempt to 'get into the shoes' of the other side, to understand the various elements forming the other side's conceptions, its fears, motivations and its personal and collective needs. Such a strategy would have tried to diffuse some of the security threats facing Israel by understanding and addressing those needs. The importance of military power would not be denied by such an approach, but a more balanced package – preserving Israel's military capability on the one hand, but with some defusing of the adversary's negative disposition taking place at the same time – would be presented. Israel would be satisfied, in this alternative scenario, with a lower level of damage to the adversary's capacity to threaten Israel, in exchange for a more substantial reduction in the adversary's motivation to threaten Israel.

Another factor that influenced the military's policy during the course of the peace negotiations was the continuing occupation. The IDF, which had played the role of unelected ruler for over a generation, had difficulty treating the Palestinians, all of a sudden, as equal partners. The long occupation had led to an attitude of lordship, and the IDF's officers found it difficult, in the words of one of the talks' participants, 'to change the disk'.[28]

The conduct of soldiers in the field also influenced the course the negotiations took. The sense of superiority that an occupying army cultivates, the opacity of a bureaucratic system which is not publicly examined, soldiers' real fear for their lives, and even instances during which some of them lost self-control and released their anger, all had their effects on the military's conduct, even though it wished to operate on a high ethical level and believed that it was practising an 'enlightened occupation'.[29] The IDF's operations as part of the war on terror also had an effect contrary to the spirit dictated by the peace initiative. The use of air force planes against civilian structures in Gaza led to the recalling of Egypt's ambassador to Israel in 2001, a consequence that was not anticipated when the operation was planned by military headquarters and by the government. Similarly, operations by low-ranking officers or soldiers, such as shots fired at the convoy or the house of security chiefs in Gaza and the West Bank Muhammad Dahlan's and Jibril Rajoub, might have influenced the latter leaders' perceptions regarding Israeli intentions to a far greater extent than what was said by government ministers and major generals at the negotiating table.[30]

But an attempt to understand how the IDF operates in this sphere also requires reference to the conservative nature of military organizations *per se*. When the military arrives at a crossroads, where it has to choose between following an old, known path and switching to a new, untested path characterized by a higher degree of uncertainty, it is generally averse to the risk involved in switching. Chief of Staff Mordechai Gur was reluctant about the peace initiative with Egypt, Chief of Staff Barak was reluctant about the Oslo Accords with the Palestinians and Chief of Staff Mofaz was anxious about a unilateral withdrawal from Lebanon. A majority within the highest echelons of the army might be politically moderate, and might support a course of compromise and dialogue, but as a body, as a collective, the military organization and those leading it are apprehensive about the risks associated with the adoption of a new path. For that reason, though it supported the political agreements of the 1990s, the IDF had difficulty internalizing the full impact of these changes, and acting accordingly.

CONCLUSION: CIVILIAN SUPERIORITY IN LIMITED CONFRONTATIONS

The Israeli case, which showed the great breadth and depth of the IDF's involvement in determining foreign policy, has context-transcending relevance. The change in the character of warfare in the present era, the shift from wars between states to intra-state conflicts and limited confrontations, brought, in its trail, a shift from the traditional relationship between the political echelon and the military echelon, which raises an essential and theoretical question not yet grappled with by theories in this field. Kemp and Hudlin have written that 'The key to good military–society relations is the respect the army exhibits for the principle of civilian control'.[31] This principle consists of two parts: (1) that civilians will determine political ends, while the military will determine the means for their attainment; and (2) that civilians will determine where the line distinguishing ends from means will be drawn. 'In other words, the military ought to carry out policy, not to determine it.'[32]

The story of the IDF and its relations with the Palestinians shows how simplistic this formula is. Even if the military does not wish to determine political outcomes, do not its intelligence branch's evaluations influence politicians' decisions when the latter formulate political ends? Equally, even if politicians do not wish to get involved in determining the means used to implement policy, can they in fact leave that determination solely to the military itself, knowing as they do that the means used in military operations have a substantial impact on the overall political results? And is the IDF's policy that political contact with the Palestinian Authority must not take place during the course of the war a political or a military policy? The hybrid situation in effect since the start of the intifada has rendered old distinctions somewhat simplistic.

The war Israel has fought against the Palestinians since 2000 is an instance of the new type of warfare, sub-conventional warfare that, at its essence, is political warfare. The war is being fought with limited use of military force, in civilian areas, in the heart of civilian populations. It is not meant to conquer territory or to destroy military units; its aims are first and foremost to break the Palestinians' will to resist, to win the hearts of the insurgent Palestinian population, and to win the battle over perception of the conflict, both at home and in world opinion. The IDF realized late in the day what the full significance of the new sort of warfare was, and developed the doctrine of 'limited confrontation' or 'the struggle over perception'.

In this type of confrontation, self-restraint and the limited use of force are more effective than an overwhelming use of force. The use of excessive force (e.g. the use of helicopters) will bring criticism from the world community; will cause random casualties among defenceless civilians; and will raise doubts at home regarding the justice of the war. The use of excessive force will only increase the motivation among some Palestinians to join the army of suicide bombers. In low-intensity conflict it is very difficult to preserve the right of 'operational autonomy', generally granted in the tactical realm – in the conventional division of labour between civilians and officers[33] – to the military in the field. In this new type of warfare, there is a blurring of the boundaries between the political and the military echelons, 'and there is an increasing interpenetrability of civilian and military spheres, both structurally and culturally'.[34] It is hardly surprising that this state of affairs invites friction between the two spheres.

Good, harmonious relations between the society and the military tend to produce a pattern not of supervision but rather of civilian *direction* of the military.[35] This less authoritative pattern can fit relations of the 'political–military partnership' type when a nation in arms is experiencing calm. But just as there is a general tendency, in wartime, for the military branch's power, within the balance of power equation, to increase (as was the case in France during World War I, or in the US during the Cold War), when this happens to a military which has a partnership relationship with the political branch, in time of war the military might cross the boundaries of legitimate activity to the point of threatening the democratic process.

In Israel, at the beginning of the twenty-first century, we have seen the combination of factors and conditions which brought about a relative weakening of civil control over the military, and a vast degree of military influence over policy. In the policy arena, these factors are: the dependence of politicians on the military alone due to the latter's monopoly of data relevant to the peace process; a relatively weak institutional framework for civilian control, which leans more on the internalization of the principle of civilian control than on strong legal mechanisms; the absence of bodies to act as coordinators between the military and political branches; and, first and foremost, the continuing political crises and the unwillingness on the part of politicians to take firm decisions regarding the fate of the State of Israel.

These are weaknesses of the mechanisms that are supposed to insulate the army from politics (e.g. the imposition of impediments to quick transitions from military careers into political life); a traditional resistance, on the part of the military, to the formation of checks and balances on military power, such as the National Security Council; a command style that cultivates a relatively high degree of autonomy in the various military ranks while at the same time it enables the civilian branch to deal directly with these ranks, even at the cost of damaging consistency within the command structure.

The fact that the IDF is a citizen army with a relatively low degree of corporatism allowed it, historically, to preserve its civilian character and gave it many advantages. But the very same attributes might, in certain circumstances, be liabilities. In a society as divided as Israeli society is today, in conditions of long term sub-conventional war, confrontation between the political and military branches is difficult to prevent. We can expect, in such circumstances, that the military will exceed the boundaries of permissible conduct for a military organization in an enlightened democratic state, while the political system, itself in crisis, will be unable to correct the situation.

NOTES

1. Yitzhak Rabin, speech on 10 June 1991, 'After the Gulf War: Israel's Defence Policy', *Yitzhak Rabin and Israel's National Security*, Ramat Gan, 1996 (Hebrew).
2. Eytan Bentzur, *The Road to Peace Passes Through Madrid*, Tel Aviv, 1997, p.114 (Hebrew).
3. Yoram Peri, 'After-word', in Yitzhak Rabin, *The Rabin Memoirs*, Berkeley, CA, 1996, pp.339–380, for a discussion of other political ramifications that the intifada had for Israel's military political elite.
4. Interview with the head of the IDF strategic planning section. This was one in a series of over two dozen interviews for a research project under the auspices of the US Institute of Peace. A more detailed version of the research, and a more detailed list of sources, appears in Yoram

Peri, 'The Israeli Military and Israel's Palestinian Policy', in *Peaceworks* (US Institute of Peace series), No.47 (2002), pp. 66.
5. Eliot Cohen, *Supreme Command*, New York, 2002. See also the declaration made by IDF Chief of Staff Lipkin-Shahak at the ceremony held in commemoration of the one-year anniversary of Yitzhak Rabin's assassination, *Haaretz* (Israeli daily), 31 October 1996.
6. Uri Sagi, *Lights in the Fog*, Tel Aviv, 1998 (Hebrew).
7. The comprehensive terms 'IDF' and 'IDF top leadership', as they appear in the present article, refer to a small group among the IDF's high-ranking officers who determine the military organization's position with respect to defence and political affairs. First and foremost among these is the chief of staff, whose status in Israel is much greater than that of the chairman of the Joint Chiefs of Staff in the US. The group also includes the deputy chief of staff; the head of military intelligence; the head of the research unit within the intelligence section; the head of the military's strategic planning section, and two or three additional high-ranking officers.
8. Amos Perlmutter, *Military and Politics in Israel: Nation-Building and Role Expansion*, London, 1969; Dan Horowitz, 'Is Israel a Garrison State?', *Jerusalem Quarterly*, Vol.4 (1997), pp.58–75.
9. Dan Horowitz and Moshe Lissak, *Troubles in Utopia: The Overburdened Polity of Israel*, Albany, NY, 1989.
10. The most eloquent exponent of this school of thought, Baruch Kimmerling, summarized matters thus: 'a militarism did indeed develop in Israel, which mutated occasionally in its form and intensity, to the point where it became one of the society's organizing principles'. See Baruch Kimmerling, 'Militarism in Israeli Society', *Theory and Criticism*, Vol.4 (1993), pp.123–40 (Hebrew).
11. Baruch Kimmerling, 'Militarism in Israeli Society', p. 131.
12. Former Prime Minister Ehud Barak repeated this thesis in his lecture as part of a daylong conference on political–military relations sponsored by Tel Aviv University's Jaffe Centre for Strategic Studies, 17 March 2003. An opposing view, much more compatible with the present article's analysis, was presented by Major General (Res.) Uzi Dayan, who had been deputy chief of staff, head of the military's strategic planning section, and head of the National Security Council.
13. The term, 'policy sphere' should be understood as distinct from the 'public sphere'. The former is the more important sphere, in which political decisions are made, whereas public discourse occurs in the public sphere. See L.W. Bennet and R.M. Entman, *Mediated Politics, Communication in the Future of Democracy*, New York, 2000.
14. Dana Priest, *The Mission*, New York, 2003.
15. State comptroller's annual report No.52a. The main parts of the unclassified portion of the report were published in *Haaretz*, 28 September 2001.
16. Interview with the head of the IDF strategic planning section, Major General Shlomo Yanai.
17. Gilad Sher, *Within Touching Distance*, Tel Aviv, 2001, p.264 (Hebrew).
18. Heading that group were the directors of the research unit within the IDF intelligence section, first Brigadier General Binyamin Amidror, followed by his successor, Brigadier General Amos Gilboa.
19. I.e., an interim agreement or a unilateral withdrawal by Israel from some territory on the West Bank in order to decrease the intensity of the confrontation between Israel and the Palestinians. See Sher, *Within Touching Distance*.
20. Amir Oren, 'The Way to Infinity', *Haaretz*, 28 September 2001.
21. On one occasion, in September 2001, 'senior officials' in the Foreign Ministry felt it necessary to make clear to the IDF that 'it had better recognize that there is a government in Jerusalem', *Yedioth Ahronoth*, 28 September 2001.
22. Ofer Shelach, *Yedioth Ahronoth*, 22 December 2000.
23. Sima Kadmon, *Yedioth Ahronoth*, 18 May 2001. A particularly sharp, though characteristic, example of the relational dynamic between the political and military branches, and one which indicated the amount of leeway the chief of staff had granted himself, occurred in December 2000, when President Clinton presented his peace proposals. Mofaz expressed staunch opposition to the proposals, calling them 'a threat to the state' (Sher, *Within Touching Distance*, p.367). The important point is that Mofaz expressed his staunch opposition to the proposals publicly, in the media, before they had even been discussed in the cabinet. See Amos Harel, *Haaretz*, 29 December 2000, and Ze'ev Schiff, *Haaretz*, 31 December 2000.

24. Amir Oren writes: 'The highest echelons of the IDF, GSS, and the Mossad are situated roughly at the "middle belt" of Israeli society, from Dan Meridor on the Right to Yossi Sarid on the Left, and neither with Benjamin Netanyahu and Ariel Sharon in the Right wing, nor with Shimon Peres and Yossi Beilin on the Left wing'. *Haaretz*, 6 January 2002.
25. An interview with the director general of the Foreign Ministry, Eytan Bentzur, July 2001. This point was made repeatedly in several interviews I conducted with high-ranking officers.
26. Eliot A. Cohen, Michael J. Eisenstadt and Andrew J. Bacevich, *Knives, Tanks and Missiles: Israel's Security Revolution*, Washington, DC, 1998.
27. Uri Savir, *The Process*, Tel Aviv, 1998, p.193 (Hebrew).
28. Uri Savir writes: 'Those who had ruled the Palestinians were now being asked to transfer their authority to their "subordinates," and this caused a conceptual and emotional crisis for them. When we dismantled the occupation ... there were many among us for whom it was very difficult to change.' (*The Process*, p.237.).
29. One example of this was the daily delays and humiliations at checkpoints, even of Palestinian leaders with VIP documents, who were supposed to be able to move unhindered as they travelled to negotiation sessions; this repeatedly soured the atmosphere around the negotiating tables. See for example Saeb Erakat's account, in an interview with Amira Hass, *Haaretz*, 26 January 2001, or Abu Ala's account in Savir, *The Process*, p.245.
30. Various IDF operations in the field were explained away as cases of misunderstanding, soldiers' errors and the like, but nevertheless led to accusations that the IDF was acting without regard to decisions made in the political sphere. See Uzi Benziman, *Haaretz*, 1 June 2001.
31. Kenneth W. Kemp and Charles Hudin, 'Civil Supremacy over the Military: Its Nature and Limits', *Armed Forces and Society*, Vol.19, No.1 (1992), pp.7–26 at p.8.
32. Douglas L. Bland, 'A Unified Theory of Civil–Military Relations', *Armed Forces and Society*, Vol.26, No.1 (1999), pp.7–25; and Charles J. Dunlap, 'The Origins of the American Military Coup of 2012', *Parameters* (Winter 1992/1993), pp.7–25.
33. Bland, 'A Unified Theory of Civil–Military Relations'.
34. Charles C. Moskos, 'Towards a Postmodern Military: The United States as a Paradigm', in Charles C. Moskos, John Allen Williams and David R. Segal (eds.), *The Postmodern Military*, New York and Oxford, 2000, p.2.
35. Bland, 'A Unified Theory of Civil–Military Relations', emphasis added.

On the Need for a Constitution

MEIR SHAMGAR

GENERAL PRINCIPLES

The legislation of a comprehensive and unified constitutional code, having an elevated and protected status, is an immediate necessity for Israel. This article describes the main contents and hallmarks of a constitution, the constitutional developments of the Israeli system of law and the main reasons underscoring the present need for a constitution in Israel.

A constitution is a statutory enactment having in most cases a theoretically elevated and practically entrenched status which defines the allocation of functions, powers and duties of the different arms and institutions of government, their main spheres of operation and the relationships among themselves and between each of them and the citizens and inhabitants. In many countries the constitution also enumerates and defines, as an essential and most important part of the provisions, the basic human rights protected by it.[1] This last mentioned part of the constitution, which includes the so-called 'Bill of Rights', covers in a number of constitutions not only the basic political and human rights but also the main basic social and economic rights of the citizen. One should add, in this context, that according to several interpretations the enumeration of basic rights is not to be regarded in any case as exclusive. It does not negate the residual existence of a wider range of rights, not included in the Bill, and which are evolving indirectly by way of interpretation, from the rights which are explicitly defined. Some constitutions even refer in their provisions[2] to

Meir Shamgar is a former military advocate general, attorney general, president of the Israel Supreme Court and lecturer in law at the Hebrew University and Tel Aviv University.

this rule of construction. In order to allay any doubts, I should add that this rule of interpretation should not lead to the conclusion that the entire series of definitions of basic freedoms and rights is superfluous. The opposite is true: The enumeration and definition of rights is deemed expedient and even crucial in order to declare and to express explicitly in the constitutional document the existence and meaning of basic human rights and to prevent thereby governmental excesses resulting from the absence of a written definition of rights. The complete lack of a Bill of Rights is apt to release the legislature and its institutions from any duty to respect basic rights in its ordinary legislation and in its governmental practices. Moreover, the existence of defined and written rights creates the legal background for a beneficial and broadening construction of the provisions of the constitution.[3] The existence of definitions of the main basic rights enables the extension, by exegesis or hermeneutics, of the meaning and contents of any given freedom already defined. In order to exemplify this proposition, I venture to put forward as an example the construction that the basic right of 'Human Dignity'[4] can reasonably be interpreted as including the extremely important norm of 'equality' and also the social right 'education'.

It should therefore be regarded as appropriate to lay down in the constitution the definition and the meaning of the basic human rights and to delimit the range and extent of the powers of the authorities accorded by the constitution. The French even found it fitting to underline in the constitution the didactic and practical characteristics of the enumeration of rights by mentioning in the Declaration of Rights of Man and the Citizen of 1789 that the National Assembly had declared these rights so that, *inter alia*:

> This Declaration, perpetually present to all members of the body social, shall be a constant reminder to them of their rights and duties. So that, since it will be possible at any moment to compare the acts of the legislative authority and those of the executive authority with the final end of all political institutions, those acts shall thereby be the more respected.[5]

The constitution is in most cases an enactment having an elevated status in comparison to ordinary primary legislation of the parliament; moreover, ordinary primary legislation is subject to the normative directives and restrictions expressed in the constitutional document. In other words, the constitutional enactment is supreme in order of the relative priority of legislative acts: The constitution is of the highest level; thereafter ranges ordinary parliamentary legislation and, at the third level, secondary legislation, namely regulations and by-laws. Even the absence (as in New Zealand for example), of an institution having the power to review such ordinary legislation, which is amending, contradicting or limiting constitutional provisions or infringing on them, does not deprive the constitutional provisions of their superiority in line of precedence and of their normative (even if only theoretical) supremacy.

Written constitutions are a means to the end of limiting governmental power and, in a democracy, even limiting the power of the elected representatives of the people in parliament.[6] The elevated status of constitutional provisions is created by the inclusion in the constitution of qualitative or quantitative preconditions for the enactment of ordinary legislation which is contradicting or infringing constitutional norms. Such conditions are expressed by the definition of the unique and exceptional situations in which such ordinary legislation can be regarded as constitutional, e.g. conditions in relation to legislation by law (as distinct from that by secondary legislation) which befit the basic norms and principles of the state, designed for a proper purpose and proportional;[7] these are qualitative conditions. The constitutional demand for a special majority in parliament is a quantitative condition.[8]

Such qualitative or quantitative legislative preconditions included in the constitution provide supreme normative principles which delimit the powers of the institutions of government, define the necessary separation of powers and safeguard human freedoms in order to protect the inhabitant from governmental excesses and acts of oppression by the authorities. The elevated status of these normative constitutional principles also prevents their circumvention by unintentional or incidental statutory steps.

The preservation and protection of the principles of liberal democracy and the promotion of their stability and certainty call for their manifest and distinct expression in the supreme constitutional enactment, so that they do not bow to the winds of opportunity or to the passing sentiments and impressions of the legislators or the public. The constitution therefore prevents, *inter alia*, legislation which contradicts basic human rights. The constitutional provisions bind both the parliament adopting them and future legislators. Thereby the rights of the people and the fundamental elements of democracy and the rule of law remain permanent and strong. By obliging the majority to respect the norms, as mentioned above, the rights of the minority are protected and the consciousness and awareness of human rights are promoted and cherished.

The adoption and enforcement of constitutional norms and provisions and their consolidation and codification in one unified constitutional document is generally regarded, especially since World War II, as a vital prerequisite of a democratic system of government. It is moreover accepted as an essential structural component in most states, even if they have not adopted a fully fledged system of democratic rule. In consequence of the above-mentioned attitudes and approaches we witness the development of the readiness to formulate the supreme rules, principles and limitations governing the powers and courses of action of the governmental authorities and to declare publicly, formally and explicitly the basic human rights and freedoms which are the dominating principles that have to be respected by the legislature and all other arms of government. To define the scope of functions of the legislature is, *ipso facto*, to limit power.

The readiness to formulate rules and limitations represented the sound and well-founded recognition of the necessity to safeguard both the principles of liberal democracy and the material rule of law as an essential proposition, by according them the legal status of elevated statutory rules which govern ordinary laws and regulations, prescribe their contents and ensure their universal observance and application.

Earlier we mentioned the need to grant elevated statutory status to the codified norms of democracy. Constitutions both liberate and bind; they provide for a framework of ordered freedom[9] within a set of rules which prevents both majorities and their elected parliamentary representatives from acting against the basic freedom of individuals, minorities, or the definition of the powers of public authorities.

Two additional remarks are important. First, there are a number of states which have laid down constitutional norms in a codified document or in a Bill of Rights without according to them supremacy over ordinary legislation; in other words, their norms are morally and socially binding but do not carry with them the quality and hallmark of legal supremacy (e.g. New Zealand and Finland[10]). It goes without saying that the effectiveness of such constitutional limitations is thereby decreased.

Secondly, the existence of a constitution does not necessarily mean that such a code will achieve its aims as described above and obtain the respect and observance owed to constitutional norms. Some totalitarian states were the progenitors of very advanced verbal promises of freedoms and human rights, but these were in fact disregarded and were accompanied by an atmosphere of public apprehension preventing any demand for their practical enforcement.

The effectiveness of the provisions of a constitution therefore depend to a large extent on the attitude of the people, their awareness of the constant necessity to defend respect for and enforcement of human rights and of the other maxims of democracy, including limitations on governmental powers, comprising the separation of powers. But the laying down of norms in a constitutional code is the logical starting point for the fashioning of public opinion; in other words, without the definitions of rights, duties and functions, the public voice favouring the implementation of the rule of law and of democracy in action lacks the basic criteria and guidelines and remains a voice in the wilderness. The public misses the background of the explicit and defined expression of the constitutional intention and of any statutory clarity.

ISRAEL – THE CONSTITUTIONAL DEVELOPMENTS

The Israeli constitution has been described as an 'emerging constitution'. However, since the accepted use and definition of the word 'constitution' includes constitutions based on unwritten rules and embraces the norms embodied in ordinary laws prescribing constitutional principles, and especially in so-called Basic Laws (part of them do not so far possess an elevated legal status) this description lacks precision. Israel already has in its Basic Laws and judgments of the Supreme Court parts of a constitution possessing components of the above-mentioned categories.

It has further been said that the constitution of Israel is unwritten. There is no constitution which is entirely written or entirely unwritten. A constitution generally regarded as written is in the form of a consolidated document which has special sanctity, but this description is not always exhaustive. A constitution generally regarded as unwritten is one which has evolved on the basis of custom or ordinary laws rather than of written law of special status. In many cases the so-called written constitution is a very complete instrument in which the framers have attempted to arrange for every conceivable contingency in its operation. In other cases the written constitution is composed of a number of fundamental or 'basic' laws which the constitution makers have framed or adopted in order to give as wide a scope as possible to the process of ordinary legislation in the development of the constitution within the framework thus set.

The Israeli constitution is best described as partly written and partly unwritten although there are as yet only a small number of norms of special preferential status from the legislative point of view. The constitutional rules of Israel are included in Basic Laws (so named and of a fundamental character), in ordinary laws including constitutional provisions, in abstract legal norms defined in judgments of the Supreme Court and in customs and practices. The constitution is thus evolutionary in character, exhibiting a gradual organic growth and development, changing from being comprised largely of ordinary laws, norms and customs to constituting, to a large extent, Basic Laws in the general sense of that term.

Because of its gradual growth the Israeli constitution is best understood in the context of its historical development. A review of this development demonstrates that the approach to the creation of a written constitution has been variegated and full of vicissitudes.

The first tentative steps were taken in the Resolution of the UN General Assembly of 29 November 1947, proposing the convening of a Constituent Assembly and the adoption of a constitution and even adumbrating some of its provisions. It may be assumed that regard was had to certain aspects of international law and to the political problems of the immediate occasion. Further developments, however, deprived this first approach of

any, except historical, significance. On 14 May 1948 the Provisional
Council of the State of Israel adopted the Declaration of Independence,
which included *inter alia* a provision that a constitution should be adopted
not later than 1 October 1948.

The Declaration of Independence of 14 May 1948 proclaimed the
establishment of the State of Israel and enunciated the basic conceptual
values of the state. The declaration also established the provisional arms of
government, which were to function until regular authorities were duly
elected in accordance with a constitution that had to be adopted, according
to the explicit wording of the declaration. The declaration stated the aims
and interests of the new state. It provided:

> The State of Israel will be open for Jewish immigration and for the
> ingathering of the Exiles; it will foster the development of the country for
> the benefit of all its inhabitants, it will be based on freedom, justice and
> peace as envisaged by the prophets of Israel; it will ensure complete
> equality of social and political rights to all its inhabitants irrespective of
> religion, race, sex; it will guarantee freedom of religion, conscience,
> language, education and culture; it will safeguard the Holy Places of all
> religions; and it will be faithful to the principle of the Charter of the
> United Nations.

After the establishment of the state, the Supreme Court of Israel ruled in
the *Gubernik* case[11] that the Declaration of Independence did not have the
force of a constitutional legislative enactment. In the eyes of the court, it
rather served as an instrument for the interpretation of the 'spirit of the
laws', namely as an abstract guideline, assisting in the understanding of
the basic aims and goals of the state, its values and concepts, and as
a document relating to 'international recognition'.

Two Basic Laws, enacted in 1992, dealt with a number of basic human
rights, namely human dignity, personal freedom, the right to property and
privacy, and liberty in the choice of occupation. They were amended by the
Knesset in 1994, by the inclusion of the following provision:

> Basic Principles: 1. The basic rights of the individual in Israel are based
> on the recognition of the value of the human being, on the sanctity of his
> life and on his being free, and they shall be respected (or upheld) in the
> spirit of the principles set forth in the Declaration on the Establishment
> of the State of Israel.

In other words, the declaration was formally accorded, by law, the status
of a fundamental and value-loaded guideline, underlying the constitutional
norms which were the statutory cornerstone of our basic human rights.
According to the majority opinion amongst legal authorities, this provision
did not amount to the transformation of the declaration into an integral
part of the written constitution or of a positive law,[12] but, as stated, instead

of such inclusion, the law giver merely recognized the elevated and binding status of the declaration as a spiritual guideline.

The first legislative enactment of the State of Israel, passed in 1948 after the establishment of the state by the Provisional State Council (i.e. the provisional parliament of Israel) was the Rule of Government and Law Ordinance, 1948.[13] According to its provisions, pre-existing law was retained: section 11 of this ordinance provided that the laws in force in Mandatory Palestine on the eve of the establishment of the state on 15 May 1948 would continue to be the law of the land, subject to any enactments of the new independent legislature and subject to such modifications as may result from the establishment of an independent state and its authorities. This meant, in other words, the adoption of the legal concept of 'succession of laws', according to which no legal vacuum remained and existing laws remained in force as long as they were not abolished, changed or amended by legislation of the new independent parliament. The ordinance provided that certain changes would arise automatically, as the inherent result of the establishment of an independent sovereign state.

The legal system of the new state did not include a consolidated comprehensive constitutional statute. It comprised remnants of Ottoman law, British Mandatory law passed before 15 May 1948 by the high commissioner for Palestine (the British head of the Mandatory government), certain Acts of Parliament and Orders-in-Council emanating from London, certain rules of common law and equity and in matters of personal status (marriage, divorce, alimony), the laws of the various religious communities, namely – and as the case may be – Jewish Halachic law, Islamic Sharia law and the canonical law of the various Christian communities (numbering about ten) formerly recognized by the Mandatory government, and in each case applying in relation to the members of such community only.

The Declaration of Independence included, as mentioned, the statement that the duly elected bodies of the state should be instituted 'in accordance with a Constitution which shall be adopted by *the Elected Constituent Assembly* not later than 1 October 1948' [italics added]. Preparations for a constitution were initiated by the provisional authorities even before the state was proclaimed. However, it became very clear that a constitution would not be forthcoming. The reason for this was, first of all, the War of Independence which raged for many months following the establishment of the state after the invasion on 15 May 1948 by the neighbouring Arab countries and the continuing strife with the local Arab habitants. The population was enlisted in the war effort, and thus a 'Constituent Assembly' could not be elected by the date – 1 October 1948 – which had been set out in the declaration. The first elections were held only in January 1949 after the Armistice Agreements.

The religious parties in the Israeli parliament objected to any constitution[14] and harboured apprehensions that certain provisions of religious law (marriage and divorce) would be regarded unconstitutional if contradictory constitutional norms are introduced. But they were not the only sceptics.

In the ongoing debate the then prime minister, David Ben-Gurion,[15] and the members of the Knesset representing his party (Mapai) expressed a negative approach to the immediate materialization of the constitutional task: His arguments were based, *inter alia*, on the fact that at that stage only a small percentage of the Jewish people (less than one million) lived in Israel and the ongoing repatriation by immigration would drastically change the composition and numbers of the population. The passing of a binding constitution at such an early stage, without the participation of the multitudes returning to their homeland, might be regarded as prejudicial. He rather supported the passing of ordinary laws including the necessary provisions for the fashioning of a democratic statehood than the adoption of a constitution. The inherent reason of the opposition by the Labour Party to a constitution was the negative approach to any restriction of parliamentary powers and preference for the British systems of absolute parliamentary supremacy and sovereignty.

But there were additional undercurrents and reasons over and above these mentioned by Ben-Gurion which found their indirect expression or echo in these arguments. Thus one should accord appropriate weight to the misgivings of political parties and their parliamentary representatives in relation to any restriction on the powers of parliament, which would be the normal *sine qua non* of the introduction of any supreme constitutional norm.

Summing all this up one may conclude that the combination of the English tradition, inherent initially in the ordinary Israeli system of law, that denied the need of a supreme law which would be binding on parliament and which would be contrary to the Blackstonian heritage of the absolute powers of parliament, the above-mentioned opposition of the religious parties to any constitution, and the reliance on the sufficiency of the democratic basis of the state in order to safeguard basic human rights were dominant factors in the considerations of most groups opposing in 1949 the adoption of a legally elevated constitutional document. The demand for a constitution was voiced at that time mainly by the right and the centre parties, but they were in the opposition and in a minority.

The government regarded it then as necessary to seek a way out of the deadlock in relation to the drawing up of a constitution. Early in 1949, after the election of the Constituent Assembly, the first law considered by the newly elected Parliamentary Assembly provided for a change in the name of the elected parliamentary body which initially carried the name and mission of a 'Constituent Assembly', and turned it by law into the 'First Knesset'.

This change of name was not a mere matter of semantics; it meant a departure from the initial determination to immediately base the newly established country on a comprehensive written constitutional document, having an entrenched and elevated status.

The compromise of enacting separate Basic Laws, stage by stage, instead of a comprehensive constitution was the solution found in 1950: The initiator of that compromise was a member of the Knesset, Jizhar Harari, and the resolution, adopted by the Knesset on 13 June 1950, still bears his name in the political jargon and is still considered binding. Such was the wording of this parliamentary resolution:

> The first Knesset charges the Constitutional, Legislative and Judicial Committee with the duty of preparing a draft Constitution for the State. The Constitution shall be composed of individual chapters, in such a manner that each of them shall constitute a basic law in itself. The individual chapters shall be brought before the Knesset as the Committee completes its work and all the chapters together will form the Constitution of the State.

Behind this resolution and the reason for its adoption lay the three divergent approaches which had become apparent in the course of the preceding discussions

(a) opposition to any written constitution mainly expounded by Prime Minister Ben-Gurion and the religious parties;

(b) support for the idea of a formal written constitution;

(c) a proposal for a 'chapter by chapter' process by trial and error and the gradual development of written constitutional norms, keeping in line with social, cultural and political developments.

The political powers opposing a constitution regarded this compromise as the achievement of an indefinite postponement or at least a material delay in the planned constitutional legislation. In other words, in 1950 the ongoing constitutional debate in the Knesset ended and a compromise was reached whereby the constitution would be drawn up chapter by chapter through enactments, by way of ordinary legislation of Basic Laws, which in time would be consolidated into one document, receive an elevated status and together form Israel's constitution.

The first of Israel's Basic Laws, Basic Law: The Knesset, was enacted in 1958, and it was followed, at a slow pace, by eight additional ones, all dealing only with the structure, powers and duties of the arms of government.[16] A number of drafts of comprehensive Bills of Rights, presented during these years to the Knesset, were not adopted. In 1992 the Knesset passed two additional Basic Laws which dealt for the first time with the basic human freedoms: Basic Law: Human Dignity and Liberty and Basic Law: Freedom of Occupation. These Basic Laws included provisions according to these statutes an entrenched status: violation of the basic rights accorded by these two laws is restricted by provisions included in section 4 of Basic Law: Freedom of Occupation and Section 8 of Basic Law: Human Dignity and Liberty.

Basic Law: Freedom of Occupation can be changed only by a Basic Law, adopted by a majority of the members of the Knesset. There is no such provision in Basic Law: Human Dignity and Liberty.

At present, Israel has a series of Basic Laws, including only two Basic Laws defining part of the human rights, but it still misses so far a complete, codified and consolidated constitution covering each and every subject which is normally included in such constitutional codes. There are as yet no Basic Laws on freedom of expression, freedom of religion, freedom of scientific research, freedom of demonstration, etc. although all these are regarded by the Supreme Court as positive law – namely as inherent ingredients of a democratic system of government; but they are not included in statutes and leave the door open, at least theoretically, to contradictory legislation.

ASSETS OF A CONSTITUTIONAL CODE

What are the factors which should be taken into account when considering the need of a constitution for Israel? First and foremost is the importance of a written and codified constitution in order to lay down the rules and maxims of a liberal democracy. Such rules should be changed or amended only by certain accepted and binding legal procedures. These should not create rigidity, but their flexibility should be accompanied by previously defined legal ways and means in order to ascertain that the legislators are aware of the fact that any proposed abolition, change or amendment of the law in force affects constitutional norms and not ordinary statutory provisions devoid of a constitutional effect. The function of democratic institutions has become interwoven and combined with the working of constitutions. The understanding of what part the constitution plays in a state's politics is essential to a correct appreciation of the working of modern democratic government. We mentioned before that the concept of a constitution is closely bound up with the notion of the limitation of government by law, namely legal restrictions by a source of authority higher than the executive arm and beyond its reach. An enacted constitution is an effective method of securing this end.[17] The limitation by constitutional provisions of a fortuitous or international change of constitutional norms, whether in relation to the structure, functions and powers of the arms of government or in relation to the definition and binding character of basic freedom can be safeguarded by constitutional provisions like section 8 of the Israeli Basic Law: Human Dignity and Liberty which provides that there shall be no violation of rights under the Basic Law except by a law fitting the values of the State of Israel, designed for a proper purpose, and to an extent no greater than required.

The need to define human rights in a constitutional code derives from their character and substance as elementary ingredients of a liberal democracy. Their inclusion in a constitutional document ensures the acceptance and safeguarding of these rights. Formal recognition of a given liberty is achieved – at the first stage – through a declaration of its existence: A given fundamental right cannot be viable without continuous, positive and reciprocal interaction between the legal and socio-moral areas. But the declaration on the existence of an abstract right is only the starting point; it must be one of the fundamental components of the law in force. The delineation of the rights in terms of the wording of the law is the basic and primary footing upon which their actual protection depends; the very existence of a statute lends tangible expression as well as stability to the political regime and its prevailing fundamental concepts. The stability stems from the existence of a statutory norm embodying the standard against which the legality of the acts of governmental agencies is measured. Therefore, it is of special significance and weight that the constitutional principles defining the fundamental rights be given explicit expression in a legislative act and not merely remain in the realm of the oral or unwritten law. In this way, it is ensured that the substance and scope of the rights will be defined in clear language, upon which the individual citizen can rest his or her demands and claims. Therein, among other things, lies the importance and value of a written constitution.

To sum up: firstly, the first component of egalitarian democracy is the transformation of abstract ideas of rights into written constitutional norms and their integration into the legal system of the country. Thereby we also promote the introduction of a common legal culture and prevent the change or amendment of ordinary laws serving as imperfect surrogates of constitutional provisions; the passing of a constitution in Israel will therefore prevent, *a priori*, amendments which infringe human rights or democratic principles.

Secondly, a constitution ensures the existence of clarity in the definition of powers, functions and rights and expresses their binding force, clearly and in unequivocal terms, as compared to unwritten conventions, customs or constitutional understandings. An important effect of the written constitution is the clarification and substantiation of the character of constitutional rights and their legal force as well as the precise formulation of the sanctions, safeguarding their rights by the legislative process in respect of matters covered by the constitution.

Thirdly, judicial review, namely the scrutiny of legislative acts by a court of law or any other similar institution constituted by legislation in order to ascertain their conformity to constitutional norms, is the natural result of the creation of binding norms: once you create binding norms, define them or accord them recognition, you are bound to ask yourself how these norms shall be enforced. In other words, is judicial review one of the alternative responses to the question of enforcement, and what is the practical meaning of these norms within the framework of the legal system? The main alternatives are two: norms can serve the legislature merely as guidelines of a political, moral or philosophical nature, or they can be legally binding. However, in order to be binding one needs the machinery which empowers one or more of the arms of government to enforce the observance of the norms.

Judicial review is the machinery which serves as the yardstick of legitimacy. It normally comes into being with the creation of a constitutional system, as the institutionalized mission which guards the constitutional norms, and ensures the observance of these provisions by the legislature. Without such supervisory institution, every norm is bound to remain at the mercy or will of its creator who may deplete it of its contents and disregard it, by his or her mere whim or under the pressure of circumstances, without adopting the procedures and ways and means laid down beforehand for any change and transformation of constitutional values.

The forms of judicial review, the institution or courts of law empowered to carry it out and the extent of such powers are normally provided for in a constitutional code. In Israel we have adopted, so far, the system of judicial review by the ordinary courts of law (as compared to special courts of constitutional review, as, e.g., in Germany or Italy). The necessary legislated provisions on this subject are to be included in one of the Basic Laws in preparation, so as to become part of the constitution.

Four, we underscored the vitality of a proper system of restraints expressed in limitation of the powers of government, in order to prevent totalitarian centralization of power and lack of balance caused by a separation of powers leading to unrestricted absolutism. Such balance and separation of powers must necessarily find its expression in the constitutional code, whose permanence and supremacy ensures the democratic equilibrium which is a vital part in forging the unity of a nation.

Five, the constitutional code is a set of comprehensive and systematically organized principles, whose unitary and coordinated order of provisions is preferable to a fortuitous and uncoordinated development of separate constitutional statutes or, even worse, to unwritten conventional rules.

Six, society's needs are constantly developing and changing.[18] Law makers therefore experience the pressure inherent in every society to introduce adaptations to fit the demands of social change. The constitutional code provides normally the opportunity and ability to create a compromise between changing needs on the one hand and the creation of entrenched written norms on the other, providing the appropriate flexibility which is not excessive and therefore not stultifying.

Seven, a constitution has a significant didactic influence. People grow up with the knowledge of their basic rights and become aware of their rights. The constitutional norms are absorbed by the people as rightful parts of their state and society.

CONCLUSIONS

The everlasting effect of the introduction of a consolidated and unified constitution in Israel is the infusion and absorption of the spirit of law, or, as we call it, the rule of law, at all levels of society. Political and social co-existence is thereby fashioned according to a system of supreme and elevated normative values and rules, which serve as universal guiding principles of the nation.

The basic human rights enumerated in a constitutional code are of first-rate didactic importance and ensure, or at least facilitate, their enforcement. They guide the people, perhaps indirectly, towards the adoption of more just and equitable rules of conduct and further the respect of human dignity and quality.

The written rules which compose the constitutional code are clearer, stronger and more binding than any customary or oral traditions. They lead to coherence instead of diffusion and safeguard the basic freedoms of the individual by more effective and lasting means. The by-products of such reality include stronger solidarity, mutual consideration and social cohesion.

In relation to the system of government, it formulates the separation of powers essential for the negation of totalitarian centralization and prevents legislation which is contrary to the basic elevated constitutional principles; except where adopted by special procedures and majorities as laid down in the code.

Democracy in Israel will be strengthened by the protection of rights accorded to social or ethnic minorities and by the negative prescription of fortuitous legislation disregarding the norms of the constitution.

The constitutional code safeguards the non-negotiable demands of human dignity. It should be mentioned that the interpretative adjudication of the Supreme Court has underscored the relative importance of 'Human Dignity' as a mainstay of the values of equality, respect for the individual and negation of any discrimination and of the right of privacy. The rule of law puts limits on the absolute power of the state, and ensures free speech, freedom of worship, equal justice, respect for women, religious and ethnic tolerance, and respect for private property.

The most perfect way to safeguard rights and duties, obligations and limitations, prescriptions and norms in Israel is by defining them clearly in written form and in this context, in a written and comprehensive constitution.

NOTES

1. The most modern British enactment of constitutional character, namely the Human Rights Act, 1998 contains only a Bill of Rights.
2. Article IX of the Amendment to the US Constitution of 15 December 1797 states: 'The enumeration in the constitution of certain rights shall not be construed to deny or disparage others retained by the people', and cf. *Richmond Newspapers* v. *Virginia* (1980), 448 U.S. 555, 579.
3. Agranat (D.P.) stated in F.H. 13/60 *A.G.* v. *Matana* (16 PD.430): 'Paying attention to the manifest constitutional contents of this law, and considering the tendency behind the shortened and general wording of the powers mentioned in it, I am of the opinion that the way to construe it should not be one of a narrowing interpretation (following, Chief Justice John Marshall in *M'Culloch* v. *Maryland*, 17 US (4 Wheat.) 316, 4 L.Ed. 579 (1819), 602: 'It is a constitution we are expounding', and Justice Frankfurter in *Youngstown Sheet and Tube Co.* v. *Sawyer* (1952) 26 A.L.R, 1378, 1399: 'Because the President does not enjoy unmentioned powers does not mean that the mentioned one's should be narrowed by a niggardly construction ....').
4. Section 1 of Basic Law: Human Dignity and Liberty. *Sefer Hachukim* (Book of Laws) 1391 (1992), p.150. Amended S.H.1494 (1994), p.90.
5. La Declaration des droits de l'homme et du citoyen votée le 27 août 1789 par l'Assemblée Constituante.
6. Vernon Bogdanor, 'Introduction', *Constitutions in Democratic Politics*, Oxford, 1988, p.3. Madison wrote in the Federalist Papers (No.51): 'In framing a government which is to be administered by men over men the great difficulty lies in this: you must first enable the government to control the governed and in the next place oblige it to control itself. A dependence on the people is, no doubt, the primary control on the government; but experience has taught mankind the necessity of auxiliary precaution' (Such precautions are expressed in the constitution – MS).
7. See Section 8 of Basic Law: Human Dignity and Liberty, which states: 'Violation of rights. There shall be no violation of rights under this Basic Law except by a Law fitting the value of the State of Israel, designed for a proper purpose, and to an extent no greater than required...'
8. See Section 4 Basic Law: The Knesset, which states: 'Electoral system. The Knesset shall be elected by general, national, direct, equal, secret and proportional elections, in accordance with the Knesset Elections Law: this section shall not be varied save by a majority of the members of the Knesset'. *Sefer Hachukim* (Book of Laws) 244 (1958), p.69.
9. Bogdanor, *Constitution in Democratic Politics*, p.4.
10. Finland: subject to section 74 of the Constitution of 11 June 1999.
11. H.C. 10/48 *Ziv* v. *Gubernick*, 1 P.D. 85, 89 (1948).
12. H.C. 7/48 *Ziv* v. *Gubernik*. H.C. 10/48 *Karbutli* v. *Chief of Staff* 2 P.D. 5 (1949).
13. *Official Gazette* No.2 of 21 May 1948, suppl. A. p.1.
14. D.H. Vol.IV (23 January 1950–29 March 1950), session 136, p.1323.
15. Ibid., session 117, p.812.
16. Basic Law: Knesset (1958); Basic Law: Public Lands of Israel (1960); Basic Law: The President (1964); Basic Law: The Government (1968) and (1992); Basic Law: The Government Finance (Budget) (1975); Basic Law: The Army (1976); Basic Law: Jerusalem the Capital of Israel (1980); Basic Law: Adjudication (1984); Basic Law: State Comptroller (1988).
17. Bogdanor, *Constitution in Democratic Politics*, p.4; Meir Shamgar, 'On the Written Constitution', *Isr. L. Rev.*, Vol.9 (1974) p.467.
18. M. Shamgar, 'The Supreme Court of Israel: Present Trends and Concepts', *Isr. L. Rev.*, Vol.20 (1985), p.175.

Presidency in Israel: Formal Authority and Personal Experience

YITZHAK NAVON

Since independence, there have been constant deliberations about the image of the institution of presidency and about the powers of the president of the state. Every now and then, a politician, a member of parliament, a scholar or a journalist would demand changes in the powers given to the president by law, in most cases calling to expand them.

My opinion is different. I claim that there is no need to add powers to the president and I think that even if he is devoid of the few powers he has it will not hinder his function – the way I see the nature of the position. I said this before being elected president and I say it now, after filling this distinguished position for five years (1978–83).

In this article I will try to give a thorough description of the Basic Law: The President (1964) pointing at some changes introduced to it. I will describe the opinions of several public figures supporting the expansion of the powers of the president and explain why I disagree, and finally I will give a subjective description of my term in office, the ways I acted, and – in my opinion – achieved my goals, in spite of the limited powers. All this evolves around one question: how the president sees his ability to function being a symbol and a symbol only. I claim he has quite a lot to do although he does not have any actual powers.

THE LAW

What does the Basic Law: The President of the State (1964) say? I shall quote only the main ideas. The law defines the president: 'A President shall stand at the head of State' (section 1). 'The election of the President of the State shall

---

Yitzhak Navon was the Fifth President of the State of Israel, 1978–83.

be by secret ballot at a meeting of the Knesset assigned only for that purpose' (section 7). 'The President of the State shall be elected by the Knesset for five years' (section 3), and can serve for no more than two terms (section 4). Since then, some sections have been changed and from now on a president can be elected for one term of seven years only.

The duties and powers of the president are defined in section 11 as follows:

> A. The President of the State –
> shall sign every law, other than a Law relating to his powers;
> shall take action to achieve the formation of a Government and shall receive the resignation of the Government in accordance with Law;
> shall receive from the Government a report on its meetings;
> Shall accredit the diplomatic representatives of the State, shall receive the credentials of diplomatic representatives sent to Israel by foreign states, shall empower the consular representatives of the State and shall confirm the appointments of consular representatives sent to Israel by foreign states;
> Shall sign such conventions with foreign states as have been ratified by the Knesset;
> (6) shall carry out every function assigned to him by Law in connection with the appointment and removal from office of judges and other office-holders ...
>> (b) The President of the State shall have power to pardon offenders and to lighten penalties by the reduction or commutation thereof.
>> (c) The President of the State shall carry out every other function and have every other powers assigned to him by Law.

Section 12 reads: 'The signature of the President of State on an official document, other than a document connected with the formation of a Government, shall require the countersignature of the Prime Minister or of such other Minister as the Government may decide.'

Section 11 A (1) – 'the President does not have the authority not to sign a law that has been approved by the Knesset and the respective minister'. The next section, 11 A (2), allegedly authorizes the president to determine the next prime minister after elections or after resignation of the government. In practice, though, he is not free to act according to his will. He summons representatives of the different parties and sees their recommendations for the position. The candidate most likely to win the support of the majority will be the one asked by the president to form the government, regardless his will. Only rarely there exists a situation where more than one candidate is likely to win a majority, and in this case the president has to decide which of the candidates is to form the government.

Section 11 A (3) – the norm is that the secretary of the government reports to the president about the government's meetings.

Section 11 A (4) – the president delegates the state diplomatic and consular representatives in foreign countries. Nowadays, he has no authority to decide who these representatives will be. It happened that I objected to a certain appointment, but it was clarified to me by Supreme Court judge Moshe Landau that I could not change an appointment made by the foreign minister and approved by the government.

Section 11 A (6) – this is also a case regarding appointment of judges. The president does not choose them; the minister of justice does.

Section 11 B – the most familiar authority of the president – pardoning criminals or commuting their sentences. The authority given by this section is actual yet not exclusive. Without the approval of the president there can be no pardoning or commuting of sentences; however the president cannot pardon or commute sentences without the approval of the minister of justice.

Section 12 defines clearly the limits on the powers of the president by saying that his signature on any official document requires a countersignature of the prime minister or any other minister determined by the government, except for a document connected with forming the government.

In short, it can be said that the powers given to the president by law are very restricted, and therefore many have suggested expanding these powers, including when the law was brought up in the Knesset, on 29 January 1963, by the then minister of justice, Dov Yosef. At the end of the deliberations and legislative process, the law was approved on 16 June 1964. Efforts by several members of parliament to introduce changes to the law were not accepted, and the law was approved as suggested by the government except for minor insignificant changes.

THE ROLE OF THE PRESIDENT

The debate regarding the nature of the role of the president started in the days of the first president, Chaim Weizmann, who complained in a letter to Foreign Minister Moshe Sharett on 13 June 1948 that he was not being provided with sufficient information about the draft constitution for the state, which was discussed by a special ministerial committee. He wished to know 'the nature of the presidency under consideration':[1]

> There are several types of Presidents: The American kind, the French, Swiss and Czech kinds and no doubt many others as well ... I haven't the slightest idea what sort of Constitution is being considered, but I should like to tell you outright that I will certainly be unwilling to be a President of the French kind. Yet the American kind is unsuitable for a State like ours, and I have no intention of demanding such a status. But you must understand that I do not want the image of a mere puppet either.[2]

In his reply to Weizmann on 20 June 1948 Sharett wrote:

> As yet there is no clear definition of the Presidency, but apparently the
> inclination is more towards the French model than the American one,
> and to make the Government responsible to the house of representatives.
> Since the system of separation of powers prevalent in the United States
> will undoubtedly not appeal to our public, giving the President real
> powers would be interpreted as his subjugation to the house of
> representatives, and this would, to a large extent, reduce the honor
> attached to his post, which would make his personal status unenviable.[3]

On 26 June Dr Weizmann wrote to Sharett:

> As to the Presidency, I am in complete agreement with you that the
> American type of Presidency is unsuitable in our conditions. But I do not
> feel that the French kind is any more desirable. I feel that the
> intermediary way approaches the Czech example ... There ought to be
> some institution which is detached from the struggle amongst the Parties
> and which stands above them.[4]

In July 1948 matters had reached a crisis. 'I cannot accept being a sort of
passive partner in an enterprise which is being run on lines which I cannot
fully accept.'[5] Weizmann thus considered tendering his resignation. He
changed his mind regarding such a drastic step, and yet he remained bitter
about having his powers curtailed. David Ben-Gurion's perception of
presidency is particularly interesting. After the death of President
Weizmann, on 26 November 1952 Ben-Gurion summoned the party
centre of Mapai to choose a presidential candidate. He said:

> The Israeli presidency, according to the existing constitution, is a living
> symbol of the state, a symbol of the unity, the integrity and the supremacy of
> the state. And since there are not many states of Israel, and it has been long
> before this state has been established, hence the symbol of the state of Israel
> is no mere word. It is a symbol not only for the existing State of Israel, not
> only for the million and half currently inhabiting it – but rather a symbol of
> the people, the entire people of Israel. And the entire people of Israel
> includes not merely the 11 million living with us today; it includes all the
> generations of the people of Israel since its establishment. And subsequently
> this symbol is awe-inspiring. It seemed to me that it is in place to request the
> greatest Jewish personality that is to be found on Earth – to make it the
> ultimate symbol of Israel. And there lives in our generation a man like this,
> who is not only great for our generation, but great among many
> generations, and great among all mankind. Knowing the greatness of the
> man and his way of life, I was almost certain he would not accept such a
> mission, but, nevertheless, I could not afford to rely on my reasoning and
> prognosis. The historic responsibility seemed so significant to me that I

considered it to be my obligation to verify whether such a thing would be possible or not – and I asked the Israeli ambassador to Washington to find out whether Professor Albert Einstein would accept the presidency of Israel after being elected, knowing he could pursue his research in Jerusalem undisturbed. Moreover, I knew that such a president as Einstein may cause us certain difficulties, and that he does not speak Hebrew. And yet! In my opinion, the symbol of the State of Israel is not similar to the symbol of any other country. In England, a very practical country, people know how to conduct symbols, and were not fearful of a personal tragedy when the man who was designated as the symbol of the kingdom was about to do something which the statesmen thought would tarnish that symbol. And, in my view, the symbol of Israel is more important than a symbol elsewhere.[6]

When Einstein's negative reply was received, the Mapai party was convened (on 26 November 1952) and Ben-Gurion spoke and offered to elect Yitzhak Ben-Zvi as president, and so it was.

Attempts to expand the president's authorities did not stop. Among the members of Knesset suggesting amendments was Dr Yohanan Bader, who sought several additions to the president's authority – the first was to authorize the president to reject a law and to return it to the Knesset, supplemented by an explanatory memorandum. However, if the Knesset reaffirms the law after an additional debate, the president is obligated to ratify it. This motion was rejected. Had it been approved, I cannot see anything in it that would have empowered the president other than delaying or expressing dissatisfaction regarding a given law. In actual fact, nothing would have been changed. Another amendment tabled by MK Bader (in 1952) proposed calling the president 'Chief of the armed forces of the state', so he would appoint the chief of staff and ratify the appointment of military officers according to recommendations of the respective minister. This motion was rejected as well. Menachem Begin tabled a similar proposition, which was also rejected. Again, I can see no reason for granting this power because it is also conditional upon the recommendation of the relevant minister, i.e. the minister of defence. What qualifications does the president have to decide about appointing a chief of staff?

Previously, the Knesset had rejected a motion by MK Landau allowing the president to participate in government meetings. Having served in both roles myself – as president and later as a government minister – I would have rejected this motion, which stems from goodwill, but could damage the image of the president, since participating in government meetings makes him unintentionally a political figure. If the president expresses his opinion about the issue under discussion he would be attacked by those who oppose his opinion, and if he keeps silent then what point is served by his presence in the meeting?

On 11 July 1977 the fourth president, Ephraim Katzir, convened several authoritative legal experts to discuss the president's authority, emphasizing the weakness of his powers regarding issues supposedly under his jurisdiction: the right to grant clemency – clemency is dependent upon the minister of justice; signing laws makes no difference; the president is given no account about the government by the prime minister. President Katzir wished to evaluate the possibility of allowing the president to dissolve the Knesset; and that the president should be informed about national security directly by the chief of staff.

The ensuing debate made their difference of opinion public. Professor Aharon Barak, the attorney general at that time, rejected the extension of the president's authority. 'Any addition of power and authorities', he said, 'is followed by responsibility, and responsibility means exposure to political criticism.' Justice Meir Shamgar rejected any extension of authority because it would cross-breed presidential government with cabinet government. Granting authority to dissolve the Knesset means, in his opinion, entering the political realm. Attorney A. Goldberg thought that the president should have a professional body advising him on the issue of clemency. Like Shamgar, he objected to the suggestion that the president participate in government meetings because he would then be identified in the public's eyes with the executive branch. 'Professor Claude Klein proposed setting up a professional body that would advise the president of returning laws to the Knesset.'[7]

The issue of presidential authority was never off the agenda. Over the years many articles have been written proposing and opposing the expansion of existing powers relying upon scholarly arguments from the formal legal field, or from the political-partisan field. Legal experts and academic professors have often made arguments in favour of or in opposition to the various aspects of the problem.[8]

A case of a clemency that preceded conviction raised a wave of debates and criticism in many circles. The issue at hand is the one known as the 'Bus-line 300 episode'. On 12 April 1984, a group of four Arab terrorists hijacked a No. 300 bus and threatened the life of its passengers. Security forces stormed the bus and killed two of the terrorists. The other two were caught and were seen and even photographed by journalists being taken away by security forces. It was later announced that these two terrorists had died. A demand was made to investigate the circumstances of their death. The minister of defence at the time, Moshe Arens, formed a commission of enquiry headed by attorney Yonah Blatman. It was subsequently decided that Brigadier General Yitzhak Mordechay, five security service men and later three police officers should be brought to trial. On 18 May 1986 the attorney general, Professor Zamir, complained to the inspector general of police that he had been receiving information which contradicted the testimonies made during the investigation, and that it seemed that there had been subornation of false evidence and disruption of legal proceedings. Hence, he asked for a police investigation. On 25 June 1986, the president granted amnesty to the chief of the security service and three of his subordinates, and subsequently to other seven security service men. The police investigation found that the security service men who were pardoned by President Chaim Herzog had killed both terrorists.[9] This was done under orders from the chief of the security service, who also induced them to commit perjury. Was the president entitled to grant clemency before they were convicted? Did he have all the details? The president's main arguments were as follows:

> I did it with the intention of putting an end to the mayhem surrounding the episode, and to prevent additional grave damage to the Security Service ... The state of events was such that the Security Service men were interrogated without any ability to defend themselves, except by exposing highly confidential secrets. In that situation I saw first and foremost the necessity to defend the public's interest and the state's security, and to act the way I did.[10]

Immense public turmoil followed the amnesty. Among the critics were those who argued, 'amnesty was used to thwart the disclosure of the truth and prevent a trial from taking place'.[11] The Supreme Court refrained from over-riding the amnesty. According to the verdict of its deputy president, Justice Ben-Porat, 'the need for exercising the authority to grant clemency prior to conviction arises when it is in order to prefer the public's interest over the principle of equality before the law'.[12]

The president of the Supreme Court, Meir Shamgar, described the use of clemency before conviction as an instrument that 'is so rare and extreme that only extraordinary circumstances, under which severe damage is expected to an utmost public interest ... and to which no other reasonable solution can be seen'.[13] The public debate continued even after the verdict of the Supreme Court.

I do not recall another example of an amnesty by the president that generated such a furious and prolonged debate as this event. Here the president's authority was exercised rapidly, although the initiative came from part of the executive branch, and without the signature of the minister of justice the amnesty would have been void. Some other cases have also raised debates, but not on such a fundamental level; there were claims about erroneous considerations on the part of the president and the recommending executive branch. In a discussion held in the government on this delicate issue I supported the decision that was made, but I insisted that a legal commission of enquiry investigate the entire episode. No one objected to my demand, but the investigation was never carried out. It now seems to me that exceptions should not be made, and that the phenomenon of amnesty preceding conviction should not be repeated.

PERSONAL EXPERIENCE

I shall now describe how I acted on my principles during my five-year term as president, pointing out the wide array of initiatives that were exercised, despite the shortage of formal authority.

On the eve of my election to the presidency (1978), Israel was inhabited by 3,500,000 Jews and nearly 600,000 non-Jewish residents: Muslims (mostly), Christians and Druzes, alongside several smaller minorities. Today the Jews number more than five million and the minorities number over a million, most of which are Muslims. A basic question is how these communities can live in friendship and understanding surrounded by Arab countries while there is an armed conflict between Israel and the Palestinians.

I have given much thought to how the president can bridge this rift; how can a Muslim Arab be a loyal citizen of the Jewish state and still express his identification with the Palestinian people? A way must be found to allow him that, as long as he breaks no law. An interesting fact is that throughout the years of Palestinian terrorism, the Israeli Arabs were not dragged into violence, except in very isolated cases. As president, I spoke with them frankly about their dilemma and about how they could express their sympathy towards their people, and yet refrain from taking the road of terror and law breaking. It pleased me to be able to express these opinions in the Arabic language. Knowing their language and culture, I felt I could speak candidly on radio and television broadcasts, and through scores of actual gatherings and dialogues.

It was customary for years that on a Muslim or a Druze holiday, their representatives would come to the president's house to receive his greetings. I changed this custom and presented myself to them, went to their communities, bringing them the blessing of the state in their language. Many thousands came to these meetings at the court of a mosque, or a schoolyard, or a sporting field and none asked what my authorities were. They saw in me a symbol of the entire state, coming to bless them on their holiday. To give such a feeling of affiliation to the state, despite the different origin and despite the conflict requires no authority; it requires a symbol. Frequent visits to Arab towns and villages gave much publicity to their unique problems and to the views I expressed about the need for peace and coexistence, the aspiration for peace with our neighbours and a demand for the government to bridge the economic gap between Jews and Arabs in Israel.

I have conducted open dialogues with school pupils who spoke candidly about their problems and feelings as a minority living in Israel. These visits offered an opportunity for relief and comfort as the citizens knew that their opinion had been made public and that their grievances were expressed. The president cannot solve their problems, but he listens, he is a conduit to exposure, and he can urge the executive branch to fix what needs to be fixed. Occasionally a small gesture can produce a fitting positive response.

I recall that when Jordan allowed Israeli Arabs to pass through on their pilgrimage to Mecca, I broadcast on the television and radio a short blessing for a successful journey. I was told that the clients of an Arab café who were there watching television stood up, applauded and loudly called: 'hail the president!' What powers are required to make such a gesture and receive such a response?

Aside from the Arab issue, Jewish society is charged with internal problems requiring appropriate solutions. The Jewish populace is composed primarily of immigrants who came to Israel from 102 countries speaking 81 languages. Different mentality, distinct and divided concepts, widely varying views about any issue: politics, culture, linguistics, traditions, family, religion, and so on. They are all united by their common distant past – expressed by the bible since the time of Abraham the patriarch, Moses and the exodus from Egypt, the granting of the Torah on Mount Sinai, King David and his heirs, the struggle against the Greek and later against the Roman conquerors – all this and more is shared by all immigrants. Whether they come from Yemen, Romania, Argentina, Morocco or the United States, they are united by the aspiration to liberty and to live in an independent Jewish state. But they are separated by 2000 years, during which they were dispersed to the ends of the earth. How can they be consolidated into one people? How do you provide them with a sense of belonging to the state? How do you make them feel at home? Here too the main key lies in the hands of the president; he can meet with all groups of immigrants, let them speak their minds, listen to them and plant within them the feeling that they are welcome and are equal to all other citizens, irrespective of their different backgrounds. It is in the president's hands to do much in the mental-emotional field, which is no less important than material aspects such as housing, education and making a living. He needs no powers to do that. It suffices that he represents the state and the unity of the people.

The Israeli society is an anthropologist's dream coming true. The special legacy of every tribe and ethnicity or group should be nurtured and respected, while seeking out and emphasizing the mutual aspects and the ancient cultural tradition. A politician who is driven by political interests will find this mission too complex. Only a figure such as the president, with no personal or political interests, can exert an influence in the desired direction. He should give proper airing to the grievances of the citizens and their needs and urge the executive branch to solve their problems.

During my term as president, the presidential residence was visited by some 5,000 people a month, with whom I conducted dialogues. Annually, this amounts to 60,000 people, and over the entire term it is 300,000 people. What were they looking for? Why did they come? Why were they troubling themselves to meet a man devoid of authority? What were they asking and what could they have received – a job? An apartment? A loan? A grant?

Connections? None of the above. They came to air their grievances, to receive support, inspiration and hope. Everything within the mental-emotional realm; nothing within the material and practical one. They can speak to the entire state through the man who represents it. Whoever seeks powers should be looking for them elsewhere. The president serves as a wailing wall of sorts, but one that responds to prayers.

In all my years in office, I did not find a community or group which did not feel underprivileged or misrepresented by the media. The president has to thoroughly examine their problems, to dive into their culture and to elicit pearls to be displayed so everyone can see them. To encourage, to plant hope, to show respect – sincere respect, not mere lip service, born out of conviction and genuine study into the real essence and the background of his visitors. Every new immigrant feels like a foreigner in his new land, speaks none of the languages spoken there and knows nothing about the state's institutions or the customs of its veteran citizens. The immigrants need moral encouragement and not just material aid, so they come to the president. He must also battle against the stereotypes of one group of immigrants against another. Ridiculing jokes and sectarian or ethnic teasing are a common phenomenon and not everyone is immune against it. But the president does not merely stay in his residence and wait to meet all these people; he goes out to see them in the places they live or in their places of gathering.

I felt obliged to visit the neighbourhoods and suburbs of the cities, remote villages along the borders, and places that are far from any hub. It is a pleasant and lasting experience to become acquainted with people and places, to feel their happiness, to sympathize with their pain, and to be captivated by the complex and amazing human mosaic of people originating from over 100 countries. Holocaust survivors, who returned from hell; people who left poor and backward countries alongside people who left the most developed and advanced countries of the world; religious and secular; rich and poor; left and right. I felt it was my duty to seek out common values to unite one with the other, as much as possible.

In meetings with pupils from the less privileged classes I invested much effort to give them high expectations, hoping they can live up to those expectations and aspire to high achievements. In my visits to remote towns and villages I made a habit of staying overnight rather than settling for a brief visit. This enabled me to conduct lengthy dialogues not only with local leaders, but also with individuals from different groups, and particularly with youths.

To test the effect of my visits to towns and suburbs, and to know what basis my expectations had, I requested the Institute of Communication at the Hebrew University to examine one prominent event. I planned a visit to a neighbourhood that was then the most notorious in Israel, the 'Hatikvah' neighbourhood. It was synonymous with criminality, drugs, army desertion, poverty, etc. The visit lasted three days, during which I visited the market and the shops, all schools, the laundry club, women's NAAMAT club, the library, the old peoples' home. I met with the founders and veterans of the neighbourhood, young couples, artists and writers, social workers, rabbis and political activists. One night I slept at the house of a Jew from Syria who was once involved in illegal immigration. That night the residents gave me a very rare and moving experience. Close to midnight I went with my companions to the streets to meet gangs, but instead my companions gave me a wonderful surprise: on a balcony of one of the houses a stage was set up, with singers and musicians, and an audience of thousands welcomed me, singing and chanting. The party lasted for several hours. That was how the residents expressed their gratitude to the president who took the trouble to visit them for three days. Poet Haim Guri who was present wrote about the occasion:

> At night thousands of youngsters – men and women – gathered next to the pita bakery. Etzel Street was closed for traffic. Coloured lights flooded the stage on which famous and admired singers stood... An enchanted celebration took place. No impresario could have arranged such a celebration. Everyone was there for his honour, and there he was greeted at midnight with cheers and applause and warmest wishes. And there he made a speech to the audience at midnight and he spoke in praise of the neighbourhood ... The party lasted until two a.m. and the cafes stayed open.[14]

The research institute that tested the results of my visit handed me its report, which included, among others, the findings shown in Table 1.

This research demonstrated what I have known all along. The president can stimulate strong feelings among large parts of the public, even though he has no powers. The neighbourhood's residents did not ask for powers nor did they expect any. They were simply happy that the state – through the president – was showing interest in them.

A loyal partner of the president is his wife. Offira, my wife, joined me in my visits to Egypt and to the United States, but also, and of no less importance, she accompanied me to the 'Hatikvah' neighbourhood and to a few other places and events. Alongside, she developed her own fields of activity. When we entered the president's residence, we brought our children with us – Na'ama, who was five years old, and Erez, who was four. They added a lot of colour, liveliness and joy, and proved an attraction to photographers.

PRESIDENCY AND POLITICS

It was customary that the person elected president belonged to the prime minister's party. My case was exceptional because I was a Labour member when elected, during the premiership of Mr Begin, leader of the Likud. Our relationship was cordial despite the differences in political views, but over

TABLE 1

AN EVALUATION OF THE EFFECT OF THE PRESIDENT'S VISIT TO 'HATIKVAH'
NEIGHBOURHOOD UPON THREE GROUPS

	Percentage of respondents with a positive tendency
Effects on the research subject himself	
Strengthened his sense of identification with the State of Israel and its goals	46
Studied positive information about the neighbourhood, which he did not know before	29
Studies about problems of the neighbourhood which he was unfamiliar with before	24
Effects on the 'Hatikvah' neighbourhood and its residents	
Giving a good feeling to the residents that someone is interested in them.	81
Adding respect and dignity to the neighbourhood	66
Effects on the general Israeli public	
Turning the public's attention to the good sides of the neighbourhood.	56
Turning the public's attention to the problems of the neighbourhood	52
Increasing the knowledge of the public about initiatives and achievements of the neighbourhood	37
Creating acquaintance between the public and special figures in the neighbourhood	34

Source: The Communication Institute, *An Evaluation of the Effect of the President's Visit to 'Hatikvah' Neighbourhood*, Jerusalem, July 1979 (Hebrew).

certain events disagreements and tension arose between us, and between me and government ministers.

The most salient of them was an issue relating to the Lebanon War, when the Christian phalanga troops brutally massacred Palestinians in the Sabra and Shatila refugee camps. Allegations were made that Israeli soldiers were involved in the massacre. Those allegations generated enormous headlines worldwide. Although I believed these were false accusations, I thought it was in order to investigate the episode. Only a legal commission of enquiry would be able to win back the trust of the people and the world. I was confident that Israel would emerge innocent from the investigation. But if it turned out that – heaven forbid – Israelis had taken part in the horrible massacre, they should be committed for trial. I expressed this opinion to Prime Minister Begin. Initially he declined, saying that the very setting up of the commission would be interpreted as a plea of guilt. I argued for the reverse. The Israeli public split over this painful issue, and massive demonstrations took place demanding an investigation, while on the opposite side there was strong resistance. I felt I should lay the entire moral weight of the presidency on the issue, and I made a public statement in the media demanding that the prime minister set up the commission. The government, which convened that evening to discuss the episode, approved a decision to set up the commission of enquiry. I was told by two ministers that my public appearance had shifted the pendulum towards that decision. There were also those who criticized me for taking a stand on a politically contentious issue. My stand was that I saw no political debate, but an issue with a moral significance of the first degree, and therefore it was not only my right but also my obligation to make my voice heard in this matter. The commission of enquiry was formed and after investigations it announced its conclusions. The essence of its formation cleared the atmosphere, and its conclusions demonstrated that Israel Defence Forces soldiers took no part in the massacre. Criticism was made of the behaviour of certain statesmen and generals, but there was no responsibility for the massacre.

I once criticized Mr Begin for calling Mr Arafat 'Hitler'. I claimed that every comparison to Hitler or the Nazis belittles the dimensions of the Holocaust and the cruelty of the Nazis. The Holocaust and its consequences are exceptional in the history of our people and in the world's history, and therefore it must not be compared to any other phenomenon, because nothing of comparison ever happened. Here again I saw not a political-partisan debate, but rather a moral, value-based one, which I found appropriate to get involved in.

The visit of President Carter to Israel caused another row between Begin and me. The question was who hosts the guest in the formal dinner and speaks on behalf of Israel. The decision was that, according to protocol, it was my duty as president to host President Carter. However, the Deputy Prime Minister, Yigael Yadin, came to see me with a request from Prime Minister Begin that he would be allowed to make a speech at that dinner in contravention of protocol. It was in the middle of the negotiations with Egypt brokered by President Carter. Mr. Begin had had scores of opportunities to make statements, not necessarily at the dinner held by the president. In the end, for the sake of peace, the three of us spoke: Carter, Begin and me.

A more substantial argument occurred after my short speech in the airport, welcoming Carter upon his arrival to Israel. I pointed out the significant difference between the Egyptian concessions and the concessions that Israel made. Israel gave very concrete things – the Sinai Peninsula, which is three times the size of Israel, airfields and oilfields. These are all things that cannot be taken back, except by force, and that was not our intention. On the other hand, what Egypt gave in return was indeed important: recognition, embassies, relationships, but in the event of tension Egypt can withdraw all of them.

Criticism of my words was raised among the government's ranks: why did I say that what we return to Egypt could not be taken back. That did not bother me much because I was not taking a political stand; I was objectively describing the state of affairs.

On other occasions, it was also argued that I was unlawfully invading the political arena. It was argued against me that in my meetings with President Saadat in Egypt, I was negotiating without proper authorization. There was no political negotiation, although we did agree to have exchange youth delegations visiting both countries, so that peace could penetrate their hearts from a younger age. I also agreed with President Saadat to raise the number of El-Al flights to Cairo, from twice a week to three times a week.

In all my public appearances in Egypt, I expressed Israel's desire for peace, good neighbourliness and mutual respect, while adhering to the accepted lines of the major parties. My visit to Egypt was an exciting personal experience that I will carry for the rest of my life. I was pleased I could speak to the Egyptian people in their own language, and that in meetings with professors and journalists I could make use of my studies at the Hebrew University in the fields of Islam, Arab language and literature. When my five-day visit ended, Saadat told me as we departed: 'You have conquered the heart of the Egyptian people. You helped me convince them that Israel indeed wants peace.'

No Egyptian asked me what my powers were as a president of a country that was an enemy just yesterday, who spoke to them in their language and was striving to tear down the curtains of alienation, animosity and stereotypes. They were satisfied that he was head of a state called Israel, with which they had signed a peace accord. By the way, I focused my activity within Israel, and only twice accepted invitations for visits abroad: to Egypt and to the USA.

When the peace accord between Israel and Egypt was signed, demonstrations erupted in the city of Yamit, as well as in other settlements that were designated for evacuation by the framework of that accord. To my surprise, nobody faced the residents, neither the prime minister nor the minister of defence nor any other minister tried to explain the evacuation decision following the peace accord. I saw my duty – unwritten and informal – to fill this void. I appeared before thousands of emotional residents. I expressed sympathy for their pain but I also applauded the importance of peace and the blessing contained within the accord with Egypt, despite the painful sacrifice that they were being expected to make. Granted, there were voices of protest, but people also listened out of respect to the president, especially as he was not a member of the government that decided to evacuate Yamit and other settlements.

I have no ability to measure the impact of my visit, but I felt that my contribution to the residents was the feeling that their protest was being heard, that their pain was being appreciated and that the state, through the president, expressed understanding of their pain while emphasizing the importance of their contribution to peace. Here, as well, it is not about the formal authority of the president, which can be defined in the articles of the constitution. It is about the sense of the president himself regarding his duty in hard times.

On occasions, a public row erupted between me and one of the ministers. I habitually visited Kiryat Shmona after nearly every Katyusha bombardment. I witnessed in many cases that bomb shelters were far from the apartments. Sometimes, the sick or the elderly were unable to reach the shelter in time while the sirens screamed and the missiles fell. After one of my visits, I criticized the minister of housing for not taking sufficient care of shelters. He replied with anger and accused me of not knowing the situation. This was not a political argument. It was an intervention in a necessary issue, which was never debated by the different parties.

I had another public quarrel, with the minister of energy and infrastructure, Yitzhak Moday, when he dealt with what was known as 'the canal of seas' project and said that he intended to bring workers from Italy to excavate the canal from the Mediterranean to the Dead Sea. I claimed that Israel had sufficient technical knowledge, hence there was no need to import workers from Italy for that purpose. The criticism was not appreciated and Mr Moday claimed that I had not properly studied the issue, but he could not claim that the president had no authority to interfere in the matter.

In the meeting of the security and foreign affairs committee of the Knesset (12 April 1983), the chief of staff, Raphael Eitan, had said according to press reports that had there been 100 Jewish settlements between Jerusalem and Nablus, rock throwing would have stopped, and those who continued throwing rocks would 'run around like drugged cockroaches in a bottle'. I publicly denounced this manner of expression.

Regarding this incident, the former attorney general, Moshe Ben-Ze'ev, wrote that none of the government ministers denounced the words of the chief of staff, 'both on account of its content and on account of the flagrant militaristic style' and he added: 'the president was therefore the only senior official figure to completely denounce the words of the chief of staff, and the chief of staff could not respond to this expression of sorrow, coming from the mouth of the president, with the words: I couldn't care less, as he did with other responses'. Mr Ben Ze'ev concluded his article by saying that the willingness of the president in the two events (Sabra and Shatila and the chief of staff's statement) to respond and to speak publicly stem from the same source: 'deep conviction in the truthfulness of his words and a will to educate the people in light of values of moral and human decency'.[15]

RELATIONS WITH WORLD JEWRY

Another aspect of the president's activity is the relationship with the Diaspora Jewry. The Jews view the president as a symbol of the State of Israel and wish to converse with him and to hear his opinion about issues concerning the Jewish people. They do not inquire what his formal authority is. I met nearly every Jewish delegation from overseas that asked to come to the president's residence and conduct a frank and warm dialogue. During these meetings I emphasized that to secure the continual existence of the Jewish people it is vital to fulfil three criteria: 1. providing Jewish education to every boy and girl in the Diaspora; 2. refraining from cross-marriages; 3. increasing the number of children in each family. These are based on the findings of demographic experts, who show a dangerous trend of decline in the number of Jews every year. In addition, I emphasized the importance of the bond between the Diaspora and Israel, which should ideally be expressed by immigration to Israel, but could have other expressions as well: investments, visits, celebration of Bar Mitzva or marriage in Israel, studies in Israel, and so on. I stressed these points in many public gatherings with Jews.

Near the end of my term, I was honoured by a formal invitation on behalf of President Reagan to visit the United States. I was there for ten days which were filled with events and meetings with administration officials, members of the Senate and the Congress, journalists and Jewish communities. I never felt limited by lack of powers in any of these meetings. I spoke about the fundamentals of our historic right over our land, our aspiration for peace, the Holocaust and its consequences, the Arab hostility and the need for reconciliation, our mission of constructing the country, settling the desert, absorbing immigration, and building a democratic moral society, which leans upon the bible's legacy as well as modern science, and further statements to refute hostile propaganda and stereotypes. I also pointed out the biblical values common to the American pioneers and the founding fathers of Israel. Everyone treated me as the president symbolizing the State of Israel and did not trouble to investigate the exact extent of my authority.

CONCLUSION

The role of the president in Israel, as defined by law, leaves wide latitude for the president's actions and enterprises, shaped by his character and inclinations. The powers granted by the law are partial, but that should not hinder his function. In actual fact, being devoid of all his authority, the president could still act on many levels by being a symbol. A symbol that can unite varying and opposing parties, a symbol that can encourage, give hope and plant faith, preach morals and point to faults. His voice will be heard because he is never suspected of partisan interests and he is trusted to act beyond political considerations.

It was an honour and a privilege to be elected to such a prominent and exciting position. When I first lost the elections for the presidency in 1973, I received a short and warm letter of consolation from Ben-Gurion, as follows:

> Dear Yitzhak,
>
> I am one of the many who deeply regret that the one man who should have been elected president – wasn't. ... I am sorry you were not elected. I believe that the Hebrew nation will yet insist on this right of yours, and that we will live to see you as the president of the nation.
>
> With deep admiration
> David Ben-Gurion

Tiberius, 24 March 1973.

Five years later, in 1978, I was privileged to be elected president but Ben-Gurion was no longer alive. Today, it is already the eighth president's term. Every president has his unique style, his preferred fields of action and his special contribution to the state. One feeling, I am convinced, is shared by all, a feeling of higher mission, and a prayer to be worthy of the people's trust.

NOTES

1. Gad Yaacobi, *The Government of Israel*, New York, 1982, p.110.
2. Ibid.
3. Ibid.
4. Ibid., p.111.
5. Ibid.
6. David Ben-Gurion, 'A President in Israel', in *Vision and Way*, Tel Aviv, 1962, Vol.D, p.138 (Hebrew).
7. Yaacobi, *The Government of Israel*, p.113.
8. Amnon Rubenstein, *The Constitutional Law of Israel*, Tel Aviv, 1974, especially the second chapter, focusing on the powers and duties of the president, p.853 and following (Hebrew). See also S.Z. Feller, *Elements of Criminal Law*, Jerusalem, 1987, Vol.B (Hebrew).
9. Ilan Rahum, *The Security Service Affair*, Jerusalem, 1990 (Hebrew).
10. Mordechai Kremnitzer, 'The Shabac Clemency – Did the Supreme Court Stand the Test?', *Iyunei Mishpat* (Tel-Aviv University Law Review), Vol.12, No.3 (1987), p.613 (Hebrew).
11. Ibid., p.614.
12. Ibid.
13. Rubenstein, *The Constitutional Law of Israel*, p.836.
14. Haim Guri, 'The Weeping and the Electric Guitar', *Davar* (Israeli daily), 7 March 1979 (Hebrew).
15. Moshe Ben Ze'ev, 'Navon's Precedent', *Haaretz* (Israeli daily), 24 April 1983.

The Government

GAD YAACOBI

THE MODERN STATE

The modern state, as we know it, began to develop on the heels of revolutions in England (1648), the United States (1776) and France (1789). Subsequently, the changes that emanated from these revolutions spread to other states in Europe and the world. The chief characteristics of the modern state are: concentration of government power, territorial unity, the application of governmental and administrative control to the entire state and all of its parts and political power spread amongst wide sectors of society rather then a monopoly of any given group or stratum. Although there are always sectors whose influence is relatively greater than others, their advantage is fluid, given to change and open to challenge by other sectors of society.[1]

All citizens irrespective of their social or economic positions enjoy civil and political rights, including the right to vote. In the running of the country, there is a considerable separation between the ruling political group, which directs the administrative apparatus, and the apparatus itself, which has an uninterrupted existence even when there are changes of government. The ruling group is represented primarily in the government

Gad Yaacobi lectures at Tel Aviv University. He was Ambassador to the United Nations and a minister in various Israeli governments.

and the parliament. In other words, there is a certain division of functions and authorities. This is discernible in the absence of a single, unified, crystallized and permanent ruling class, secure in a position consecrated by tradition and rooted in the customs of generations and sanctified rights. In fact, a multiplicity of new sectors constantly develop and, given fair opportunity, compete with each other, overtly or secretly, for influence and power.

The state that embraces these characteristics developed in the wake of technological and economic developments that began with the Industrial Revolution. These included the development of a broad market economy and social processes that changed the class structure, and were both the cause and the consequence of the development of socio-political ideologies and approaches based on rationalism and secularism. This eventually led to the dissemination of the democratic principles that called for equal rights and the freedom of every citizen to elect representatives as well as the development of mass media.

THE RULE OF LAW

The fundamental principle that acts as a central pillar to the existence and operation of a modern democracy is the rule of law. One of the first appearances of this principle as an institutionalized foundation of the state is in the Platonic dialogue 'Crito'.[2] The story tells of Socrates, who was brought to court for a transgression that to the best of his understanding and knowledge he had not committed. This is what he argued in court. But he was found guilty and sentenced to death. As he sat in prison, waiting for the sentence to be carried out, his friends proposed to help him to escape. Yet he refused. True, he said, he was not guilty, but he had been given a fair trial. He had expressed his arguments before the judges and now he must accept the verdict and sentence. If he were not to accept them, the foundations of the rule of law and the order of society would be shaken. Socrates continued to sit in prison until given the poison prescribed by the law, which he duly drank. In accordance with his philosophy, Socrates considered this his duty. As citizens enjoy a system of rights, so must they comply with duties. All these are based on the law, the rule of which is the foundation of organized society – in other words, of the state.

Rule of law in a democratic regime means the existence of rules laid down by society, through its elected representatives and its authorized institutions, so that the society can function and exist within a single political framework. These rules lay down the standards of what is and is not allowed and bind the behaviour of individual members of the framework. The modern state is based on the foundations of both organization and freedom. The organized existence of the state and society is conditional upon the rule of law, while the individual's freedom is guaranteed by it. These rules are, in fact, a summary of the human, public and political experience of society. The rule of law is the fundamental principle upon which a country can and must function.[3]

THE PRINCIPLE OF CONSTITUTIONALITY

When a constitution exists, the parliament cannot pass legislation that clashes with it. But even in Israel the Knesset cannot pass legislation contrary to the iron rules that appear in several articles of the Basic Laws, which form the basis for the future constitution of the state.[4]

However, the primary importance of the rule of law in its formal sense lies in its relation to the executive branch. The meaning of the legality of the regime applies in particular to the legality of the administration or, in other words, to the executive branch. The executive branch may not act unless its action is drawn from the instructions of the law. An action with no legal basis is null and void, and is contrary to the principle of the rule of law in its formal sense. The executive authority is subject to the law and has no rights, powers or immunities except for those granted it explicitly by the law.

As to actual implementation of the law, the gap between the letter of the law and the extent to which it is actually applied and realized in a particular democratic state indicates the degree to which the rule of law prevails and tells something of the nature of the national and social culture. Concerning the duty of the authorities to maintain the law, the executive government is charged with the implementation of the state's laws, by means of its offices and branches, as stated in Article 1 of the Basic Law: The Government. The duty of making the law public is meant to ensure that it is known to every citizen in order to enable the application of the rule of law to everyone. For this reason, all rules and regulations are published.

The principle of equality before the law applies both to the state authorities and to the individual. Former minister of justice, Professor Amnon Rubinstein, has discerned two connotations to the principle of 'equality before the law':

> The first is formal and refers to the fact that the courts of law will implement the law impartially and without discrimination between litigants. This connotation does not apply to distinctions made by the law itself ... the second connotation, the essential one, does not deal with its equal implementation but with the law itself.[5]

The principle of the rule of law is tightly bound, both formally and in its fundamental nature, with the principle of the 'separation of powers'. The principle of the 'separation of powers' is the norm for the very foundations of constitutional democracy, even when in the course of time infringements between the various authorities might manifest themselves. For example, if the Knesset interferes in those areas designated to the executive or judiciary branch in a way not prescribed by the law, it attacks the principle of the 'separation of powers' and thus acts against the principle of the rule of law. The same is true when the executive branch performs judicial or legislative acts that it is not authorized to perform. The judicial authority, when it lays down general norms or individual procedures that do not emanate from the law, is also liable to contravene this principle.[6]

PUBLIC INVOLVEMENT

Several basic conditions are prerequisite to the existence of a democratic regime. These include the awareness by most of the people of the affairs of state and a desire to be involved in them. There must also exist a certain intellectual capability that cannot develop sufficiently when the majority of the people subsist at a low standard of living and education or when the majority of the citizens hold extreme religious beliefs. Extreme social and cultural gaps are capable of undermining the necessary foundation for the existence of a democracy in the long run and may even cause it to eventually disintegrate.

Excessive centralization may turn a democracy into a purely formal structure and process, without any real content. A fundamental requirement of democracy is the existence of a multiplicity of power centres and the right of free public competition for representation within the political institutions. This is one of the paradoxes of the democratic system: on the one hand, it is based on broad political awareness and on the possibility of constant competition for political power; on the other hand, this power, which is the subject of competition, must not turn into the main goal of democracy. Only if this power does not appear as a supreme value can the competition for it be preserved within legitimate boundaries, without penetrating or destroying every nook of social existence. Democracy is, consequently, based on openness and equal opportunity on the one hand and on constraints and limitations on the other; only through the maintenance of a balance between the two can it function.

The realization of democracy in theory and in practice necessitates the existence of motivation for active citizen participation in the political processes. This motivation emanates from the political system that prevails in a given society and from the political culture that results from the educational system and the national-spiritual heritage. In the absence of real motivation for participation in political processes, which is frequently referred to as 'the desire for influence and power', democracy cannot function. In its positive connotation, this is the desire to participate in formulating the future shape of and the course taken by the state and the society.[7] In its most sublime form this represents a renunciation of exclusive devotion to one's personal affairs in favour of public affairs. Without this, the state and society are not led and cannot maintain a government of representatives.[8]

THE QUEST FOR PERSONAL POWER

Within the complex motives for wanting to participate and to be elected, there is the personal aspiration for power. Separating the desire to act for society from the personal aspiration for power is no simple matter, for the two motives complement one another. As long as a balance between them exists, the system is positive. But when the aspiration for power turns into the main goal, the governmental-political system starts to decay and becomes negative.

It is clear that even those who consider power a means are not free of the drive to amass influence and power. The conclusion depends on the relative proportion of the various motives. Whether the conclusion is positive or negative depends on how people reach positions of government influence. In other words, on whether in the process of realizing their aspirations they generate negative phenomena that might outweigh the positive actions they might perform when finally achieving the reins of power. The balance between the essence of the motives and the manner in which influence is amassed in order to realize them, between the road taken to the power centres and the manner in which they are used in implementing policy influences to a great extent, for better of for worse, the essence of the regime and its policy.

The aspiration to influence and participate in government with the aim of moulding the shape of the society and the state is essentially positive, but the individual must control the means to its realization. It must also be rooted in democratic processes and in social norms so that it does not act as a boomerang. Individuals, when realizing their aspirations, must be aware of their own limitations as well as the societal restrictions placed upon them to avoid becoming drunk with the idea of power; a condition deleterious to their intentions, to society as a whole and in the final analysis to themselves.

DEMOCRACY AND DEVELOPMENT

Our democratic system is in an ongoing process of being formed. Democratic values have not yet been internalized by all of Israel's citizens. The obligations of the citizen in a democratic society as well as the rights democracy confers on the citizen are not accepted conventions. The very patterns of behaviour of Israeli democracy are also in the process of being crystallized. The Israeli government itself is still not particularly meticulous as regards the rule of law and democratic norms of governance.

Our political culture is in *statu nascendi* (in the process of being created) and because of this we are still struggling to create a public recognition of the vital need to fashion a properly run democratic culture. It is, therefore, incumbent upon the government to excel in its ability to produce a vision, to generate conviction and to determine goals, aims and long-term objectives. It must have the ability to map out a future and define the ways by which it might be realized. It must function as a coordinated entity, leading the populace as a whole, as well as organized civil society, in a common endeavour dedicated to achieving clearly defined goals. It must act with constancy and consistency, with continuous reference to its aims and the ways and means to achieve them. It must be true to these aims and persistent in seeking their realization. It must function within a collective sense of responsibility and attain an authority that derives from the character of its prime minister and cabinet, from its policy and its performance and from the degree to which the citizenry is convinced of the justice of its direction.

Four principles should be a guiding light for the leadership. First, the leaders must take responsibility for and avoid contradictions between their language and their actions. The government did not conduct itself according to this principle with regard to the Lebanese War when it said the military action was an anti-terror operation, but it really intended to replace the Lebanese government. Second, they must seek the widest cooperation of the representatives of the various sectors of organized civil society in formulating and implementing policy. This is how the 1985 National Unity Government conducted itself when it created the economic-social advisory board composed of representatives of the government, the Histadrut and the major employers on its way to implementing the stabilization plan. Third, they must always sacrifice the present in favour of the future. For example, if the government tries to improve the income of its citizens by lowering taxes and increasing salaries without any consideration for increased productivity it will inevitably create inflation in the future that will damage the economy and the citizens. Fourth, they must constantly strive for the qualitative and quantitative growth of the country and its economy, primarily through the development of its human capital by way of investment in research and education.

Every democratic government should excel in the pursuit of these principles. But even more so the Israeli government, which presumes to be the government of the entire Jewish people and which has had to function, for most of its existence, in circumstances of unvarying pressure and urgency. The Israeli government frequently has to make critical decisions regarding security and foreign affairs as well as economic and social policy, usually in conditions of crisis and emergency. Israel requires, therefore, a government of great quality and moral authority. A government founded on the widest possible democratic and public participation in the election of the Knesset as well as on a very great degree of decentralization of administrative power, in addition to policy principles that do not require continuous direct intervention in the economy.

Because of all this it is important that the composition of the government includes the foremost individuals leading the various parties. Since Israel has a parliamentary-cabinet system rather than a presidential system, it is inevitable that the ministers will be party activists dependent on the voters they represent. On the other hand, the government cannot be composed only of political operatives that have reached organizational and establishment power by attaining the political manoeuvring skills that enabled them to succeed.

The government must be composed of individuals with leadership abilities, possessed of creative imagination, knowledge and experience. They must be trustworthy and prudent in the matters of state entrusted to them, not only in the national sphere, as required by their membership in the government, but also in the ongoing management of their ministries. This ambitious and desirable goal is a far cry from the present situation in Israel. We frequently encounter discordance between the deeds and decisions of the government and the laws and norms characteristic of a civilized democratic state.

ISRAEL'S SYSTEM OF GOVERNANCE

Israel finds itself in a paradoxical situation. Its government is at one and the same time both too strong and too weak. It is too strong because of the degree of its involvement in every area of life, because of the dependence this has produced amongst Israel's citizens and economy and because of the narrow base of public involvement. It is too weak in those areas that obligate it to be more qualitative and authoritative. In planning and initiation, in its internal decision making processes, in its ability to perceive and define current and potential circumstances and to conduct and actualize policy according to national goals.

The dominance of government in Israel's national life derives from historical causes and objective circumstances. The historical causes originate in the development of the pre-state Jewish settlement in the land of Israel that was dependent almost completely on centralistic national and public institutions. These same institutions amplified their intervention during the early days of the state with regard to the absorption of the mass immigration, the creation of new settlements, development towns, public education institutions, a national water, electricity and energy system as well as industry and air and shipping infrastructures.[9] The social political reality and the nationwide proportional electoral system contributed greatly to this reality. The objective circumstances for strong centralized government derived from the extremely small size of the country, the level of defence expenditure, the extent of external aid and a situation of recurring crisis that required immediate centralized decision making. The tendency for centralized power to control the economic, political and social life of the country found fertile ground in Israel's cultural milieu and political tradition as well as various national-ideological rationalizations.[10]

The weakness of Israel's government is also a consequence of historical causes and objective circumstances. The way in which the political leadership of the various parties developed did not always enable the finest individuals to emerge, and often caused distortions in the ways in which the ministerial representatives of the various parties were chosen. The want of organized procedures of decision making has weakened the governmental cabinet as an entity while strengthening its individual members. There is also poor instruction to and coordination between the various governmental ministries. The coalition structure is an added burden, working against the more desirable development of a government functioning with vision and conviction and working with integrity, coordination, constancy and dependability within a framework of collective responsibility for the realization of its policy aims.[11]

THE ELECTORAL SYSTEM

The nationwide proportional electoral system employed in Israel since its inception has had a far-reaching impact on the structure of Israel's governmental system as well as its mode of behaviour. Over the years there have been many attempts to replace this system with a regional-district system and a proportional-regional system. But none of these attempts have succeeded.

The proportional electoral system determines that the number of seats in the parliament reflects the number of votes a party list received in the elections. For example, if a party wins half the votes it will occupy half the seats in the parliament. Thus its representation will reflect the number of its supporters amongst the electorate. This system enables small collections of voters spread out across the country to join together to garner enough votes to be represented in the parliament. During the electoral campaign the parties put forward a list of candidates as well as a party platform. At the end of the campaign the voters choose their preferred party. When the votes are counted the parties divide up the seats according to the relative proportion of the votes they received.

The regional-district system divides the parliamentary seats between the various areas of the country: one seat for each area. The seat dedicated to a particular area is awarded to the candidate that received the most votes in that area, even if he only received one vote more than another candidate. If there are three candidates in an area and one receives only 34% of the vote and the other two split the remaining 66% evenly the first will be awarded the seat in parliament unless the law determines there be a second round run-off in order for one candidate to achieve at least 50% of the vote.

The proportional-regional system integrates many of the characteristics of the proportional and the regional systems. Firstly, the country is divided into districts, but their number is smaller than the number of seats in the parliament. The candidates in these districts compete *within the district* on the basis of the proportional system. As a result several candidates are chosen from each district. If a district sends ten candidates to parliament and four parties compete then if one of them wins half the votes it will send five candidates to parliament. If another party wins one-fifth of the votes it will send two candidates to parliament. And so on. Secondly, a certain number of candidates will be elected according to the present nationwide proportional system. In other words, there will be two lists from which the voters will elect their candidates, a local list and a national list.

An election campaign conducted according to the individual-district system is usually a confrontation between two 'governments' over who will lead the country. Even when there are more lists the choice is usually between two major parties. The party that wins the majority leads the country for that term of office and the party that loses is left in the 'shadows' and becomes the opposition that prepares for the next election campaign. In this system the government is chosen in tandem with the parliament and is not formed after the parliament is elected as a result of bargaining between numerous parties.

In this system the future government is always already extant. Indeed, one knows who will be in the next government even before the elections – the cabinet or shadow cabinet of one of the two major parties. There may be some changes after the elections as a consequence of coalition considerations or second thoughts on the part of the prime minister regarding a particular minister, but these will be very minor.

This is not the case regarding the Israeli system. And the differences are most significant. In countries that operate according to the regional system the various public power centres join forces before the elections on the basis of preliminary compromises and within a common organizational framework in order to achieve agreed upon aims by way of cooperation in the government. In Israel's case this joining of forces takes place only after the elections, in the course of forming the coalition.

Yet Israel has also created certain political associations before the elections, such as the Likud or Labour, but neither of these has the power to create a government without a coalition, even if there is the appearance that the electorate can choose between two alternative future 'govern-ments'. Paradoxically, then, only the opposition parties can remain loyal to their platforms. They may not be able to implement their platform but they can remain faithful to it in their pronouncements in the Knesset and to the public. This is not the case for parties in the governmental coalition.

It is not a common sight in other countries to see the types of coalition we have in Israel, where we may see in the same coalition a religious party, a socialist party, a liberal party and an ultra-nationalist party. The gaps between the stated positions of these parties are as wide as the ocean yet in the coalition they act as one in foreign and defence affairs, the economy and even as regards religious coercion.

Yet although this is the picture in reality, even large pluralistic parties like Labour or the Likud request the support of the electorate before the elections on the basis of their stated platforms. The voters know for whom they vote and to what they are giving their support. The coalition is formed despite the fact that all the elements that compose it still *formally* preserve the distinctiveness of their respective parties. They have all sharpened their political organizations and have all made their pitch to the voter on the basis of denigrating the positions of the opposing parties while celebrating the virtues of their own party. In the end the government is formed from parties that are completely different in their thinking, in their philosophy and in their spoken word but partners in the execution of policy.

It often occurs that thanks to its being a counterweight a very small party dictates a policy that totally contradicts the positions of the majority and their obligations to their voters. The regional electoral system on the other hand greatly limits the gap of internal conflict between speech and action, even though in politics this never completely disappears. Because even in this system sometimes a small party can constitute a counterweight – such as the Liberals in England –it is drastically less likely.

POLITICAL STRUCTURE

The electoral system also has a great impact on the political structure of society and the parties themselves. In contrast to the proportional system, which by its nature encourages the proliferation of small parties holding a wide range of very narrow views and inflexible political positions, the regional system encourages larger more inclusive and conciliatory parties. Such parties include a much wider range of ideas and personalities.

In the regional system the party constitutes a much looser ideological and organizational framework in which mutual compromise enables it to arrive at a consensus that will win the support of a majority or a least a significant minority of the electorate. This framework enables every group to democratically influence every member of the organization, trying to change its perceptions and policy.

The electoral system influences the structure of the government as a matter of course and as a consequence the very structure of the regime in its totality. The proportional system has a built in incentive to induce both the public and the Knesset to splinter into ever-smaller political groupings. Because of this any one party is prevented from achieving an electoral or parliamentary majority, forming a government solely from its own representatives and attempting to realize a comprehensive platform. It is also difficult for another party to gather a significant minority of voters that may in the course of time constitute a significant alternative to the party in power. This forces the majority party to perform its duties faithfully, since if it does not its majority could turn into a minority and the minority into a majority.

Any electoral system must have four goals. It must extend the ability of the electorate to increase its influence on the make-up of the parliament and by way of this on the parliament's activities. It must erect as few barriers as possible between the electorate and their representatives. It must enable the establishment of a government that has the trust of the majority of the people and as a consequence is capable of managing the affairs of state in an efficient manner. It must also enable the existence of a large well-defined minority that criticizes the government in parliament, and is capable of earning the trust of the majority to manage the affairs of the country. A democracy that does not have these fundamental elements is not functioning properly. Its citizens do not feel that they have any real prospect of participating in shaping the future of the country. Its government is not discharging its main responsibility, namely the formulation and execution of policy.

The economic structures of Israel (and governmental intervention in the economy), the centralized control of the appointment of senior figures in the parties and the electoral system have increased Israel's political centralization. The electoral system in itself is but one element of Israel's political culture. In order to improve the quality of Israeli democracy in the future we must strive to change the present situation in several principal directions.

CHANGING THE DIRECTION OF ISRAELI DEMOCRACY

First, we must deepen and cultivate normative democratic culture in Israel. This should begin in childhood, from nursery school through elementary and middle school and into high school. It should continue on in adult life in the form of initiatives in civil society. But without democratic behaviour within the political system itself all this will be in vain. As long as so-called higher godly commandments and public statements by rabbis lacking any respect for the nature of democracy are placed above the law and democratic norms, our democratic standards will continue to be eroded, at first just formally, but then, more dangerously, with regard to how the broad spectrum of Israel's citizenry views its very way of life.

Second, we must have electoral reform: from the nationwide proportional system to a regional proportional system. The proportional nationwide electoral system encourages the existence of numerous small parties, giving them great financial and political advantage. It enables relatively small parties to be a counterweight that dictates to the government (Knesset and cabinet) a policy unacceptable to most of the electorate. The proportional regional system, on the other hand, would minimize the gap between word and act, between platform and actual performance. It would decrease meaningless divisions and increase the opportunity to crystallize coherent policy.

The electoral system influences the structure of the government and by doing so the very nature of governance itself. It influences both the Knesset and the public. The current nationwide proportional electoral system increases the enfeeblement of effective political power. This finds its expression in the government in the inflation of ministers and the sub-division of ministries. In the Knesset and amongst the citizenry it finds its expression in the fact that no one party is capable of winning the trust of a majority of citizens, creating a parliamentary majority, establishing a government based solely on its representatives and realizing its political platform. It also makes it difficult for a different party to coalesce a *significant* minority of voters in order to constitute a viable alternative to the party in power.

A new electoral system must achieve three aims. It must increase the influence of the voters on the composition of the Knesset and thus on its activities. It must decrease as much as possible the partition between the voters and their elected officials. It must establish a government that enjoys the support of the majority of the people and is capable of managing the affairs of state in a stable way. A democracy that does not possess these three elements cannot function properly. Its citizens do not feel that they can participate meaningfully in shaping the future of the country. Its governments cannot fulfil their primary duty of determining and implementing policy.

Third, we must minimize the centralistic character of the political system. The centralistic character of the political system derives from the status and power of the executive branch in conjunction with the nationwide proportional electoral system. It makes the openness of the system questionable, and the equal opportunity to sustain free democratic processes within the system problematic. The *essential* political pluralism of Israeli democracy is thrown into doubt because of these issues.

There are several directions that might be taken to assist in the development of an essential democracy in Israel. These include: statutory procedures for internal party elections, statutory clarity regulating party behaviour external to political activities and the minimizing of political appointees in the civil service.

Fourth, we must enhance the principle of collective governmental responsibility. This has two connotations: the responsibility of the entire government for the behaviour of every one of its individual members and the responsibility of every individual member for the behaviour of the government. In recent years this principle has been watered down: ministers have frequently criticized governmental policy as well as their ministerial colleagues publicly. The principle of secrecy regarding governmental deliberations has also been violated. Recent prime ministers have not insisted that these principles be honoured. It has not been a practice to censure ministers for leaking sensitive information.

It would be advisable to make obligatory the principle of collective responsibility that has been so honoured in the breach. Every minister has the right to disagree on particular points of policy, but after the government has debated the point and decided to act on it every minister must take responsibility for and defend it. Even if they have not taken part in the determination or the shaping of a position, the ministers cannot free themselves from their association with it. If they wish to cease being responsible for a particular policy there is only one acceptable way for them to do so: to resign from the government. If they do not do so the prime minister must insist that they draw the proper conclusions. This is the meaning of collective responsibility according to the letter and the spirit of the law.

Fifth, we must augment the principle of ministerial responsibility. The law gives the prime minister the right to dismiss a minister. But the real key to maintaining ministerial responsibility is to cultivate a behavioural culture that increases the expectation that the ministers will conduct themselves properly. This depends, first and foremost on the prime minister, cabinet and Knesset members as well as the leaders of the various parties.

Sixth, we must clarify and change the essentials of the relationship between the government and Knesset. To begin with, the government must be sensitive to the opinions of the opposition, despite the fact that its main job is to oppose the government, to lay in wait for its mistakes and blunders, and to embarrass it. The criticism of the opposition may sometimes uncover an error made or about to be made by the government. The government is so involved in immediate tasks and pressing problems, so involved with itself that often its members lack the necessary leisure to examine its policy from every angle by listening and being sensitive to the public and to differing perspectives.

It has frequently been the case that ministers have heard honest reservations about a point of policy in Knesset committee hearings that have caused them to reconsider decisions already taken or at least to widen their perspectives on matters within their ministerial purview. Knesset debates also provide the minister with the opportunity to learn which arguments their critics will use in future battles for public opinion. This may be useful in shaping an information campaign as well as in formulating responses to his critics.

A reciprocal relationship between the Knesset and the government is necessary for the proper conduct of the affairs of the country. This is not in its fundamental nature a relationship of mutual annoyance, even if some ministers might view it as such as a consequence of their short-sightedness and narrow-mindedness. Dialogue and debate between the two branches of government is necessary in order to limit the distortions and misguided actions that can often occur within the governmental process. The various Knesset committees must also be more open to the media and the public. In contrast to the government, the strength of the Knesset derives from its openness to the public, except, of course, with regard to matters relating to national security or the vital interests of the country. Subsidiary legislation not requiring the approval of the Knesset or one of its committees must also be limited. Such legislation in Israel is much greater than in most other parliamentary democracies and is often not substantiated or properly elucidated.

Seventh, we must clarify the significance of the coalition and its way of doing business. The coalition structure of the Israeli government diminishes its ability to function with constancy in determining policy. The British government, composed of representatives from only one party, also includes ministers with different views, styles and temperaments, but they act in the name of one party with a prime minister chosen by that party.

The coalition structure of the Israeli government sometimes resembles a federation of frameworks whose political interests are at cross-purposes. Each party is headed by an individual in constant competition with his colleagues even if they are all members of the same government serving the same country. In other words, the major defects in the operations of the government are rooted in the multiparty coalition character of the government. This all too frequently obligates the government to act as a coordinating committee between various interests and different view-points, and not as a central body determining wide-ranging multi-dimensional policy. This structure encourages a situation whereby the activities of the government are a product of the ministers heading the various governmental offices, rather than as a consequence of a 'national administration' dedicated to directing the ministries in conjunction with wider national goals formulated as part of a multidimensional analysis.

Moreover, this coalition structure forces the government to adopt a conservative strategy that in the name of pragmatism is often too short term and which requires frequent improvisations. The requirement of reciprocal compromise prevents necessary initiatives and long term planning. Since the very existence of a coalition has been a prerequisite to sustaining a functioning government in Israel, every government has refrained as much as possible from making decisions on controversial subjects. This constraint reinforces a tendency towards continuity and routine that averts confrontations. It is easier, as regards the maintenance of the coalition, to deal with the small details of practical problems rather than issues that require decisive resolution.

These are only several of the necessary steps that need to be taken to change the direction of Israeli democracy. In addition to all of these we require an essentially different national strategy that influences the public and democratic way of life of the country.

CONCLUSION

Israel's democracy is based on formal procedures and constitutional elements, yet even now fissures are appearing that threaten it. Some of these derive from the very composition of Israeli society and some derive from Israel's security situation and from the fact that a great number of our leaders have a military background that affects their way of thinking and their behaviour. Changes in these areas as well as the reforms already mentioned will go a long way towards strengthening Israel's democracy.

The continued existence of an open, free and culturally dynamic Israeli democracy depends on the quality of its leadership, the extent of its education, its regional and international frame of reference and a system of governance that enables the emergence of qualified and independent minded elected representatives.

I believe that this is possible if we do what needs to be done. The vital key is a worthy leadership that understands that it will earn the trust of the public and will lead it towards better days only if it liberates itself from outmoded thinking and concepts. This will be a leadership that understands that 'the future begins now' and that its fundamental responsibility lies beyond immediate political exigencies and needs; that its fundamental responsibility is to be focused on the long term future.

NOTES

1. James Bryce, *Modern Democracies*, London, 1921.
2. John Burnett (ed.), *Plato's Dialogues*, Oxford, 1953.
3. Ronald Dworkin, *Law's Empire*, London, 1986.
4. See Meir Shamgar's article in this volume.
5. Amnon Rubenstein, *The Constitutional Law of Israel*, Tel Aviv, 1974; 2000 (Hebrew). See also John Rawls, 6. 'Liberty, Equality, and Law', in Sterling M. McMurrin (ed.), *The Tanner Lectures on Human Values*, Cambridge, 1987, pp.1–87.
6. Michel Troper, 'The Development of the Notion of Separation of Powers', *Israel Law Review*, Vol.26 (1992), pp.1–15.
7. Cf. Terrence E. Cook and Patrick M. Morgan, *Participatory Democracy*, San Francisco, 1971; Roland J. Pennock and John W. Chapman (eds.), *Participation in Politics*, New York, 1975; Sidney Verba, Norman H. Nie and Jae-On Kim, *Participation and Political Equality*, Cambridge, 1978; Carole Pateman, *Participation and Democratic Theory*, Cambridge, 1979; Richard Dagger, *Civic Virtues*, New York, 1997. See also Norberto Bobbio, *The Future of Democracy*, Cambridge, 1987.

8. Cf. Hanna F. Pitkin, *The Concept of Representation*, Berkeley, CA, 1967; Ronald J. Pennock and John W. Chapman (eds.), *Representation*, New York, 1968; A.H. Birch, *Representation*, London, 1971.

9. Dan Horowitz and Moshe Lissak, *The Origins of Israeli Polity*, Chicago, 1978; Raphael Cohen-Almagor, 'Cultural Pluralism and the Israeli Nation-Building Ideology', *International Journal of Middle East Studies*, Vol.27 (1995), pp.461–84.

10. David Ben-Gurion, *Israel: Years of Challenge*, London, 1964; idem, *Rebirth and Destiny of Israel*, London, 1959; idem, *Reflections*, London, 1970; idem, *Uniqueness and Mission*, Tel-Aviv, 1971 (Hebrew); idem, *Vision and Way*, Tel Aviv, 1953 (Hebrew).

11. Ehud Sprinzak and Larry Diamond (eds.), *Israeli Democracy Under Stress*, Boulder, CO and London, 1993.

The Knesset

NAOMI CHAZAN

The Knesset, the central political institution in Israel's parliamentary democracy, exemplifies the confusion that characterizes the Israeli political arena at the beginning of the twenty-first century. During the 54 years since the inauguration of the first Knesset in 1949, Israel's parliament has undergone profound changes in its power, public standing, and influence. None have been more dramatic than those that have occurred during the past decade.

The Knesset today is more representative than ever before; it also enjoys less popular esteem than at any previous point in its history. Its legislative activity has risen substantially just as its centrality in regulating policy has eroded. As a deliberative body the Knesset retains its pre-eminence, but it has had an adverse effect on political culture and norms of good governance. Many of the heretofore unique roles of Israel's parliament are now shared by the judicial and executive branches; at the same time, its position as the key political institution in the country may be more pronounced today than at any point in the past.

The paradoxical patterns of parliamentary evolution in Israel reflect both major shifts in Israeli society and institutional functions, as well as significant alterations in popular expectations and the rules of the political game. These developments have not received the attention they deserve. Few studies of the Knesset have been undertaken recently; the last

Naomi Chazan, former Deputy Speaker of the Knesset, is professor of political science and African studies at the Hebrew University of Jerusalem.

authoritative book was published almost 40 years ago.[1] This essay can only begin to identify major processes and highlight crucial topics for future study and action.

Specifically, the first section deals with the Knesset as a representative institution. The second examines its formal and informal structures. The third section elaborates on its operations and role performance, and takes a closer look at its standing in the eyes of the public. The conclusion attempts to assess the relative power and influence of the Knesset today; it also offers some suggestions on how to improve upon its performance and conduct and deal with its progressively enigmatic character.

REPRESENTATIVES AND REPRESENTATION

Assemblies are, first and foremost, representative institutions. They are the concrete symbol of the people's will and hence the structural bedrock of modern democratic governments. Increasingly, the composition of parliaments mirrors the various identities and aspirations of their citizens.[2] Israel has traditionally been considered to house one of the most representative bodies in the world. The Knesset became truly reflective of the diversity of Israeli society during the past decade. This heterogeneity, however, has been accompanied by growing inter-party fractionalization and the impairment of parliamentary capacities.

Israel's single constituency proportional representation electoral system, with its exceedingly low threshold (1.5%), has been widely known for the multiplicity of parties it generates.[3] The average number of parties voted into the Knesset in the 16 national elections held since independence is 13.[4] Until the 1990s, alongside the large number of parties (none of which ever commanded a majority of the house) it was always possible to discern at least one, if not two, dominant parties (Labour and/or the Likud).

This picture changed with the introduction of the direct election of the prime minister in 1996 (subsequently rescinded in 2001). The dual ballot system employed in 1996 and 1999 drastically reduced the size of the major electoral alignments, increased the number of sectarian and single-issue formations, and generally undermined party cohesion and durability. Significantly, the effective differences between the parties increased and ideological polarization intensified.[5]

The 2003 general elections, conducted under the old/new pure proportional representation system, did indeed witness a mild drop in the number of parties (from 15 to 13), but had little impact on their disparate character. The Likud emerged as a pivot party without which no government could be formed (a throwback to the heyday of Labour hegemony in the 1950s and 1960s), while the size of the Labour faction plummeted to an all time low. But most parties continued to articulate the narrow interests of particularistic and frequently conflicting constituencies.

The party scene has consequently been unsettled for over a decade, mostly as a result of incessant (and irresponsible) tampering with the electoral system.[6] Power has vacillated between the centre-right and the centre-left in each one of the last five elections, increasing political volatility and precluding governmental or parliamentary continuity.

The highly inclusive yet inchoate party map is apparent in the changing personal characteristics and backgrounds of the members of the Knesset (MKs). Until recently, Israeli parliamentarians, like their counterparts elsewhere, were disproportionately drawn from the more established sectors of society. For the first two decades, most elected representatives conformed to a standard profile: Ashkenazi, male, urban resident (or kibbutz member), and secular. Representation of women and Arabs was abysmal. This pattern shifted during the 1970s and 1980s as more Sephardi and religious members – some hailing from development towns – were elected to office.

The Knesset only became truly representative of the key segments of Israeli society in the last few years. By 1999, 30% of the 120 members of the Knesset were Sephardi, 25% were orthodox, 11% were Arab and 9.2% were recent immigrants from the former Soviet Union. With the exception of women, who remain sorely under-represented in Israel (a meagre 14.1% in 2003 when a record 17 women were elected), the composition of the Knesset reflects the main elements of Israeli society more faithfully than almost any parliament in the democratic world.[7]

These changes can be attributed more to the rise of particularistic parties than to significant shifts within veteran electoral alignments. Indeed, the politicization of social schisms encouraged by the dual ballot improved societal representation at the expense of a commitment to broad national worldviews and pursuits. The new parliamentarians are more committed to promoting narrow interests than to forwarding general societal goals.

The narrowing perspective of elected representatives has plagued established parties as well. Candidate selection has undergone a purported process of democratization during the past decade. Primaries were introduced in the Labour party in 1992 and adopted by the Likud and Meretz (a social-democratic civil rights party) prior to the 1996 elections. Even when primaries were abandoned in all but the Labour party on the eve of the 1999 elections, with the notable exception of the ultra-orthodox formations, other representative bodies (party councils, conventions) assumed the task of candidate selection. In all these parties provisions were made to guarantee adequate representation of women, new immigrants, geographical areas and minorities.

Democratization of selection procedures consequently exacerbated the dependence of individual MKs on narrowly construed but extremely well organized groups within their own parties (but hardly to the party ideology *per se*). More to the point, the new rules have given extraordinary advantages to those who have access to money, organizations or media visibility (and preferably to a mixture of these resources).

As a result, many of those who won prominent places on their party lists were either well connected, well healed or well publicized. The relationship between qualifications, experience and electability was shattered.[8] In the last three elections too many members entered the Knesset with no prior experience in the public arena, with few relevant skills, and with little understanding of the issues at hand. Some had attained high media visibility (all too often, notoriety), but lacked any explicit political agenda. Others, especially in the 2003 preliminary party races, gained their positions through a mixture of chicanery and outright bribery.[9]

Representative turnover in Israel has always been high, averaging 33% (40.4 members) after each national election.[10] There would therefore be nothing unusual in the large influx of new members after recent elections if not for their problematic background and the fact that many veteran politicians chose not to enter the fray, were ousted in the internal party ballots, or survived and subsequently resigned in desperation. In 1999, 31 new MKs were elected (25% of the Knesset), but 20 of the most able members left of their own volition in mid-term. In 2003, 37 fresh representatives gained seats, all too often at the expense of experienced parliamentarians. Some parliamentary rotation is undeniably necessary for innovation, but the developments of the past decade have depleted the Knesset of its most competent human resources and left Israel's parliament with a majority of unschooled politicians.

The personal characteristics and capabilities of members of the Knesset have aroused considerable public concern in recent years. So, too, has the disproportionate number of rabbis, ex-military men and party function-aries in the house.[11] These issues have also preoccupied party leaders, who have attempted to adjust selection procedures to attract and reward competent candidates from all walks of life. In 2003, the second Sharon government went so far as to propose legislation that would require all parties with over 15 seats in parliament to hold primaries. The question of candidate selection cannot, however, be so neatly divorced from the changing nature of the political arena. The current composition of the Knesset is as much an outcome of the fragmentation and diversification of Israeli politics as of internal party dynamics.

The constricted interests of political parties and the variable capabilities of elected representatives carry added weight in light of the growing size of coalition governments in the past decade. During the Ehud Barak and Ariel Sharon administrations, the number of ministers and deputy ministers soared, reaching a record 40 on the eve of the 2003 elections (when a broad national unity government commanding the backing of over 80 MKs was in office). Since so many members of Knesset hold ministerial posts, in effect the actual number of potential full-time parliamentarians has been scaled down substantially. Parliamentary work today is in actuality conducted by, at best, between 80 and 90 backbenchers.

Opposition MKs, many with ministerial experience, have a distinct advantage under these circumstances: they can devote more time and attention to their work than their overburdened and frequently inexperienced colleagues in the coalition should they be so inclined (many ex-cabinet members are not). Since there is such a clear inverse correlation between the size of the government and the parliamentary capabilities of its constituent party representatives, all recent governments have suffered from problems of parliamentary ineffectiveness and lax party discipline.[12]

The Knesset is, undeniably, a microcosm of the wide range of political opinions and the unique multiculturalism of Israeli society. But in recent years the Israeli parliament has become a paradigmatic example of the representational conundrum: as its membership has become increasingly representative, the ability of individual members to represent broad popular currents has diminished. In the absence of defined mechanisms and norms of accountability between elected officials and their constituencies, MKs mirror society but are decreasingly its emissaries in the decision making nexus.

STRUCTURES AND PROCEDURES

The operation of the Knesset is largely determined – like parliaments elsewhere – by its internal structures and procedural guidelines. In recent years, despite multiple attempts to buttress the professional capacities of the formal organs of the house, the locus of parliamentary power has shifted sharply to informal mechanisms. As a result, the binding rules of procedure have been eroded, frequently replaced by makeshift provisions enacted on an *ad hoc* basis according to need.[13]

The Knesset is a small unicameral assembly. Its size promotes inter-action and a measure of intimacy, but of necessity imposes a severe workload on its members and limits specialization. As the issues brought before the chamber have become increasingly complex, it has sought to compensate by the augmentation of professional services in lieu of an increase in its membership.[14] Efforts to establish an upper house in order to introduce a modicum of stability, protect various groups and interests, enhance efficiency and provide checks on assembly activities have failed repeatedly. In 2002 the Israel Democracy Institute hosted a conference on the subject in the Knesset. The reaction of parliamentarians was resoundingly negative, partly for substantive reasons (a second house is not reflective of social-democratic norms), but also on personal grounds (a bi-cameral structure would curtail their powers and reduce their status). Knesset members guard their position jealously, justifying their reluctance to concede some of their powers in terms of the need to maintain the legislature as the institutional expression of the popular concept of democracy.[15]

The formal structures of the Knesset therefore remain the plenary, the parliamentary committees and the party factions. The speaker of the Knesset, usually selected from the ranks of the prime minister's party, is responsible for all the activities within the house and is the ultimate arbiter of disputes on issues of process and comportment. Together with his deputies in the presidium he determines the agenda and presides over plenary sessions.

The speaker of the Knesset is, by definition, a political creature. Until recently, the incumbents of the third highest office in the country were elder statesmen determined to maintain a measure of objectivity and to protect the Knesset as an institution from incursions by other branches of government. This tradition has changed in recent years as unstable coalitions have sought, and received, substantial assistance from the recent holders of the speaker's chair. Thus, despite the formalization of the role of the leader of the opposition in 1999, in reality the government, through the person of the speaker of the Knesset, has sought to exert undue influence on the workings of the house.[16]

The bulk of the work of the Knesset, as of most legislatures, is conducted in its committees, which are responsible for monitoring government operations, preparing bills for approval by the plenary, and investigating questions of public concern. The Knesset has 12 standing committees, the most prestigious being the Foreign Affairs and Defence Committee, and the most powerful the Finance Committee. A relatively large number of select committees (such as the Committee to Combat Drug Abuse, the Committee on the Rights of the Child, and the Committee on Foreign Workers) have been established in recent years, mostly to placate restless backbenchers and to silence opposition discontent. Parliamentary investigation panels have also proliferated, providing a platform for individual members seeking an outlet for action and media salience.[17]

Members and parties vie with each other over committee placements and chairs at the start of each new Knesset. Decisions are made by an informal organizing panel set up by the factions, which is charged with dividing everything from committee chairs and placements to office space, usually on the basis of a strict party key.[18] Since most veteran politicians in the coalition move to ministerial posts, backbenchers have the opportunity to achieve prominence as chairs of key committees and members of high profile panels. Competition among opposition members over plum committee assignments is generally even more intense and personal.

Committee chairs usually rule their domains with an iron fist, controlling the agenda, deciding if and when to permit member participation and dictating the list of invited officials and specialists. Despite the high-handed techniques adopted by most committee chairs in their ongoing attempts to safeguard their standing and status, their tenure is increasingly fleeting. Given the absence of any seniority rules, high turnover rates, inexperience and lack of continuity in personal composition, committees encounter increasing difficulty in functioning smoothly.

The proliferation of parliamentary committees, reaching as many as 20 in the late 1990s, means that individual MKs have multiple committee assignments (ranging from at least two in the opposition to up to six in the coalition). Committees tend to meet at the same times when the plenary is not in session. The rate of absenteeism is consequently enormous. Most meetings are attended by a handful of members, and the full number is mobilized only for crucial votes. Experts appearing before the committees view this conduct with a disdain bordering on derision, and have further impaired their operations by frequently refusing to attend their sessions. Under the circumstances, it is surprising that some committees succeed in working at all.[19]

Regardless of the faltering operations of the committee system, and despite the failure of recent attempts to totally reform their structure,[20] the parliamentary committees nevertheless remain the place where most of the serious work of the Knesset is conducted. They are the home of those 20 or 30 MKs who see themselves first and foremost as parliamentarians and policy advocates. The other 60 working MKs (some 30 are ministers or deputy ministers) appear only sporadically or cannot be bothered to attend committee meetings at all. This phenomenon, which has plagued the Knesset since its inception, has become more pronounced as the number of committees has proliferated and as it has become clearer to many politicians that most committee work, by definition very demanding, remains unnoticed and hence electorally unrewarding.

For all members of Knesset, the party faction is the focus of their political activity within the house. Party formations possess formal status: arrangements regarding participation in debates, private member bills, committee placement, parliamentary positions and participation in delegations are computed on the basis of faction size. All the party formations have representation in the Knesset (House) Committee, charged with overseeing the day-to-day operation of the parliament.[21]

Factions receive funding, office space and services from the Knesset. Their coordinators, operating behind the scenes, follow debates in the plenary, try to influence the agenda, monitor committee meetings, mobilize members for votes and generally safeguard their interests. In many respects the faction coordinators, most of whom are highly experienced women, are the movers and shakers of in-house activities.

Faction meetings, usually held on Monday afternoons before the opening of the plenary, are better attended than any other forum in the Knesset. Not only are issues of legislative strategy and floor tactics discussed in these gatherings, but in many instances major political issues are aired and policy positions consolidated. Some of these sessions receive wide media coverage (especially in the larger parties). They have become the place where ministers and ministerial aspirants reign.

The party formations are the connecting link between the individual MK and the formal structures of the Knesset. Traditionally, party discipline has been the primary means of maintaining a modicum of stability and predictability in decision making. The effectiveness of this tool has been blunted in the past decade. Individual members, whose margin of manoeuvrability is severely constrained, often prefer to gain public visibility by flaunting party dictates rather than scoring brownie points for good citizenship in inner circles. They are willing to risk loosely imposed penalties meted out by the faction (usually the denial of floor time) for the opportunity to grab a headline in tomorrow's newspaper: the greater their breach of discipline, the higher their media exposure. Factions retain their centrality in Knesset life, but their contribution to its effectiveness has diminished.

Increasingly, therefore, the staff of the Knesset has become the repository of expertise and specialization. The clerk of the Knesset, charged with overseeing the administration of the house, together with his deputies, the directors of the standing committees, and the legal advisor and her staff, constitute the institutional mainstay of the Knesset. These functionaries form a mini civil service that ensures some continuity, especially in times of political instability. Here, too, however, the by now familiar pattern of structural erosion has surfaced. Dominant speakers and committee chairs have sought to either constrict or cow Knesset officers, rendering them weaker and more timid than at any point in the past.[22] These Knesset potentates have isolated some of the leading house officers or forced their removal in order to increase political control over procedure and outcomes.

The formal structures of the Knesset therefore provide the framework for parliamentary activity, but its pace and nature is in actuality determined in several distinct informal – and frequently underestimated – settings.

Major decisions are made, in the first instance, through a series of unofficial consultations. Faction whips, who have no official standing, gather periodically to discuss issues of common concern (ranging from recess dates to member benefits) and to iron out differences. In the past few years, the speakers of the Knesset have consulted this forum on delicate votes and procedures.

The management executives of the coalition and the opposition, respectively (consisting of the faction whip and senior members of each constituent party), meet weekly to discuss the legislative agenda and to deal with ongoing matters. Voting procedures on sensitive issues are negotiated by *ad hoc* groups composed of a small number of coalition and opposition members (commonly dubbed 'agreement teams'), often pre-empting guidelines established by the Knesset committee.[23]

Particularly knotty problems are ironed out in frequent meetings between the speaker of the Knesset and the cabinet minister charged with coordinating between the government and the Knesset (a new portfolio created formally only in 1999).[24] In effect, these unrecorded discussions have had a direct bearing on the outcome of critical votes, ranging from the budget to major debates on peace and security.

A second set of informal structures revolves around representatives of organized interests and a growing number of voluntary organizations. The industrialists, chambers of commerce, banks, insurance companies, farmers' cooperatives and professional associations all employ lobbyists on a full-time basis. During the past decade almost all groups active in civil society (articulating diverse concerns ranging from women, minority and animal rights to environmental, social justice and religious pluralism causes) maintain a regular presence in the corridors of the Knesset.[25] On critical legislative matters, all of these interests engage the services of one of the six leading legislative strategy and lobby firms (all established during the past ten years).[26]

Lobbyists now have recognized status in law. They are granted standing entry permits to the Knesset, full mobility in the house, and dining privileges, provided they conform to a few basic guidelines on transparency and disclosure.[27] In effect, these professionals control the outcome of most major legislative initiatives. They are the main source of information to harried MKs, they regularly take part in committee meetings, and they nurture close relations with key politicians, staff members and journalists. As certified specialists whose income depends on success, they are fast becoming an indispensable source of detailed knowledge on the various facets of the Knesset.

The third circle of informal structures centres on the media. Since the mid-1990s all plenary debates are televised; for the past few years cameras have been allowed into committee rooms. The extent and nature of coverage can literally make or break political careers. The omnipresence of the electronic media and of a group of veteran parliamentary correspondents has come to determine not only main elements of MK behaviour, but also key agenda items.[28]

The informal bodies and the formal structures of the house converge in the Knesset cafeteria. The members' dining room is where critical information is transmitted, deals are struck, and futures determined.

Since 2003, party activists (especially Likud central committee members) have made it their second home. Savvy MKs either regularly spend time in the cafeteria or dispatch their assistants to eavesdrop. Those who absent themselves from this arena do so at their peril.

The growing dependence on informal structures has also affected parliamentary norms. *The Knesset Rules of Procedure*, which details the form and the guidelines of debate and conduct, is ostensibly the law book of the house. Every truly skilled MK is familiar with its detailed regulations and able to invoke its more obscure provisions to suit the occasion.

The speaker and his deputies have traditionally served as the guardians and interpreters of these rules and, by extension, of the institutional autonomy of the Knesset. Their commitment to this task has visibly faltered in the past few years. They have made numerous questionable rulings, allowed members to flaunt the regulations, and in some instances simply ignored explicit provisions under pressure. The Interpretations Committee, the final judge of Knesset procedure, was convened only sporadically during the 15th Knesset, and did not meet even once in its last two years. The failure to defend the rules of the game (out of ignorance or political utility) has contributed directly to the growing chaos in the chamber and to the erosion of the parliamentary process.[29]

The structural and procedural framework of Knesset activities is more open to the public today than in the past. It is also more exposed to outside pressure and manipulation. The structures established to safeguard the Knesset as an institution and facilitate its operation have been subjected to multiple assaults for reasons of political expediency and personal aggrandizement. Consequently parliamentary efficacy has been curtailed and decision making capacities circumscribed. The prominence of the Knesset as the crossroads of political interaction has solidified in the process.

ROLES AND PERFORMANCE

Knesset performance of key parliamentary tasks (law making, government scrutiny, communication, deliberation and socialization) follows a variable pattern. Where the Knesset fulfils its functions reasonably well, it competes directly with the executive and the judiciary. In the spheres of activity that are virtually unique to the Knesset, its record is, to put it mildly, unsatisfactory.

Legislation

The Israeli parliament is one of the most active lawmaking bodies in the world. Since 1992, the legislative initiatives of it members have stepped up considerably. By 2003, in fact, the Knesset reached the point of what can only be described as hyper-legislation. Paradoxically, although members of

Knesset excel themselves in the prime parliamentary task of lawmaking, too many of their initiatives are unnecessary or trivial, while others are unreasonable or prohibitively costly. Legislative frenzy cannot be equated with superior legislative performance.

During its first four decades the Knesset moulded the legal codex of the country.[30] In coordination with the government, it gave the fundamental norms of Israel's democracy legal shape, defined the rules of individual and administrative behaviour, established the guidelines for the allocation of goods and services, and delineated the powers of public institutions and their limitations. In the course of this period 85% of all legislation emanated from the government, but MKs played a critical role by revising proposals between the first, and second and third, readings and suggesting innovative amendments.[31]

Even in its formative years it was clear that the members of the Knesset took their legislative role seriously. Immense efforts were invested, especially in the Constitution, Law, and Justice Committee (whose members included some of the best legal minds in the country), in systematically covering all relevant topics needed for the regulation of public life in the country. Since the Knesset is also, formally, the country's Constituent Assembly, special attention was devoted to drafting the Basic Laws, which carry constitutional weight.[32] Not surprisingly, given the difficulty of achieving a consensus on constitutional matters between secular and religious parties in successive governments, Israel's first, and to date only, Basic Laws on human and civil rights (passed in the last days of the 12th Knesset in 1992 over government opposition) were initially presented as private members' bills. The only major structural political reform, the introduction of the dual ballot system, was also an initiative of individual members completed in early 1992 (as was the decision to abandon the experiment nine years later).[33]

The inauguration of the 13th Knesset in the summer of 1992 marked the turning point in lawmaking trends. During its tenure (1992–96), 3,607 private member's bills were proposed (up from an average of 336 between 1949 and 1992); 213 passed all three readings (in contrast to an average of 41 in the past). Fifty-four per cent of all laws originated from individual members. The same pattern repeated itself in the three-year term of the 14th (1996–99) Knesset, when 2,702 private bills were presented, and 140 passed (54% of all legislation). The 15th Knesset (1999–2003) approved a total of 440 laws, of which a record 239 were private members' bills (54.3%).[34]

There are many reasons for the steep rise in MK legislation, most notably governmental laxity on the legislative front, increased pressure from specific constituencies, new needs emanating from rapid economic and technological change, and rising competition among MKs in an era in which their every move is critically scrutinized. Nevertheless, the Knesset has actually lost its legislative monopoly during this period.

The High Court under the Aharon Barak presidency assumed an activist role, questioning the constitutionality of some laws, reinterpreting others and continually requesting legislative clarifications or corrections.[35] This involvement has evoked bitter criticism in the Knesset, reaching unprecedented intensity in 2003 when the speaker, Reuven Rivlin, accused the court system of being undemocratic. The relationship between the Knesset and the judiciary is now at its nadir.

The executive branch, only partly successful both in thwarting the rising legislative output of individual MKs (from the coalition as well as those of the opposition) and in assuring majorities for its own initiatives, has found other ways to impose its will in the legislative sphere. In some cases, it has simply ignored new laws and failed to ensure their implementation. Increasingly, it has resorted to substituting policy decisions and administrative regulations for laws where possible, thereby relieving itself of the tedious and enervating task of mobilizing backing in the recalcitrant parliamentary arena. More significantly, it has used the annual 'Arrangements Law', tagged on to the budget, as a mechanism for cancelling private member's bills, postponing their implementation and introducing totally new legislation which it would not be able to pass through regular channels. Since the budget debates constitute a vote of confidence in the government, this is one of the rare occasions that the coalition can effectively impose party discipline.[36] Thus the government has become an independent lawmaker by skilfully bypassing the parliamentary process.

These measures, however, did not slow down private legislative productivity. In 2002 the first Sharon government rammed through a bill prohibiting the adoption of private member initiatives costing more than five million shekels unless these received the support of at least 50 members of the house. This order has been extended for the duration of the 16th Knesset, and will probably result in a substantial decrease in the number of bills approved in the current session. Such a step will have a mixed impact: it will curtail highly costly and populist proposals; at the same time it will reduce the prospects of passing necessary social reforms and render private initiatives either incidental or marginal.

In many respects Israel has reached a legislative impasse. On the one hand, the Knesset has over-performed in its lawmaking capacity, passing some irresponsible bills that have had extensive social and economic consequences.[37] On the other hand, many of the most progressive social and normative legal instruments originated in private member's bills (most notably in the field of women's rights, the handicapped, consumer affairs, environmental protection, social justice and domestic violence). Usurping the lawmaking powers of the Knesset does not solve the problem and undermines the position and authority of the legislature. Curtailing its legislative functions arbitrarily threatens to sacrifice the contribution inherent in many of these initiatives. Unless a reasonable balance is found in the near future, the lawmaking scene threatens to become chaotic, adversely affecting the division of powers between the legislature and its judicial and executive counterparts.

Supervision

One of the key roles of the Knesset, like most modern assemblies, is to monitor the activities of the government. In this respect, the parliament is the public's watchdog over the executive and the key institutional check on its use (or abuse) of power. The Knesset possesses multiple tools to scrutinize government activity, and has added some innovative instruments to its oversight arsenal in the past few years. Nevertheless, the effectiveness of the parliament in this area, as in lawmaking, is being overtaken by other bodies (especially the state comptroller[38] and the media).

In theory, an integral part of the job of individual members of Knesset is to monitor government activities. The standard technique at their disposal is the parliamentary question. Each MK is allotted a quota of regular questions (which must be presented in writing and are answered in the plenary) and oral questions aired in the chamber (usually used to embarrass the government or to affect policy on a pressing issue).[39] Members can also present more detailed direct questions, asked and answered in writing. Only about 20% of MKs have actually used their full allotment in the past decade, as there is usually little glory to be garnered in employing this instrument. Some have never asked an oral question; many are simply unaware of the direct question option.[40] Too many of the parliamentary questions that are actually posed are culled from the press and prepared by industrious parliamentary assistants eager to bolster their MK's performance statistics.

The government's attitude towards parliamentary questions is consequently at best cursory and, more frequently, dismissive. Some ministers just do not answer questions, or do so after so much time has elapsed that they are no longer relevant. Most senior ministers send their deputies to read responses prepared by the very officials whose behaviour is queried. The Knesset secretariat contributes to this practice by scheduling answers at the close of long sessions, when the interrogator has already left the building. The responses that are received are all too often equivocal and at times downright misleading. The parliamentary question, by its very nature a substantively diffuse and sporadically utilized instrument, has generally proven to be an extremely blunt tool of control over the administration.[41]

To compensate for these weaknesses the Knesset introduced a ministerial question hour in 1997. Unlike the British weekly tradition of the prime minister's question time, which is a critical tool of parliamentary supervision, the Knesset question hour (used very intermittently) involves only one minister, who answers questions on a predetermined list of topics. The prime minister has never participated in this new, and generally ineffective, ritual.

Determined MKs can exert some influence over administrative action if they employ another new device: the request for a rapid debate in committee. The presidium may approve up to five such proposals a week, and the relevant committee must present its findings in writing to the plenary within two weeks. The rapid debate procedure has halted some administrative actions and helped to expose cases of blatant administrative wrongdoing. Unfortunately, it has been employed by only a handful of MKs since it was first introduced in 1999.[42]

The parliamentary committees are, in fact, the locus of the most consistent scrutiny of the government (if only because they meet regularly and deal with a defined set of topics and administrative bodies). However, with the notable exception of the Finance Committee, which has the power to authorize expenditures, the monitoring activities of the standing committees tend to be superficial. The expertise at their disposal is still inadequate, and they cannot impose sanctions on truant officials.

Discussions on the performance of specific ministries usually offer an opportunity for confrontation between the coalition and the opposition rather than for close scrutiny. Thus, for example, the Foreign Affairs and Defence Committee, whose work is primarily of a supervisory nature, has evolved into a debating forum.[43] The ever popular (and usually well publicized) committee visits to projects and installations can sometimes make a dent, but without adequate follow-up, their efficacy is ephemeral. Even the State Control Committee, charged specifically with monitoring government performance, depends almost exclusively on the *State Comptroller's Report* as its sole guidebook. Committee oversight remains a major parliamentary pursuit; it is questionable whether, given its highly retrospective quality, it constitutes an adequate means of placing checks and balances on the executive.

The proliferation of parliamentary investigation committees is, to some extent, a response to the weaknesses inherent in its more institutionalized mechanisms. These panels do not, however, possess the quasi-judicial authority of governmental investigation commissions. In most instances, they produce detailed reports with policy recommendations that gather dust on bureaucrats' shelves.[44] In many respects, the use of this device is misplaced: it confuses policy oversight with policy making, and therefore actually constitutes an intrusion into the realm of the executive as opposed to a monitor of its activities.

The guardians of the Knesset as an institution have been aware of the continuous erosion of its supervisory powers. They therefore introduced a clause into Basic Law: The Government that enables 40 members to convene an emergency debate requiring the presence of the prime minister. Though employed only sporadically, these deliberations have focused on major political and economic issues. They inevitably end with a vote endorsing the government's position.

The no-confidence vote continues to be the ultimate means of calling the government to order. Its effectiveness has diminished during the past decade, first because an amendment was passed in 1992 requiring an absolute majority of 61 members to bring down a government, and then, as part of the reinstatement of the single ballot, with the adoption of the constructive vote of no-confidence.[45] The opposition continues to introduce no-confidence motions almost every Monday afternoon when the Knesset is in session. This tedious ceremony is clearly not a real check on the administration; it rarely even attracts media attention.

Israel does not differ substantially from other democracies (with the notable exception of the United States) in its limited capacity to scrutinize the administration. Nevertheless, despite growing competition for primacy with other bodies, the Knesset, justifiably, doggedly persists in performing this role.

Communication

The functions of the Knesset also include maintaining regular communication with the public. This task is extraordinarily time-consuming and frequently thankless. Yet it is essential in meeting the uniquely parliamentary charge of representation of individual and group interests and, subsequently, regime legitimation.[46] Members of Knesset have increasingly faltered in performing this role.

The bulk of the correspondence reaching MK offices consists of demands for explanations on votes or positions, requests for assistance, advice on anything from policy to comportment, and, inevitably, judgements on performance. The volume of these appeals – both from individual citizens and organized groups – has grown enormously in recent years. Most often, they involve intercession with the authorities, a clear indication of rising administrative inefficiency.

In the wake of growing MK pressure, the Knesset augmented the resources available for communication with the public. The number of parliamentary assistants was increased from one to two in 1995 (still leaving members of Knesset with much less administrative support than their counterparts elsewhere). The special budget granted members for communication with the electorate was more than doubled (and its name changed to reflect its purported purpose: contact with the public). In 1999 the Knesset Committee voted members a new account to enable them to open parliamentary bureaus outside of Jerusalem and to employ additional staff. And, to relieve some of the load, an *ad hoc* Knesset committee was created to deal with public complaints.

Despite these substantial attempts to facilitate the interaction between elected officials and their constituents, only a few MKs devote much energy to communicating with the public at large. The daily work of the staffs of those members who still define their job as serving citizens is almost entirely consumed with dealing with specific requests.[47] Most MKs, however, have preferred to concentrate on meeting the needs of narrowly defined groups, party members or, in some extreme cases, friends and family. Their expense accounts are reflective of this trend: they spend a great deal of their special budget on season's greetings, wedding and bar mitzvah presents, fancy brochures and, increasingly, on themselves (purchasing everything from palm pilots and TV sets to digital cameras and clothes).[48]

It is difficult to escape the conclusion that the Knesset is failing miserably in carrying out one of the few roles that no other governmental body can perform consistently: communicating with Israel's (admittedly demanding) citizens. Not only do members tend to respond to the concerns of particularistic groups and individuals at the expense of the general interest, they also, in the process, compromise the representative function of the Knesset as an institution. Their poorly honed sense of accountability may contribute directly to the loss of faith in government structures, and, in the long run, in the country's democratic order.

Deliberation

Parliaments are, by definition, the locus of discussion on national affairs. The Knesset has, through its deliberations, always played a central role in setting the public agenda and defining the terms and nature of political discourse. It continues to do so today, although its debates have become as shallow as they are raucous.

The Knesset offers multiple opportunities for discussion of major issues. The key tool is the urgent motion for the agenda. Members vigorously compete with each other to raise attractive topics and receive precious floor time. They are, however, more diligent in publicizing their initiatives than in actually participating in the debates, which tend to be the last item on the weekly schedule of the chamber.

Some members take advantage of their right to raise regular motions for the agenda, which allow them to expand on a topic and to receive a more detailed answer from the relevant minister. The quota for regular motions is, however, severely constricted, and MKs must decide whether to use their allotment for legislation or debate. All motions end in a vote, and those which are not removed are transferred to committee or lead to a general debate in the plenary. Except in unusual cases, the ensuing discussions are poorly attended and usually yield broad declarations rather than any constructive recommendations.

The subjects of deliberation do, indeed, focus on the key issues of peace and security, the economy, social justice and religious-secular relations. In recent years, however, the topics approved for debate have tended to minimize major questions and given undue prominence to marginal matters. Thus, two motions on local council disputes will be scheduled in the same week that ten motions on the peace process or Arab-Jewish relations are rejected.[49] To compensate for this substantive imbalance some members take advantage of the first reading on proposed legislation or register reservations to laws in the second reading in order to voice their opinion on other issues entirely. The inevitable result is that specific bills rarely receive the attention they are due, while critical political matters, which intrude in every debate, are not debated systematically.

In order to encourage greater participation and to broaden the range of issues discussed, the Knesset introduced a new procedure of one-minute speeches every Tuesday afternoon. At least 20 members regularly take part in this intriguing 30-minute exercise. But a closer look shows that these are precisely the same MKs that are active in presenting motions and intervening in discussions on legislation (although those who talk incessantly are not always the same members who actually have something useful to say). In reality, some 30% of MKs account for over 80% of the speeches in the Knesset.[50]

Knesset deliberations nevertheless play a crucial role in shaping public discourse. In the absence (with a few notable exceptions) of outstanding orators, like some who occupied the chamber in the Knesset's formative years, vital issues are treated superficially, sloganeering is common and speeches are delivered in impoverished language (if not in gratingly poor Hebrew). A palpable inability to listen as well as to proclaim has resulted in decisions that have almost everything to do with the political affiliation of the speaker and very little to do with the merit of the case. The Knesset has become a platform for a series of pronouncements rather than for any real substantive exchange.

The key problem in the performance of the Knesset as a deliberative forum lies, however, in the dynamics of its discussions. Sessions are either unbearably dreary or impossibly unruly. Truly innovative ideas, especially on social issues, are presented before an empty house, while speakers dealing with matters of life and death are prevented by hecklers from completing a sentence. In the past few years, the avowedly rambunctious plenary has often been transformed into a verbal battlefield in which extremists on both sides of the political spectrum prevail. Since the socio-political situation deteriorated in the wake of the breakdown of Israeli-Palestinian negotiations and the resurgence of violence, some sessions have turned into veritable brawls.[51]

There is no replacement for the Knesset as Israel's main deliberative forum. Almost every topic of public concern is discussed within its confines. Instead of elucidating issues, some debates are arid and others obfuscating. More tellingly, the Knesset has made a negative contribution to Israel's political culture. Its failure to demonstrate ways of dealing reasonably with highly divisive questions, especially in times of stress, has adversely affected political debate and behavioural norms.

Socialization

The malfunctioning of the Knesset in its communication and deliberation roles means that it has not been able to satisfactorily perform the broad societal tasks attributed to legislatures in mature democracies: public education and socialization to binding political values. Members of the Knesset in recent years do not act as role models and are not perceived as such. The public image of the Knesset has consequently plummeted, and with it the faith of many Israelis in the regime it symbolizes.

The norms of conduct that have evolved in the house have never been particularly worthy of emulation. For years, MKs have been berated for everything from poor work habits, absenteeism and laziness to rudeness, incivility, lack of collegiality, ostentation and arrogance. Their behaviour in plenary sessions and committee meetings – now transmitted electronically into the home of every citizen – is carefully scrutinized and almost uniformly decried. The Knesset has been viewed for some time as the antithesis of the model of desirable comportment.[52]

This problematic image has been further tarnished in recent years as a result of changes in the terms of employment of MKs and rising incidences of gross misconduct. In retrospect, 1996 proved to be a critical turning point. In that year, in line with the recommendations of a public commission set up to review the salaries and working conditions of MKs, the Knesset instituted major changes in the benefits granted to its members.[53] Salaries were hiked by 33% in exchange for a complete prohibition on all outside employment. Phone and office equipment budgets were increased, and expense accounts augmented. Since then MKs have accrued additional benefits, including cars and beefed up allowances for everything from language lessons to furniture. The gap between the lifestyles of MKs and those of the average citizen has grown palpably, and with it the frequency and tenor of public criticism.

The actions of individual MKs have added fuel to this discontent. Despite the fact that their every move is examined through a magnifying glass, the press is replete with stories of minor abuses and major legal infractions. Two high profile party leaders were convicted on criminal charges and others are under investigation for bribery and embezzlement.[54] The most recent scandal occurred in the chamber itself, when at least four MKs were accused of voting twice (for themselves and their immediate neighbours) in the course of the ballot on the economic reform programme. Criminal charges have been brought against two of these members. The country's lawmakers have set a poor example of how to uphold the law.

The Knesset has not always succeeded in regulating itself and its members. The Ethics Committee of the Knesset, charged with disciplining MKs for breaches of its own rules of procedures and norms of official conduct, has few tools to implement its decisions. It can monitor behaviour, reprimand members and impose minor sanctions, but it has not been able to enforce its already weak behavioural guidelines.

The Knesset Committee, responsible for all matters related to the house and its members, is the supreme internal arbiter of MK comportment since it possesses semi-judicial standing on questions of parliamentary immunity. Its record in this regard has been, at best, uneven. During the past decade the Knesset Committee has acceded to requests to limit the procedural freedom of particular MKs (brought before the committee by their political opponents in the house). At the same time, it has provided a haven for other members by refusing to lift their immunity to allow the authorities to bring them to trial on criminal charges.[55]

Parliamentary immunity in Israel is probably the broadest in the democratic world.[56] The purpose of immunity is to protect the legislature and its members from undue political pressure. Recent decisions of the Knesset Committee have seriously confounded this logic. By safeguarding the personal interests of individual MKs, the committee has directly contributed to the growing public clamour to drastically circumscribe their immunity. More seriously, by constricting the ability of other members to perform their jobs for purely political reasons, it has exposed the Knesset to intrusions in its affairs, thereby severely compromising its institutional autonomy.

There is a growing awareness within the Knesset that the house has not been able to effectively police itself. It has therefore developed a practice of outsourcing key regulatory tasks. The creation of external public commissions (usually chaired by retired justices) to deal with matters related to salaries and perks is indicative. But in this most delicate area it has refused to take the additional step of forgoing its right to amend commission recommendations, still leaving the final word in the hands of the MK guild in the Knesset Committee. The Knesset presidium, significantly, has also established an outside commission to redraft its ethical code. The speaker of the Knesset has proposed the creation of an external panel to adjudicate requests to remove the parliamentary immunity of its members. And, reluctantly, he brought the police into the house to investigate the double vote fiasco. Ironically, the Knesset seems to be protecting its powers in those areas in which it would substantially improve its standing by relinquishing control. At the same time, it appears eager to forfeit its authority on ethical and immunity matters, which are the basis for its operations and the key to its institutional independence.

Most members of Knesset, to be sure, are honest and law-abiding. The recent antics of some MKs, however, have tainted the reputation of the house as whole. The Knesset today does not constitute an instrument of socialization (except in the negative sense), its educational capacities are meagre, and its mode of operation furnishes a major disincentive in efforts to attract competent political recruits.

The public has judged MKs and their performance harshly. Recent opinion polls consistently show extremely low levels of support for the Knesset and its office holders. The most comprehensive – and damning – study was commissioned by the Knesset itself in 2001.[57] Members of the Knesset received an appalling overall rating of 4 (on a scale of 10). Only 8% of the public think that MKs deal with the concerns of the general public; barely 15% feel that they care about maintaining contact with the electorate; and just 18% are convinced that they prepare properly for debates. The findings depict a picture of a public totally alienated from its representatives, who are seen as lazy by 80% of the respondents, motivated primarily by a quest for money and status (76%), and at least somewhat dishonest (71%). Seventy-six per cent consider the level of debate in the Knesset to be below average, and only 16% take any pride in the media appearances of their parliamentary emissaries.

Under the circumstances, it is hardly surprising that popular esteem for the Knesset is at an all-time low. Barely 10% of a representative sample of the public express satisfaction with the Knesset as an institution, and only 17% take any pride in its operations (50% are actually ashamed of their parliament). The Knesset receives a grade of 3.9 from the public.[58]

The status of the Knesset in comparison to other governmental bodies has noticeably declined. The Israel Defence Forces and the High Court of Justice have traditionally garnered high approval rates (90% and 85% respectively). The overall confidence of the public in the Knesset went down from 41% in 1995 to 14% in 2000 (only the political parties evoke greater distrust).[59] More disturbingly, although 54% of the public still believe that the Knesset strengthens Israel's democracy, a growing proportion (44%) think that the Knesset actually harms democratic government in the country. In the latest public opinion poll, the judiciary, the executive branch and even the media are perceived as nurturing democracy more effectively than the parliament.[60]

These catastrophic findings mean that the Knesset has failed abysmally in its most fundamental democratic function: mobilizing consent for the system of government. Israelis have developed such an intense dislike for their legislature and tend to be so cynical about its members that they evince little knowledge and even less appreciation of its positive achievements.[61] Since the Knesset is in fact a mirror of Israeli society, the growing disenchantment with the legislature implies that the public is actually disillusioned with itself. If, as some experts claim, parliaments are important in the long run for what they stand for, and not necessarily for what they do,[62] then the picture of democracy in Israel is very grim indeed.

The functional balance sheet of the Knesset is far less devastating than popular attitudes make it appear. To be sure, its performance record in most spheres has declined. But Israel's legislature is still a vibrant lawmaking body and a persistent (if not always effective) monitoring organ. Its strengths lie in those spheres where its powers are increasingly curtailed by other branches of government. Its weaknesses are most pronounced in those areas in which it possesses, by definition, a virtual monopoly. From this perspective, the way the Knesset fulfils its multiple roles is an accurate measure of the equivocal nature of governance in the country.

CONCLUSIONS AND RECOMMENDATIONS

The recent history of the Knesset is symptomatic of the chronic maladies infecting democratic government in Israel today. The parliament has undergone a severe deflation in human resources, organizational capacities, role performance and public standing. It has forfeited portions of its institutional autonomy and voluntarily relinquished others. The lines between the Knesset and the other branches of government have become increasingly blurred. Nevertheless, for better or for worse, it continues to be the pivot of political life in the country.

As such, the changes evident in the structures and functions of the Knesset during the past decade have highlighted the tremendous contradictions that are part and parcel of the contemporary Israeli experience. The policy impact of the legislature persists and, in some instances, has grown; but the Knesset is not the main policy arena in the country. The Knesset mirrors the multicultural character of the country, yet it provides a regular platform for division and discord. Its centrality as the locus of public interaction is in inverse relationship to its popular standing. The only consensus members of Knesset have consistently nurtured is the lack of consent to their behaviour and actions. The Knesset's influence has been most widely felt under unstable governments; relative coalition stability has reduced its political efficacy.[63]

The Knesset thus magnifies one of the major paradoxes of Israeli politics: the shifting location of power in the country. The Knesset's power is greatest precisely where its performance is weakest, and its power is circumscribed when it is most effective. As an institution, it epitomizes the elusive nature of power structures in the country.

Any attempt to reform the Knesset and improve its capacities there-fore requires a thorough revamping of all branches of government. In a parliamentary democracy, the legislature is the heart of the political system; changes in its organization and procedures necessarily affect other bodies as well. With this in mind, any political reform package must commence with legislative reform. Some preliminary, and interlocking, suggestions that emerge from this analysis are in order.

First, it is evident that representation without accountability is inherently destructive. This problem cannot be resolved without adjustments in the electoral system either through the introduction of a mixed constituency cum proportional representation system or through the merging of candidate selection with general elections by adding a personal preference to the ballot.[64]

Second, the structures of the Knesset actually hinder its task performance. The size of the house must be increased, either, preferably, by adding members to the existing chamber or by establishing a second house. The committee system is distorted, and needs to be revised to reflect the changes in the executive.

Third, if it wants to maintain its autonomy and improve its public image, the Knesset has to tighten its rules of procedures, draft a binding code of conduct and increase the disciplinary sanctions at its disposal.

Fourth, the Knesset cannot provide effective checks on the government as long as it lacks supervisory power. Instituting hearings on major government appointments is an important way to increase control; so, too, is the augmentation of independent sources of information and expertise.

Finally, the Knesset is exposed to popular pressures, but has not developed mechanisms of interacting with the public. Making more information available is important, but so too is devising other, innovative, avenues of communication.

Fortifying the Knesset is the first step in confronting the dilemmas of political reform in the country. Its reconstruction and rehabilitation is the essential structural precondition for revitalizing and strengthening Israel's floundering democracy.

NOTES

1. Asher Zidon, *The Knesset*, New York, 1967. The latest Hebrew edition was published under the title: *Beit Hanivharim: Moreh Netivei Haknesset B'hakika U'vemimshal*, Jerusalem, 1971. Also see Shevah Weiss, *The Knesset: Performance and Output*, Jerusalem, 1977 (Hebrew); Shmuel Seger, *Israel's Parliamentary Regime*, Jerusalem, 1988 (Hebrew); and Gregory Mahler, *The Knesset: Parliament in the Israeli Political System*, Rutherford, NJ, 1981.
2. Rod Hague, Martin Harrop and Shaun Breslin, *Comparative Government and Politics: An Introduction*, 4th edn., London, 1998, p.184; David Olson, *Legislative Institutions: A Comparative View*, Armonk, NY, 1994, p.1.
3. There are have been numerous attempts to increase the threshold from the 1.5% instituted since the 1992 general elections. Two bills, one proposing a threshold of 3% and another a threshold of 5%, are currently pending. Such a move is important: it will decrease the number of parties without affecting representation of divergent opinions and sectors.
4. Computed from figures published on the Knesset website. See www.knesset.gov.il/history /heb/. In general, all relevant information on parties, votes, committees, members of Knesset, legislation, debates, and votes can be found on this site.

5. Avraham Diskin, *Jerusalem's Last Days: Guidelines for Examining the New Israeli Democracy*, Jerusalem, 2001, pp.52–85 (Hebrew). On the issue of effective diversity of parties see Table 19, p.85.

6. There are now further attempts at electoral reform. These efforts, as in the past, are being conducted on a piecemeal basis without giving sufficient attention to their effects on other institutions. Experience has shown that structural changes are significant only if carried out comprehensively and simultaneously.

7. Avraham Brichta, 'The Knesset as the Representative of the Public', in Efraim Torgovnik (ed.), *The Knesset in the Israeli Democracy*, Tel Aviv, 2001, pp.45–9 (Hebrew). Also see Diskin, *Jerusalem's Last Days*, p.95.

8. For an overview of these issues, see Asher Arian and Michal Shamir (eds.), *Elections in Israel – 1999*, Jerusalem, 2001 (Hebrew).

9. At least four members of the Likud are under investigation for corruption in the internal party elections. Some Labour candidates unabashedly employed vote contractors, and complaints have been issued to the police. Other candidates are also under investigation for flaunting the electoral laws.

10. This figure was computed from data provided by Dr Shiela Hattis-Rolef of the Knesset library. Dr Hattis-Rolef is responsible for the statistics appearing on the Knesset website, www.knesset.gov.il, and was extremely helpful in supplying additional information and analysis.

11. In the 15th Knesset (1999–2003) there were 23 rabbis and 17 retired career officers in the Knesset. Fully one-third of the Knesset had gained office through avenues that are totally blocked to women.

12. Several attempts to introduce the Norwegian law, which requires ministers to resign their seats while in government, allowing the next person on the list to enter parliament, have failed to garner a majority. Ministers are extremely reluctant to accede to what they perceive as an attempt to reduce their status and power. Since the Norwegian formula saves the seat for the minister should s/he leave the cabinet (thus ensuring the smooth operation of the coalition in parliament and increasing government stability and party discipline), it continues to attract a good deal of academic and political attention. For a useful discussion, see *The Knesset and the Executive, an Upper House, and the Electoral System*, Jerusalem, 2000, pp.7–21 (Hebrew).

13. The official structures and rules of procedure are encoded in *The Knesset Rules of Procedure*, Jerusalem, 2003 (Hebrew).

14. The restructuring of the Knesset library, the establishment of a Centre for Information and Research, and the academization of parliamentary assistance provide some notable examples.

15. See Gregory Mahler, *Comparative Politics: An Institutional and Cross-National Approach*, Upper Saddle River, NJ, 2000, pp.71–8. For a general analysis, see *The Knesset and the Executive, An Upper House, and the Electoral System*, pp.25–42.

16. For details on the amendments to Basic Law: The Knesset related to the standing and privileges of the leader of the opposition, see *The Parliament*, No.26 (December 1999), pp.1–4 (Hebrew). For a comparative discussion, see Jean Blondel, 'Opposition in the Contemporary World', *Government and Opposition*, Vol.32, No.4 (1997), pp.462–86.

17. The special investigation panels are usually the foothold of opposition members. Some examples in the 15th and 16th Knesset: the Investigation Committee on Violence in Sports; the Investigation Committee on Commerce in Women; the Investigation Committee on Social Inequalities; and the Investigation Committee on Traffic Accidents. The recommendations of these committees, however important, are not binding on the authorities.

18. Hardly any research has been done on the organizing panel (*Hava'adah Hamesaderet*) whose decisions determine how each Knesset will operate, and consequently define the nature and lines of internal conflicts.

19. See for example, Reuven Hazan, 'Political Reform and the Committee System in Israel: Structural and Functional Adaptation', *Journal of Legislative Studies*, Vol.4, No.1 (1998), pp.147–53.

20. The latest attempt at committee reform was made in the heyday of the 15th Knesset. The proposals were never seriously debated, and the Knesset dispersed before any decisions were made. Many of these recommendation were raised by Reuven Hazan, a summary of which may be found in Reuven Hazan, 'The Knesset Committees and Supervision over

the Executive Branch', in Torgovnik (ed.), *The Knesset in the Israeli Democracy*, pp.106–9 (Hebrew).

21. The Knesset Committee is akin to the Ways and Means Committee in the US House of Representatives. Once again, there is almost no research either on the Knesset Committee or on party factions and how they operate.

22. The Legal Advisor to the Knesset Law, enacted in 2000, sought to enhance the autonomy of the Knesset *vis-à-vis* the executive branch and, simultaneously, strengthen the professionalism of the administration. In retrospect, the pattern of political pressure and professional equivocation has persisted.

23. These teams first emerged in the 12th Knesset to manage the protracted budget debates. They have since been assembled not only on the budget, but on virtually every single sensitive vote. Shoshana Kerem, formally deputy clerk of the Knesset and an authority on the rules of procedure, has been extremely helpful in clarifying the role of the agreement teams.

24. Prior to 1999 ministers were sometimes charged with liaising with the Knesset, but more often this task was given to one of the deputy ministers. The decision to establish a separate cabinet portfolio was made not only to meet specific political needs, but also as a result of the growing awareness of the importance of direct government involvement in Knesset activities.

25. For the phenomenal growth in voluntary associations, see Benjamin Kidron, Hagai Katz and Mihal Bar, *The Third Sector in Israel 2000*, Beer Sheva, 2000, esp. pp.1–43 (Hebrew).

26. The first, and still the leading, lobbying company is Policy, owned by Boris Krasny. Its *Handbook of the Knesset and the Government*, Tel Aviv, 2003, updated annually, is the authoritative guide to the Knesset and leading government institutions and players.

27. See amendments to The Law of the Knesset and its Domain – 1996. Efforts to legislate a new code for lobbyists, proposed by Yehudit Naot, failed in the 15th Knesset.

28. For the self-perception of the role of parliamentary correspondents, see Haim Shibi, *The Image Mask*, Tel Aviv, 1999 (Hebrew).

29. The most notable breach occurred in March 2003, when the Knesset Committee convened in the midst of the vote on the economic reform package and decided to combine votes on numerous reservations requiring a separate ballot in order to 'save time'.

30. Proposed legislation undergoes at least three readings (four for private member bills). During the first reading any MK can participate in the debate. Between the preliminary reading and the first reading, and then again between the first and the second and third readings, the legislation is discussed (and frequently revised) in committee and amendments are considered. Those that are accepted are raised as revisions in the plenary during the second reading, which is followed – except in rare cases – by a vote on the bill in its entirety in the third reading.

31. The standard analysis of these early efforts is Shevah Weiss and Avraham Brichta, 'Private Members' Bills in Israel's Parliament', *Parliamentary Affairs*, Vol.23, No.2 (1969), pp.21–33. This work needs revision in light of recent developments. Also see Hazan, 'Political Reform and the Committee System in Israel'.

32. The classic text on the topic is Amnon Rubinstein and Barak Medina, *Israel's Constitutional Law*, 5th edn., Tel Aviv, 1996 (Hebrew).

33. See Gideon Allon, *Direct Election*, Tel Aviv, 1995 (Hebrew).

34. All figures on the performance of MKs (legislation, parliamentary questions, motions for the agenda, voting percentages, attendance) can be found in the periodic *Statistical Activity Report of the Knesset* (Jerusalem: The Knesset) and posted on the Knesset website.

35. There is an entire literature on judicial activism. For a useful discussion from a parliamentary perspective, see Torgovnik (ed.), *The Knesset in the Israeli Democracy*, esp. pp.119–61.

36. For a good analysis of this tool, see David Nahmias and Eran Klein, *The Arrangements Law: Between Economics and Politics*, Jerusalem, 1999 (Hebrew).

37. The most blatant example is the Large Family Law passed in 2000, which substantially increased allowances to families with a large number of children, thus favouring ultra-orthodox and Arab families, at the cost of over one billion shekels a year.

38. See Eliezer Goldberg's article in this volume.

39. The quotas are agreed upon in the Knesset Committee at the outset of each Knesset, according a strict party key, and are given to each MK individually. Opposition members enjoy a slightly higher personal quota than coalition members.

40. See *Statistical Activity Report of the Knesset* for details. The pattern of decreasing use of the parliamentary question is evident over the past seven years.

41. There is a dearth of research in this area. For one of the few discussions, see 'Parliamentary Questions as a Means of Monitoring the Executive Branch', *The Parliament*, No.25 (December 1999), pp.5–9 (Hebrew).

42. The rapid debate is not dissimilar to the European interpellation, but does not carry the same weight.

43. The sub-committees of the Foreign Affairs and Defence Committee (and especially the sub-committee on the secret services), where most of the serious discussions take place far away from the public eye, receive a steady stream of information and their members are highly knowledgeable, but they have virtually no powers.

44. For one example, *see Report of the Parliamentary Investigation Committee on the Murder of Women by their Partners*, Jerusalem, 1996 (Hebrew).

45. The constructive no-confidence vote, designed on the basis of the German Bundestag precedent, requires the mobilization of an absolute majority of the house in favour of an alternative candidate. It virtually precludes the possibility of toppling a government in a no-confidence vote.

46. For a useful discussion, see Mahler, *Comparative Politics*, p.87.

47. For one of the only (and by now outdated) analyses, see Eric Uslaner, 'Casework and Institutional Design: Redeeming Promises in the Promised Land', *Legislative Studies Quarterly*, Vol.10, No.1 (1985), pp.35–52.

48. The detailed list of expenditures is posted on the Knesset website, www.knesset.gov.il, annually.

49. The considerations of the presidium in the approval of motions for the agenda do not always follow set criteria. Many MKs exercise their right of appeal before the Knesset committee, which tends to approve coalition members' requests.

50. Computed from *The Statistical Activity Report of the Knesset*, 1995–2003.

51. The use of epithets – ranging from 'Nazi' to 'fascist' and 'racist' – became so commonplace that the Knesset Ethics Committee issued a memorandum listing unacceptable terms and imposing sanctions on transgressors.

52. Teachers regularly admonish students to behave by reminding them that the classroom 'is not the Knesset'.

53. The full report of this commission (known as the Ariel Rosen-Zvi Commission) and subsequent public commissions to assess the working conditions of MKs (especially the Yitzhak Galnoor Commission), is available on the Knesset website, www.knesset.gov.il/docs.

54. The most notable case is that of Aryeh Der'i, who served a prison sentence for receiving bribes, and Yitzhak Mordechai, who has been convicted of sexual harassment.

55. Limitations on the procedural freedoms have been imposed only on Arab MKs (most notably Hashem Mahmeed, Azmi Bishara and Ahmed Tibi). Avigdor Lieberman and Naomi Blumenthal avoided criminal trial by successfully invoking their parliamentary immunity.

56. See the Law of Immunity of Members of Knesset: Their Rights and Obligations – 1951, with its 29 amendments passed up to January 2003.

57. 'The Knesset Index: Public Perceptions of the Legislative Branch', available at www.knesset. gov.il/mmm/data/docs.mdd.htm.

58. Ibid., p.11.

59. These findings conform to those of the democracy index project surveys conducted by the Israel Democracy Institute. For a summary, see *The Parliament*, No.25 (November 1999), p.16 (Hebrew).

60. 'The Democracy Index', *The Parliament*, No.40 (June 2003) (Hebrew).

61. 'The Knesset Index', p.5 shows that most people surveyed do not have more than a cursory knowledge of the inner workings of the Knesset. The study shows that the level of knowledge about the Knesset is not a significant variable in explaining attitudes towards the institution and its members.

62. Hague *et al.*, *Comparative Government and Politics*, p.184.

63. Some of these patterns are evident in European countries as well. For an interesting analysis, see Gabriel Almond and G. Bingham Powell, *Comparative Politics: A Theoretical Framework*, New York, 1996, pp.139–40.

64. Gideon Rahat has done important work in this area. See 'Proposals on Electoral Reform and Candidate Selection Methods' (Draft paper, Jerusalem, 2003).

The Attorney General in Israel: A Delicate Balance of Powers and Responsibilities in a Jewish and Democratic State

ELYAKIM RUBINSTEIN

Israel, a Jewish and democratic state, is riddled with internal divisions and copes with security threats that pose a constant challenge to the rule of law. Almost every word in the above sentence raises social as well as legal dilemmas. What is a Jewish state? What is a Jewish and democratic state? How does one cope with the frictions between Jews and Arabs; between Jews in matters of state and religion; between political left and right, during periods in which political as well as security issues are in the focus of public attention; between veterans and new immigrants; between haves and have-nots; and even between ethnic groups within the Jewish population – 'tribes' and sectors of all kinds. How does one deal with real and critical security challenges in a democracy that properly sanctifies civil rights? All of these are part of the daily challenges facing the attorney general, a role almost unique in the world, which during the 55 years of Israeli statehood has become a central part of public law in Israel. Both in the Attorney General's Office, and – of course – in the Supreme Court, an attempt is made to find the golden path described by such Jewish sages of old as Maimonides, and we always try to apply fairness.

The law is the framework within which the state functions. Jewish sages teach us that 'Rabbi Hanina, the deputy High Priest says: "Thou should

Elyakim Rubinstein was the Attorney General of Israel (1997–2004). He has been a Justice of the Supreme Court of Israel since May 2004.

pray for the peaceful existence of the Kingdom, because without its fear, one person would be swallowing the other alive"'.[1] As Rabbi Hanina watched the destruction of the Jerusalem Temple and the internal hatred within it, he called for peaceful law enforcement.

The Attorney General's Office is called upon to make difficult decisions and to account for them. Criticisms come from almost every part of the political system. Some criticism is legitimate, while some comes from interested parties who worry about being investigated or about their own economic or other interests. While public and media criticism forms part of the general discourse, there are normative ways of testing the judgement of the attorney general. The main path is via judicial examination, and the overwhelming majority of our decisions have met this test when faced with it. Some of the decisions that are scrutinized publicly have not ever been tested in court. Criticism of the courts, including the Supreme Court is legitimate. But in this context I would say that the motive, the measure and the style of the complaints are important, and excessive criticism may destroy the delicate balance required.

This article describes the role of the attorney general in Israel's legal system. The position is complex, combining, *inter alia*, the responsibility for the criminal prosecution in the country, as well as for legal counsel to the government and other functions. The duties of the attorney general, the tradition the role carries, as well as the difficulties connected with the discharge of these duties are discussed below. This includes the modalities of appointment, the main responsibilities, the principal spheres of public law involved and some proposals for change.

THE ATTORNEY GENERAL – APPOINTMENT AND TENURE

Until 2000, there was no fixed procedure for the appointment of the attorney general, except for one article – Art. 5 in the Law of Government Service (Appointments), 5719-1959, which stipulates: 'The Government may set the modalities and terms for the appointment of the Attorney General and if it has not done so, the provisions of this law will apply'. In addition, a government resolution in 1960 stipulated that the candidate for the position of the attorney general would be proposed to the government by the minister of justice, that the minister would not propose to the government a candidate who is not qualified to be appointed a Supreme Court justice; and that the position of the attorney general would be vacated upon death, resignation or appointment of another person. The rule was, then, that the government appointed the attorney general upon a proposal by the minister of justice.

In 1997, a major public fury erupted after the two-day tenure of an attorney general (Ronnie Bar-On) who resigned because of public pressure pertaining to his political affiliation with the governing party. It was followed by a criminal investigation on allegations of breach of trust by the then prime minister and minister of justice, for making the appointment with the illegal motive of helping a politician who was under investigation. The file was closed later on grounds of lack of evidence. The decision withstood a petition to the High Court of Justice aimed at achieving a criminal indictment filed against the prime minister as well as others.

One of the results of this controversy was the appointment of the Shamgar Committee, named after its chairperson, former chief justice and former attorney general, Meir Shamgar. The committee was appointed by the minister of justice in February 1997. Its members included three former ministers of justice, David Libai, Moshe Nissim, the late Haim Zadok, as well as Professor Ruth Gavison of the Hebrew University of Jerusalem.

The committee report was submitted in November 1998. It described the functions of the attorney general, underlining his professional independence and the required integrity. It described the role of the criminal prosecution, the public interest involved and the independence necessary for the discharge of the attorney general's duties.

The main operative recommendation of the Shamgar Committee was a major change in the mode of appointment of the attorney general. Its recommendations in this respect were adopted by the government on 20 August 2000. The central change is the establishment of a professional public permanent committee that will propose to the government the candidates for attorney general. The committee is chaired by a former Supreme Court justice appointed by the chief justice, and includes a former minister of justice or attorney general appointed by the government; a Knesset member elected by the Constitution and Law Committee of the Knesset; a lawyer elected by the National Council of the Bar Association, and an academic versed in public and criminal law, elected by deans of recognized Israeli law schools. Candidates for attorney general may be proposed by the prime minister, the minister of justice, or both, or by a member of the committee. A candidate must be eligible to become a Supreme Court justice. The committee, by consent of at least four of its members, may submit to the government one or more names, and the government may appoint someone only from among the proposed candidates. The new system is aimed at minimizing the possibilities of politicization of the attorney general's position and at attaining the best possible results. My successor as attorney general, Meni Mazuz, was appointed early in 2004 through the new process. Mr Mazuz served before as deputy attorney general.

Until the government revised the appointment process, there had been no limit of tenure to the attorney general's position, and former incumbents served between three and almost eight years. The 2000 resolution stipulates a non-renewable tenure of six years (or until the age of 70, the earlier date prevailing), with a possible extension of six months.

The government's power to terminate the attorney general's tenure is very limited, but includes the existence of substantial, prolonged differences of view between the government and the attorney general that prevent efficient cooperation. Other possibilities include the case of the attorney general having committed an act unfitting to his position, his being no longer medically fit for his duties, or the situation in which a criminal investigation is opened or an indictment is submitted against the attorney general.

ON THE ATTORNEY GENERAL'S FOUR HATS

In Israel, the reader of daily newspapers will almost inevitably find news pertaining to the attorney general. The title of the position in Hebrew is 'the legal counsel to the government' as it was translated during the British period, 1917–48. This does not properly convey the position's powers and responsibilities. That is why the Shamgar Committee, dealing in 1997/98 with the attorney general, suggested changing its title to 'Chief Legal Counsel' (the proposed change was not accepted, mainly for reasons of tradition).

The attorney general in Israel:

- heads the criminal prosecution;
- represents the state and the government in all litigation, both criminal and civil;
- is the ultimate and exclusive legal counsel to the government;
- represents the public interest.

Fulfilling all these missions – in effect wearing four hats – is a formidable challenge. It requires a strong sense of commitment and responsibility as well as humility. Following is a brief discussion of all four functions.

Criminal Prosecution

The attorney general heads the criminal prosecution of the country in its entirety. There is one criminal prosecution authority for all of Israel. It is naturally divided into functional divisions and units, but Israel's size as well as tradition, have not necessitated the creation of divided criminal jurisdictions.

The attorney general's responsibility with respect to criminal prosecution includes both policy issues and specific cases. Policy includes setting priorities – for instance violence of various kinds, in the family, at home, in school and on the street. This is, by definition, a central priority. Other priorities are shaped by social and technological changes – such as matters connected with intellectual property, and developments in technology that create the need for new areas of criminal enforcement.

The central arm of the criminal prosecution is the State Attorney's Office, headed by the state attorney. It includes the headquarters in Jerusalem, as well as eight district attorneys' offices. The state attorney's headquarters deals with all Supreme Court litigation, including appeals of district court decisions, administrative and constitutional law cases and international law matters. The district attorney's offices deal with criminal prosecution and civil and administrative litigation. The Police Officers Investigations Department, in charge of criminal investigations against police officers for acts committed within or during the performance of their duties, is also part of the State Attorney's Office. Other arms of the criminal prosecution include: the police prosecution service, including 11 prosecution bureaus dealing with the quantitative majority of criminal cases; the economic and fiscal prosecution units – income tax, customs and value added tax; anti-trust authority; securities authority; and also specialized units of various government ministries – Transportation, Industry and Commerce, Environment, some of them employing government lawyers and some prosecuting through private lawyers accredited by the attorney general. The criminal prosecution also includes the municipal criminal units, both through municipalities' employees or through external lawyers. The fact that in the criminal sphere all prosecutors are personally accredited by the attorney general gives them professional independence in resisting possible pressures by politicians. We have introduced changes in the process of accreditation, enabling a better screening of the candidates for prosecutorial positions.

While the overwhelming majority of criminal cases constitute 'classic' crime, public attention, within the lively framework of Israeli democracy, is constantly attracted to investigations concerning public figures, and to issues within the public debate, such as offences related to the freedom of speech. These cases all come to the desk of the attorney general.

Investigations concerning political figures – and during my tenure, I have had to open investigations concerning a president, prime ministers and ministers, Knesset members and mayors – are discussed and decided upon at the Attorney General's Office, together with the state attorney and other senior officials. Naturally, decisions to open investigations as well as the legal conclusions following the investigations are taken in consultation with the state attorney, the state attorney's lawyers, the relevant district attorney, as well as deputies to the attorney general. The ultimate responsibility lies with the attorney general.

The freedom of speech issue looms large in our work. The political debate in Israel, including questions related to the disputed territories and the relations with the Palestinians, are also a constant feature in our work. Complaints keep piling up on the attorney general's desk, and usually the argument amounts to: 'What I say about you is within the boundaries of free expression, whereas what you say about me is a criminal offence'.

The attorney general has also dealt, before 2004, personally with many decisions of a specific nature in the criminal sphere. There are about 270 references in Israeli law to special legal powers of the attorney general, some of them in rather common use. Proposals for certain changes in the powers of the attorney general were suggested partially in order to relieve the heavy burden of these responsibilities. These will be discussed later.

Representation

The attorney general and his associates represent the government in criminal matters and, additionally, in all other areas pertaining to state and government litigation: civil, labour, international, fiscal, administrative and constitutional. I shall refer separately to the last two headings in the next section. By convention and tradition, the government cannot be represented by outside counsel without the agreement of the attorney general, which is very rarely given. This is a necessity: but for this tradition, we might have found ourselves in a representational jungle in which various ministries and senior functionaries would hire their own representation, under their own policy, charging the government the fees, and expressing contradictory positions in important cases. We often see what happens in public authorities that are not under the attorney general's direct supervision. The existing policy has definitely proven itself over the years.

Legal Counsel to the Government

By convention, the attorney general is the only legal counsel to the government, and his advice to the government is binding. This means that the government cannot accept binding legal counsel from anybody else without the consent of the attorney general. This convention is aimed at preventing a situation in which, as in court representation, a number of ministries would each present their own legal advice without having a single authority that could make a decision.

There are natural differences of view, including in terms of legal interpretation of laws, between the legal advisors of the various ministries. It is the role of the attorney general (or one of his deputies) to provide the interpretation binding upon the government.

The role of legal counsel in the government ministries is, *inter alia*, to serve as 'gate keeper' for the proper functioning of the government in terms of the law and the basic principles of the Israeli legal system. That is why a written directive by the attorney general instructs the ministries to abide by legal opinions; the legal advisor's opinion binds the ministry; the attorney general's advice binds the government subject, of course, to court decisions.

In accordance with a directive by the attorney general, when there are differences of view within a ministry, the minister, the director general or the legal advisor may apply to the attorney general for his legal opinion, and that will be binding.

The attorney general regularly issues legal directives which are binding upon public authorities.

On the Public Interest

By law, the attorney general is entitled to join any case between non-governmental parties, private or public, to represent the public interest. This is based on statutory provisions, and reflects the basic confidence of the legislature in the attorney general as a fair and objective authority.

In this respect, it is common for the attorney general to join cases which present a 'public' case. This is done not only in sensitive matters of children's custody or status, but also in matters affecting governmental or public funds and property. Typically it could include questions of labour disputes, insurance and pension matters which transcend the limits of the specific case and could affect wider circles of the population.

ON ADMINISTRATIVE AND CONSTITUTIONAL LAW AND THE HIGH COURT OF JUSTICE

The Supreme Court of Israel, in its capacity as the High Court of Justice, deals as a court of first and last instance in matters of administrative and constitutional law. While administrative cases have always been part of the court's jurisdiction, the policy adopted for the last quarter-century has been of waiving the requirement of standing, or *locus standi*, in submitting petitions to the High Court of Justice, thus widening the court's scope of supervision and involvement. Petitions can be submitted by private or public petitioners, who do not have to show any personal connection to the case. The wide open gates of standing have been accompanied by a broad interpretation of the idea of justiciability. In general, the court has seen almost everything as justiciable, though it has sometimes refrained from dealing with certain issues for institutional reasons, explaining that the court was not the appropriate institution to deal with them.

In the mid-1990s, a constitutional jurisdiction was added: the court decided, in a 500-page decision in the *Mizrahi Bank* v. *Migdal* case,[2] that it had the power of judicial review over legislation. This case has become the Israeli *Marbury* v. *Madison*.[3] While the court has offered evidence of this approach since the late 1960s, the full-fledged legal basis for it was laid in 1995, following the promulgation in 1992 of the two basic laws dealing with civil rights, Basic Law: Human Dignity and Liberty, and Basic Law: Freedom of Occupation.

While Israel does not yet have a full-fledged formal constitution, it has, based on a Knesset resolution of 1950, promulgated Basic Laws which are to be finally incorporated into a formal constitution. So far, 11 Basic Laws have been enacted, mostly concerning the various state authorities, but also – as mentioned above – on civil rights.

Until 2003, there have been only three cases in which a law or parts thereof have been declared void by the court, which has applied a cautious and measured policy concerning judicial review.[4] The annulled pieces of legislation were by and large of secondary importance.

Meanwhile, since the court has for many years sat as a court of first instance in all administrative law matters, the burden on it in this regard has been almost unbearable. As a result, the court has worked with government representatives and legislators to transfer some of the areas of administrative law to the district courts, which was achieved.

In addition, in 2003 a debate erupted around the question of whether the power of judicial review should be limited to the Supreme Court or be made available to all courts (which has been the case so far). It appears that we are tending towards limiting it to the Supreme Court.

The attorney general is called upon to defend the government and public authorities in issues of administrative and constitutional law. In the State Attorney's Office, a division that includes 20 lawyers deals with the cases, in addition to lawyers in the district attorney's offices who appear in administrative cases in the district courts.

While in most cases we would defend the government, fully or partially, at times a different stand will be taken and the attorney general will state, from the legal point of view, that he will not defend a certain administrative decision or even a law. When it happens more often with regard to administrative matters, including government resolutions, we inform the government or other relevant authorities that we will not defend a certain decision, or that it should be amended to accommodate the law.

For instance, when the Treasury planned in 2002 to reduce family social allowance by 80% based on military service, which would have affected specific groups in the population, we informed it that this could not be defended, and the cuts had to be drastically reduced (to 20%; and even that has been challenged in court). We informed the Israel Land Authority on more than one occasion over recent years that we could not defend decisions on land allocation that appeared not to be based on reasonable criteria. Our position was accepted by the courts. I should add here that, by and large, our positions generally have been respected and accepted by the Supreme Court. We can basically look back with professional pride.

ON A JEWISH AND DEMOCRATIC STATE AND ISSUES WITHIN ISRAELI SOCIETY

A Jewish and democratic state, the way Israel defines itself, presents a major challenge. The Jewish aspect is Israel's *raison d'être*. The Jewish people have had an abnormal existence since having been expelled from their country mainly following the destruction of the Second Temple in the first century. Zionism is all about the return of Jews to their ancient homeland. The Israeli Declaration of Independence of 1948 describes milestones of Jewish history, including the persecutions and massacres, culminating in the Holocaust of 1939–45, an attempt to liquidate the Jewish people in its entirety.

But the Jewish state is democratic; the Zionist movement developed democratic institutions from the very beginning, 50 years before the establishment of the state. This was strongly demonstrated in the development of the Jewish community during the British Mandatory period. Israeli democracy has developed into a very real phenomenon. Equality for the Arab minority is one part of democratic life. It is provided for in the Declaration of Independence.

A major part of our work has been dedicated to issues connected with the polarization of Israeli society, within the framework of the Jewish and democratic state. Questions of equality, state and religion, security and civil rights are constantly discussed, whether towards government resolutions or legislation, and in response to High Court of Justice petitions. The Supreme Court has played a role in all these issues and the attorney general's representatives express our opinion while arguing the various cases.

As for equality and Israeli Arabs, including the Druze and Circassians, in my view equality is a basic right and should be implemented. Its implementation is not easy, but we have to act diligently and continuously towards it. I saw my role in this regard as including an ongoing struggle for equality in budgets and appointments. While there are sensitivities and problems in this respect, and at the same time it is our duty to preserve, in the area of law, the Jewish and democratic character of the state of Israel, the struggle for equality for minorities must continue.

One of the main areas of polarization in Israel is connected with state and religion issues. This applies mainly to intra-Jewish aspects, but also to the relationship with other religions, and within those religions too. The Attorney General's Office is called upon to deal with these issues in the framework of High Court petitions and finds itself deeply immersed in them. My own approach in this respect is to strive for 'the golden path'. It is my strong belief that in most of these issues – the character of the Sabbath as a day of rest, questions of conversion and 'who is a Jew?' etc. – there is no need to push ideological disputes to the extreme, and understandings can be reached. In my view, this can be attained without coercing anyone to give up their religious beliefs.[5]

May I add here that I am very supportive of the completion of the Israeli constitution. In my view, this is possible; the reservations raised derive mainly from apprehensions concerning the constitutional interpretation by the court, rather than the text itself, and this is well understood by the court, too.[6]

CIVIL RIGHTS AND SECURITY

The pendulum between civil rights and security keeps shifting, in particular throughout difficult periods of security threats and of terrorism, during which we bury our dead – and I speak as a person who has dedicated almost a quarter of a century to ploughing in the field of peace.

When I was a young man, security was the focus – the country was struggling for its survival and, serving for years in the Ministry of Defence, I personally witnessed it. But years have passed. The common collectivist ethos in Israeli society has, at least partially, been replaced by an individualistic ethos that has merged into the worldwide era of human rights. Both have great importance. The ethos and security of life is a part of it. There is no sense in rights without implementation of the basic right to a safe and secure life. But human rights are a central theme in democratic existence. How is it possible to combine the two? Sometimes there are more dilemmas than solutions and the saga continues. We – my colleagues and myself – have seen ourselves both as trustees of security and as trustees of rights. We must oppose the use of security reasons to denigrate rights, but we also have to understand and grasp the terrible effects on Israeli society and the tremendous fear aroused when buses explode and people are killed in cafes, in markets and in bus stations.

Our positions, both when we advise the government and the Israel Defence Forces and security agencies and in court, have aimed for balance. We have tried to enable and assist the government to provide security within the frame of the law, while constantly insisting on issues of rights, on proportionality and on the need to apply all measures cautiously and in accordance with international and domestic law. In this respect, numerous discussions and deliberations have taken place in the Attorney General's Office, opinions are given to the government and positions in court cases are decided upon and shaped.

What greatly contributes to the complexity is the fact that the Palestinian Authority has not developed a valid legal system, and no true rule of law has existed in it. In term of the terrorism, as well as 'classic' crime, the Palestinian Authority has been a jungle, with various organizations and gangs operating on their own, and trials sometimes unfortunately beginning in the morning and ending with an execution in the afternoon. I have raised this subject many times and, in my view, the establishment of a functioning legal system there is a must for a safe future of good relations between us.

APPOINTMENTS, FINANCIAL SUPPORT, LAND ISSUES

A major part of the attorney general's work is preventing excesses and aberrations in public administration, namely, appointments to public office, the allocation of budgets and government financial support, as well as public land. These are complex issues. The Babylonian Talmud (Tractate Sabbath 11, A) describes in the third century the complexity of running a state and a government by stating that had all oceans been of ink and if all reeds were pens, if all skies were parchment and all people scribes, still it would not be possible to grasp the full depth of authority. And as Rashi, the great eleventh century commentator, put it, the authority must pay attention to a number of foreign states, to taxes, to a number of wars and a number of trials, all in one day. The complexity was understood by those ancient sources. What shall we say today in the modern state and government? My colleagues and I have seen our role as gatekeepers in all the areas mentioned above.

As far as government appointments are concerned, a form of revolution has taken place over recent years. The number of positions that can be filled without an appropriate screening has been significantly reduced. This has happened due to changes in legislation and to court decisions, and due to our own opinions given to the government. Most government appointments, as well as appointments in government companies and in statutory authorities, now undergo a screening process, either at the Civil Service Commission or at a special statutory committee for the examination of appointments to government companies and authorities, headed by a retired judge who acts as the representative of the attorney general.

We cannot argue, in this respect, that we have achieved all our goals – it is a dynamic area, political pressures always exist and surprises may always appear – but we have been doing our best under difficult circumstances of competing political trends.

The same applies to budgets and government financial support. Political pressures of all kinds exist inside the government, with conflicting and competing interests. Some years ago, we declared that no double support by the government can be given, namely, that two government money sources could not be used for the same purpose. This might sound obvious, but great pressure has been applied to change the decision, or at least to postpone its implementation. We have resisted this.

Another example is public land, where we insisted on fulfilling our role as trustees of the public, with a responsibility to generations ahead. Land is

a one-time resource, and the just allocation of it is crucial. This proposition
was recognized by the Supreme Court.[7]

THE ATTORNEY GENERAL AND THE GOVERNMENT DECISION MAKING

A debate has long existed regarding the question of whether the attorney
general should participate in Cabinet meetings. Until 1977, the attorney
general participated in these meetings only by invitation, when legal issues
were under discussion.

In 1977, Prime Minister Menachem Begin, who had had a legal
education and possessed great respect for the law, began to invite the
attorney general (then Aaron Barak – later justice and chief justice of the
Supreme Court) to participate in government meetings. It started whilst
there was temporarily no full-fledged minister of justice, but continued
when a minister of justice was appointed who was a renowned jurist but
distant politically, as well as personally, from the prime minister. The
tradition has been maintained continuously ever since. Moreover, in the
1990s, the late Prime Minister Rabin agreed to the request of the attorney
general that he be invited to the meetings of the 'Inner Cabinet' or
Ministerial National Security committee, which he had not attended
before.

When I was appointed in February 1997, this tradition continued.
It should be noted that, between 1948 and the second half of the 1990s,
most (but not all) ministers of justice were well-known jurists, experienced
in law and government. This changed towards the end of the 1990s, when
ministers were appointed who, while being seasoned politicians, were not
legally trained or possessed only a formal legal education. But a definite
need exists for an authoritative legal voice at the government table.
In November 1998, the Shamgar Committee suggested a return to the pre-
1977 convention of inviting the attorney general to government meetings
only when legal issues requiring his advice were to be discussed. The reason
given was the need to avoid, as far as possible, the constant contact
between the attorney general, who is the chief criminal prosecutor, and the
ministers – political people, who might at times themselves be under
investigation. When the recommendation was issued, I immediately asked
the then prime minister and minister of justice if I might be excused from
sitting in on government meetings. My request was rejected and I have
continued the post-1977 tradition ever since.

Respectfully, I must state here my opinion that the attorney general
should attend government meetings. A meeting of the board of directors of
a major corporation without a legal counsel in attendance would be
inconceivable. The government is, at the very least, the national board of
directors. It deals with the most vital and most important issues of national

interest. Experience shows that there are almost always meetings of the Cabinet (and the National Security Ministerial Committee) that include issues of a legal nature, and sometimes more than one such issue in a meeting. There is seldom a government meeting in which I was not called upon to offer an opinion on legal aspects pertaining to security issues, government appointments, budget, land issues and other matters. This might have happened on my own initiative or at the prime minister's or ministers' requests. This is even more the case during times of military conflict, such as the period we have experienced since October 2000. An attorney general should indeed be sensitive to the need to avoid excessive contact with ministers or political people. As mentioned before, being the chief prosecutor and sitting around the government table with ministers and even prime ministers who may be under investigation is not the most pleasant or comfortable situation. But the solution lies in the use of self-restraint and common sense, and in avoiding as much as possible any discussion of investigations around the table or even informally. It lies in the attempt to fulfil one's role as counsel to the government and its gatekeeper and watchdog on the rule of law whilst keeping a professional distance, without losing the ability to maintain a positive, appropriate and correct interpersonal relationship with the ministers. It will only be fair to add that my successor decided to shrink his participation in government meetings, and he has been chosing which meetings to attend.

It is interesting to observe and to note the attitude of prime ministers and ministers to positions expressed by the attorney general at the government table (or elsewhere, for that matter) – and I speak here of issues of counsel rather than criminal matters in which the attorney general acts totally independently. The attorney general's counsel is accepted as binding when he declares that a certain proposal is illegal – in such instances his position would be honoured without exception. However, when a proposal is described by the attorney general as inappropriate but not illegal, that will occasionally be ignored due to political considerations. This would not constitute a violation of the law.

Due to apprehension concerning political intervention in criminal matters, I have generally refrained from consulting on such matters with the government or with ministers. This has been my approach despite recommendations by the Agranat Committee (1962)[8] and Shamgar Committee (1998)[9] on consultations by the attorney general with the ministerial level on criminal cases that may have security, political or public significance. I have believed this to be a healthier approach under the prevailing circumstances, since thereby the attorney general avoids the perception – even if inaccurate – of political considerations being injected into the criminal prosecution decision making.

MINISTERIAL RESPONSIBILITY AND INTERACTION

The minister of justice in Israel, is – naturally – a politician, a member of the government, including, by law, the Ministerial Committee for National Security. The minister serves as the chairperson of the Ministerial Committee on Legislation, a focal organ of the government in legislative and parliamentary issues. He is, by law, the chairperson of the highly important statutory Judges' Selection Committee, which selects all judges in the country, from the magistrate's courts to the Supreme Court. The minister is also in charge of the administrative functioning of the Ministry of Justice. Aside from the State Attorney's Office and the ministry's legislative divisions, this includes, *inter alia*, the Land Registration Office, the Public Defender's Office and civil legal aid.

The minister of justice is not in charge the functions of the attorney general in their substance. He is ministerially responsible for the actions of the attorney general, including answering for them in the Knesset, but cannot in any way intervene in the attorney general's professional decisions. No such attempt has been made by any of the four ministers with whom I have worked since 1997. I can unequivocally state that even though some ministers tried to speak to me – on rare occasions – about pending cases, and I advised them to refrain from it, there has been no political intervention in my decision making over the years.

SHOULD THERE BE A CHANGE IN THE POWERS OF THE ATTORNEY GENERAL?

Over the years, ideas have occasionally been raised concerning the powers of the attorney general. A repeated suggestion has been that powers be divided so that the criminal prosecution would be under the state attorney, while the other powers of representation and counsel in all non-criminal matters would remain with the attorney general. The main reason given for the suggested change is protecting the decision making process in criminal matters from the image of political influences. The Shamgar Commission, examining the idea, recommended that the current situation, whereby powers are unified under the attorney general, should remain intact, mainly in order to avoid weakening the attorney general's position altogether.[10] With respect, this is my view too, and in fact it is basically the common view of the state attorney and the deputies to the attorney general.

My colleagues and I have been opposed to the idea of a separation between the roles of the attorney general in the area of counsel to the government and those related to criminal prosecution. Some of those who support it sincerely believe that the duality of being both the chief prosecutor and the chief legal counsel to the government is unhealthy. But some of those who promote the idea may be interested in weakening both the prosecution and the counsel, by politicizing the position of the attorney general, and reducing the checks and balances of legal supervision that exist in our system. Israel has had a long and positive tradition concerning the powers of the attorney general. The combination of these powers is what gives the position its authority in a very difficult environment. The separation will mean, first, that the counsel to the government will become political, and the attorney general will change with every new prime minister. It is easy to predict the effect of this on public confidence. It may look better from the perception of the criminal prosecution, but may shed doubts on matters concerning appointments, budgets, land issues and basically all administrative issues, through the apprehension of a politicization of legal counsel in these areas, in contradiction to the tradition of independence that has been so carefully developed and maintained over the years.

It will also mean splitting the State Attorney's Office and the District Attorney's Office: the criminal prosecution would be under the state attorney and the other litigating attorneys in civil and administrative matters under the attorney general. This would weaken the system and create frictions over jurisdiction instead of the solid and by and large harmonious structure that has been erected over the years, with great effort and with a very positive tradition of public service.

In my view, the problems in the existing system and the enormous workload of the attorney general may be substantially mitigated by avoiding over-exposure to the politicians – as indeed I did – and by certain changes in the specific powers of the attorney general. I strongly believe that the proposed separation should not take place. I can speak about this objectively, since my own tenure is now over.

I should take the opportunity to commend the state attorney, the deputies to the attorney general, the lawyers at the district bureaus and at the counsel divisions – these are able, non-partisan, loyal and honest civil servants who would make any country proud. That is why we were all stunned when the investigation of a leak during the election campaign early in 2003, regarding proceedings initiated by us in South Africa, dealing with an inquiry into Prime Minister Sharon's campaign financing, led to the suspicion of a deputy district attorney who later admitted the leak. The explanation given by her was ideological. This was an exception, which in my view only underlines the quality of the legal service where no serious violations of the law have happened throughout the 55 years of its existence.

POWERS OF THE ATTORNEY GENERAL: PROPOSALS FOR CHANGE

Having said this, there are means by which the burden on the attorney general could be somewhat eased. The attorney general's powers in legislation are vast as mentioned before. While many of them are rarely used, there are quite a number that constitute a huge burden. While in the area of stay of proceedings – the power to stop criminal court proceedings after indictment – some of the powers have been delegated to the deputies of the attorney general (formerly they could deal only with misdemeanours; now they also deal with certain types of felonies), many powers in this sphere and others were, until recently, exclusively in the hands of the attorney general. One example is the power to submit to the Supreme Court an opinion on a request for a retrial, thereby starting anew the proceedings in a criminal case that had formerly been exhausted and closed. This put a serious load on the attorney general who, while assisted by drafts prepared by the State Attorney's Office, had himself to review vast volumes of material before finalizing the opinion.

Other powers common in the work of the attorney general are indicting a minor after one year has lapsed since the commitment of the alleged offence. Bringing a minor to trial together with an adult also requires a personal determination by the attorney general. Submitting a request to a court to detain a person beyond 30 days before an indictment was subject to personal approval by the attorney general. My custom was to invite the police officers investigating the case, as well as prosecutors, to present the case to me before I made my decision, and this too was highly demanding on my schedule.

Another example is the appeal to the attorney general when criminal cases are closed by district attorneys for what is perceived as lack of public interest to pursue criminal proceedings (namely, that there appears to be evidence that an offence has been committed, however the circumstances seem to the district attorney to be inappropriate for criminal enforcement). A similar power, with regard to other kinds of decisions, to close a file, rests with the state attorney and with other senior officials of the State Attorney's Office. It is also highly time consuming.

The above are a few examples. There are many other powers vested in the attorney general that placed tremendous demands on his time. There have been discussions in 2002–03 between myself, the state attorney and my deputies regarding relieving the attorney general of a part of these powers by creating modes of delegation to other senior functionaries. All of these ideas required legislation, which was indeed introduced during the last period of my tenure as attorney general, and passed the legislative process shortly after the appointment of my successor.

CONCLUSION

The burden on the attorney general and his colleagues is enormous. But they have to fulfil their duties, trying to combine law and humanity. The Prophet Hosea (2, 22) speaks of the alliance between the Almighty and the Jewish people as including 'justice and law, kindness and compassion'. And, as the prophet Micah says (2, 8) this is 'practising justice and loving kindness' – a universal command. The effort to achieve tolerance, to strive for a golden path based on positive values, on true justice for all, is a goal that, perhaps, can never be fully attained. The road is paved with obstacles and difficulties, but I would like to believe that our efforts have always been true and fair.

NOTES

The article is partially based on my essay, 'Legal Advice to the Government and Law Enforcement – Functions and Complexity in a Polarized Jewish and Democratic State', *Mechkarei Mishpat* (Bar-Ilan University Law Studies), Vol.17, No.1 (2001), pp.7–16 (Hebrew).

1. *Wisdom of the Fathers*, 3, 2.
2. High Court of Justice (H.C.) 6821/93, *Mizrachi Bank* v. *Midgal*, P.D. 49 (4), 221.
3. *Marbury* v. *Madison*, 5 U.S. 137 (1803). This is the well-known case in which the United States Supreme Court established its judicial review power.
4. High Court of Justice (H.C.) 6055/95, *Sagi Tzemach* v. *Minister of Defense*, P.D. 53 (5) 241; High Court of Justice (H.C.) 1715/97, *Israeli Association of Investment Brokers* v. *Minister of Finance*, P.D. 51 (4) 367; High Court of Justice (H.C.) 1030/99, *MK Chaim Oron* v. *Chairman of the Knesset*, P.D. Tak-el (Takdin) 2001(1), 839.
5. For further discussion, see Asa Kasher's article 'A Jewish and Democratic State': Present Navigation in the Map of Interpretations, *Israel Affairs*, Vol. 1, No.1, special issue: *Israeli Democracy at the Crossroads*.
6. See Meir Shamgar's article in this volume.
7. High Court of Justice (H.C.) 3939/99, *Kibbutz Sde Nachum* v. *Israel Land Authority*, P.D. 56(6), 25.
8. Report of the Agranat Committee, at p.25.
9. Report of the Public Committee on the Appointment of the Attorney General and Other Matters Relating to his Office (Jerusalem, 1998) (Hebrew).
10. Ibid., at pp.52–6.

Particularistic Considerations and the Absence of Strategic Assessment in the Israeli Public Administration: The Role of the State Comptroller

ELIEZER GOLDBERG

The State of Israel is a relatively young state and in the 50 years since its establishment has experienced far-ranging social and political upheavals. The shared national basis notwithstanding, each part of Israeli society brought its own cargo of culture, customs and tradition. Israel is a young state living an intensive existence, and is continually developing normative systems intended to delineate the boundaries of the permitted and prohibited, as well as guidelines, not always self-evident, regarding what is and is not legitimate.

Over the years, the State of Israel underwent a transformation of values, accompanied by political and social change, which deeply affected the public administration and the public sector.

This process was accompanied by value-centred tensions and conflicts that moulded the operative norms of the public sector, and influenced both the practical issues and the issues of principle which commanded the state comptroller's attention.

Success in the processing of values and their inculcation within a mandatory normative system is essential for maintaining the stability of any society, including the Israeli society: 'Consolidation is the multifaceted process by which democratic structures, norm and civil society are firmly

Eliezer Goldberg is state comptroller and ombudsman of the State of Israel.

established.'[1] This article will depict the connection between these developments and the emergence of particular operative modes which epitomize the Israeli public sector, and the challenges they raise for state audit.

The basic and leading assumption in this article is that Israeli society is still undergoing the process of formulating a consensual set of values and norms accompanied by a conflict over the power to determine the dominancy of ideas and groups. One of the results of this process is the allocation of resources on a particularistic basis. The combination of this process with the need to provide solutions to problems, which are perceived by policy makers as urgent and critical, results and is very often aimed at giving short term relief rather than in the setting of long range programmes based on a strategic perspective.

Indeed, over the 50 years of existence of the State of Israel, a remarkable system of values has developed, written and non-written, as well as a trustworthy institutional framework for law enforcement, which also includes the state comptroller. But at the same time one can also discern the phenomenon of legitimizing the violation of the rules in circumstances perceived as 'justifying' such violations. This phenomenon is expressed both in practice and in the public discourse.

The phenomenon is closely related to the 'ideologization' of activities in the public sector, i.e. perceiving activities in terms of ideology. Many areas are perceived, often justly, in terms of national missions. The terminology surrounding them has this character too, and this impacts positively upon the motivation for action. Yet it also has a retarding effect on the willingness to create and fortify a consensual system of values. Quite simply, the achievement of national goals can prompt a disregard of rules that are defined as appropriate operational norms. Such disregard may be conscious and volitional, or incidental and unintended. Where tension exists between the realization of national goals and rules that 'disturb' such realization, it should not necessarily be assumed that the norms should invariably prevail. Quite often they are considered as being of secondary importance, or even an obstacle to the promotion of goals regarded as crucial – be it a national imperative or even a particularistic imperative in the guise of national goals.

The need to provide immediate solutions for national imperatives or even for community-related needs engenders a sense of urgency. This, in turn, occasionally affords express or implied 'legitimacy' for violation of the normative system which has developed over the years and which the law enforcement institutions have laboured to assimilate and to channel the organs of the executive branch into strict compliance within it.

The geopolitical situation of the State of Israel, i.e. the repeated states of crises in which the state finds itself, strengthens that sense of urgency and provides legitimization for 'breaking the rules'. Inevitably, this thwarts the internalization of a consensual commitment to compliance with rules.

Rehashed terminology is sometimes used to justify divergence from the rules. Terms such as 'reverse discrimination' or 'affirmative action' now belong to the political-social discourse.

It is stressed that affirmative action by way of preferential treatment is not necessarily illegitimate. Moreover, Israeli law even recognizes the need to create apparatuses for amelioration of discrimination, e.g. the obligation to provide suitable representation for both genders, for handicapped people and for the Arab population in the public service as well as on the boards of directors of government corporations. However, an essential condition for such ameliorative action is its execution in accordance with clear rules and with lawful authority. *They cannot become an instrument exercised exclusively in accordance with subjective considerations of the executive power*, even if the protagonists of a particular goal believe that their actions are performed on behalf of the entire public in order to 'rectify an historical aberration'.

PARTICULARISTIC CONSIDERATIONS IN THE ACTS OF GOVERNMENT

Against the background of these historical and evaluative developments, there must be an awareness of the damaging phenomenon of public servants being guided by particularistic considerations. In doing so they exploit the governmental power conferred on them, acting in absolute defiance of the rules that are fundamental to the legal normative conceptions accepted in Israel. This unacceptable phenomenon is expressed repeatedly in the reports of the state comptroller, as well as in Supreme Court judgments discussing the misallocation of state resources, whether through the absence of clear criteria or by slanted interpretation of these criteria.

Regarding the rules incumbent upon the public authority and the definition of its public liability, the matter is crystal clear. On more than one occasion the Supreme Court has emphasized the duty of trust owed by a public authority to the entire public and its obligation to act in accordance with equality-based criteria, without any bias, whether in terms of the individual or in terms of the sector. The reason is that the authority

> is formed exclusively in order to serve the public; it has nothing of its own. Whatever it has - has been given in trust. It has neither rights nor obligations in addition thereto, or which are different and separate thereof. All of its rights and obligations derive from this trusteeship or were conferred upon it under statutory provisions.[2]

In the same vein, the state comptroller's reports have stated that a person

> elected or appointed as a public servant, by nature becomes a trustee for the public. Together with his duty to diligently discharge his duty with devotion and efficiency, he must also act in good faith. Good faith means that the public trust cannot be compromised, regarding the public servant or regarding the body employing him. Public trust is the life source from which the executive branch draws its vitality and its authority to discharge the variety of functions imposed upon it.[3]

The Supreme Court dealt with the fundamental principle guiding the exercise of the public authority's responsibilities, *inter alia*, when discussing the allocation of land rights. The court said the following:

> Public lands must be administered in accordance with national criteria. The adoption of such criteria is incumbent upon public authorities in all their dealings, and all the more so in matters which concern the treatment of property belonging to the entire public.

> Translating these criteria into operational modes indicates, *inter alia*, the obligation of behaving fairly and equally and in accordance the principles of proper administration.[4]

Experience indicates that those vested with power are not deterred from disregarding the rules dictated by this conception, thereby violating the principles of equality and the duty of trust owed to the public. In fact, quite often the holder of power finds himself in a conflict of interests, torn between the broad public interest and his desire to act on behalf of a particularistic or party interest, in the guise of a relevant consideration. This receives expression at many levels, including the direct allocation of financial resources, the allocation of land and appointments of persons to positions in the public service, all such decisions or appointments being based upon preference for a particular political or particularistic identity. It also affects the operational modes practised in the public administration in the broader sense, as will be described below.

It should be emphasized that the phenomenon of preferential treatment for particular sectors does not characterize any particular branch; it is a broad phenomenon, and as old as the state itself. I will mention a few examples taken from state audit.

The state comptroller published a report on grants given to certain institutions from the budgets of the local municipalities, with the direct involvement of then serving minister of the interior. It was suggested that a particular sector merited 'extra-budgetary' support, after previously having been discriminated against with respect to the allocation of resources for satisfying its particular needs. According to the minister of interior, the claim of this sector's representatives was that:

> its educational and cultural needs are of a special nature, the kind of which are not satisfied by general institutions, and as a result, they and their children have been discriminated against for years, when compared with other sectors of the population. The representatives claimed that the time has come to change direction and to make this sector equal to the other sectors of the population ... the Minister referred to his intervention in issuing grants for this sector as 'reverse discrimination'.[5]

The state comptroller's response was that 'it is inconceivable that parallel, circumventive tracks and illegitimate norms should be established for channelling money to institutions. There are fixed principles and criteria for state budgetary allocation and acquiescing to this situation would divest them of any substance', and that if there was substance to the claims of discrimination, then 'they should be responded to as dictated by law and by the principles of reasonableness and equality'.[6]

In another case, the Israel Lands Authority joined a local authority in a non-tender allocation of land to an *Amuta* (non-profit organization) comprising army personnel from a particular unit. Ultimately, the allocation did not take place, *inter alia*, due to the intervention of the state comptroller. Nonetheless, the state comptroller's audit revealed that the Land Authority had improperly approved the allocation of the land, and that the municipality was responsible for altering planning definitions in order to reduce the price of land. These factors, combined with the fact that both the minister in charge and the mayor himself were senior retired army officers (the latter having served in the same unit), pointed to the motivation for these initiatives as well as the problems involved therein.[7] In another report the comptroller dealt with rental apartments that had been built by the Construction and Housing Ministry. It emerged that the definitions of the entitlement conditions created preferential treatment for a particular sector of the population, that particular sector being represented by the head of the ministry. These kinds of particularistic preferences can also be identified in many other areas, e.g. channelling money to educational institutions, or to commemorating the legacy of the social, cultural group to which those in charge of the allocation are connected, etc.

Another illustration of the exploitation of governmental power for particularistic purposes is the appointment of 'cronies' to positions in the public service. Such prohibited appointments compound particularistic preference with party preference.

Both the state comptrollers and the courts have frequently addressed these phenomena, both in relation to concrete cases and as a matter of principle. When adjudicating a petition which attacked a particular appointment as being politically motivated, the court stressed that:

> any contesting of the validity of a political appointment, claiming it to have been politically motivated, will encounter considerable difficulty. The difficulty relates to the manner of proving the influence of political considerations. An authority is presumed to have acted lawfully and a person claiming that a particular action was done unlawfully bears the onus of proving it. In order to discharge this evidentiary burden, a vague intuition based upon conjecture alone is insufficient.[8]

The difficulty is therefore evidentiary, as almost any decision can be presented in a guise of relevant considerations, and distinguishing the wheat from the chaff is not so easy. Consequently, one can query the presumption that the authority always acts lawfully unless proven otherwise. Conceivably, such a presumption supplies the governmental authority with an 'insurance certificate', licensing it to act upon unlawful motivations in the guise of legitimate considerations. A preferable position could be that in certain cases, where the temptation to act out of party preferences is great, the onus shifts to the authority to present the data in order to demonstrate that it acted on the basis of relevant considerations. Should it fail to do so, then the opposite conclusion will be drawn. The aforementioned presumption enables the abuse of government power for particularistic goals, and facilitates the breach of the basic trust which the holder of any public position owes the public as a whole.

Without expressing an opinion on the problematic nature of the aforementioned approach, it is clear that where a sense of particularistic identification influences the objective considerations of the public servant, it impairs his ability – and inevitably his duty – to consider comprehensive societal considerations. This removes the very basis of the fulfilment of his duty of trust.

The state comptroller stands sentinel, ensuring adherence to the principles of trust and equality, the cornerstone of any ordered society.

THE ABSENCE OF A STRATEGIC PERSPECTIVE

A more frequent flaw, repeatedly mentioned in the reports of the state comptroller, is the absence of a strategic perspective in the execution of governmental actions. Unfortunately, it cannot be defined as a local defect, limited in scope; it is a characteristic trait, wherein lies its severity and its negative long-term ramifications. As stated, it has been referred to in numerous reports, and most recently in the report published by the state comptroller concerning the treatment of development towns over many years.[9] These cities and towns were established during the first years of the State of Israel, and recently arrived immigrants were settled there. The leaders of the state were confronted with the challenge of dispersing the population throughout the country, and these townships were intended to serve in the realization of this policy. Unfortunately, over the years most of these areas became characterized by a socio-economic level below the average Israeli level; the central question that arose was, why?

The conclusion emerging from the entirety of data presented in the report was that the difficulties faced by the development towns, sometimes even their failures, were not necessarily the result of the lack of resources. Quite the opposite – resource investment was extensive. The miserable reality reflected the lack of a comprehensive perspective and clear policy in the treatment of these towns over the years which could have enabled the adjustment and regulation of resource investment in accordance with clear, long-term goals.

The absence of operative patterns based on a long-term conception is also expressed with respect to the realization of extensive reforms in the public administration. Like other states in the Western world, Israel also planned a comprehensive programme in this area. Thus, back in 1986 a special committee was appointed to structure the reform, and in 1990 the government approved its recommendations in principle. Yet at the close of the decade its central recommendations had not been implemented.

The non-implementation of the recommendations did not reflect a change in policy, for the government that had approved them, as well its successors, never adopted decisions revoking previous decisions and replacing them with others. The conclusion is that this was not a solitary, one-time occurrence, but rather part of an operational mode which repeated itself. This is a mode which does not necessarily perceive long-term goals as preceding or taking preference over immediate interests and short-term political gains; in fact it sees a justification for preferring the latter:

> The main reason for the ongoing problematic nature of the public administration is its unwillingness, or perhaps inability, to call a halt to piecemeal reforms, and to introduce in their stead substantial and fundamental changes, as occurred in most of the democratic states. This contention is particularly valid with respect to the civil service, which despite the changes engendered by ongoing events, still awaits programmatic and comprehensive reform.[10]

The facts indicate that the Israeli government has no organized process for determining long-term national priorities. This is of far-reaching importance with respect to the allocation of national resources in accordance with a comprehensive long-term perspective, which is required precisely due to the magnitude of problems confronting Israeli society.

Conceivably, the absence of a 'macro' thought pattern is also connected, *inter alia*, to an unwillingness to confront the need to decide fundamental, controversial issues. Furthermore, it enables a flexibility which in political terms is regarded as advantageous.

It seems to be that there is a thread connecting all of these factors with the formation of the national budget. Determination of the national budget means adopting a decision on the level of a worldview. This is not a neutral decision based upon the technical allocation of a given quantity of resources. Accordingly, it is naturally affected by pressures from a variety of political and social groups. There is an inherent tension between the fundamental democratic interest in the equal allocation of the national budget and other legitimate forces interested in promoting particular social goals at the expense of others. When relating to equality in resource allocation, one must remember that equality is an elusive concept. There may be more than one correct definition. The definition is largely subjective and the decision in parliament will reflect a legitimate result of the democratic process. Even so, the budget does not express a result flowing from a strategic perspective regarding national needs, but rather needs measured by short-term, if not immediate indexes. The vagueness of various budgetary sections (and in many executive branch decisions) also serves the particularistic mode which characterizes the public administration in Israel, in as much as vagueness allows 'flexibility'.

The Minister of Health of the government serving in 1994, stated it as follows:

> I can say with almost absolute certainty that our government today has no serious process, at a cabinet level, regarding what is referred to as national priorities. It does not exist, as a system ... as a system it does not exist in the cabinet, in a procedure for organized discussion in the cabinet framework, to determine national priorities which subsequently dictate or lead to budgetary consequences.[11]

THE ROLE OF THE STATE COMPTROLLER

The state comptroller fulfils his role primarily by exposing defects in the audited bodies; such exposure is intended to accommodate the process of rectification and, occasionally, even substantial reform. In principle, the process of reform belongs entirely to the sphere of activities of the audited body. The question is therefore asked: should the state comptroller himself initiate reforms or thrust his full weight as a partner to their formulation?

In the international conference of INTOSAI (International Organization of Supreme Audit Institutions), held in October 2002 in Seoul, this was the prevailing spirit, indicating a trend towards broadening the range of state auditing. Many members supported this approach, which contends that state audit

> may include being consulted by government when reform initiatives concern issues directly relevant to the expertise and values of SAIs

(Supreme Audit Institution), serving on committees with government agencies (preferably as an observer), and engaging in constructive dialogues with government agencies to address performance shortfalls and management weaknesses.[12]

In the decision adopted by INTOSAI it was determined that:

SAIs should ... Recognize that the advisor role, without getting directly involved in the decision making process, should be:

- Based on relevant audit work augmented by the auditor's institutional knowledge and professional judgment. This advisor role includes a range of management functional areas where the SAI has long-term demonstrated expertise (such as financial management and accounting or strategic planning and performance measurement) and/or involves values that are of vital concern to the SAI, including transparency accountability, governance and propriety.

- Started during the early strategic planning stage and continue through implementation.

- Considered in the context of the broad audit function with great caution exercised to maintain SAI independence.[13]

This trend may reflect an attempt to renew and broaden the scope of state auditing, deepen its influence, introduce new values and confer additional powers which it has not to date possessed in free states. However, there is a danger of crossing the boundaries, which may disturb the balance of powers between the branches of government; in other words, broadening the power of the comptroller in a manner that oversteps its boundaries and invades the realm of the executive branch.

Finally, the operative modes of the public administration in Israel directly affect the sense of accountability, which must accompany every public servant. The importance of actualizing the accountability of public servants cannot be overstated. It is a central tenet of a democratic worldview, and of the government's responsibility towards its citizens. This concept too developed gradually, with the deepened understanding of the duty of trust owed by the public servant.

In this context, the pertinent questions are: who is perceived to be accountable? To whom are they accountable? What are the standards or values against which accountability is measured? What are the means for its realization?[14] The answers to these questions are obviously culturally dependent. Clearly, in democratic states the government, and the civil service carrying out its policies, are accountable to the public, to the tax payers. Indeed, in certain cases accountability is imposed by the force of law. However, it is not the power of law that should 'convince' the civil service to fulfil the obligation of accountability. It is rather the inherent conviction that this obligation stems from basic democratic values and the ability to transform this conviction into daily behaviour; the assimilation of the idea that the power given to the executive generates from the public, to whom it is committed and responsible. The level of accountability is not static. It varies from society to society and may also develop over time, in any given society.

The inevitable conclusion is that the Achilles' heel of the Israeli public administration, as described, weakens the vitality of such accountability. It is therefore one of the major tasks of the state comptroller to deepen the awareness and commitment to these values by developing and posing higher norms of behaviour for the civil service, which coincide both with the local law and with universal standards of good governance.

CONCLUSION

Against the background of the comments above, it will be understood that it is the state comptroller's role to disseminate the understanding that there is no conflict between compliance with norms and the achievement of goals. Moreover, illegitimate channels of action ultimately intensify public conflict and tension, to the extent that their perpetrators and the causes they represent lose their legitimacy for large parts of the public. The state comptroller must therefore concentrate on delineating and buttressing the normative borders between the appropriate and the inappropriate, between the permitted and the proscribed.

The internalization of these values ultimately impacts upon the overall patterns of administrative conduct, as well as upon the decision making process, the broader context and considerations surrounding their adoption. The auditing process should be focused on sensitive issues of principle, on developing and sharpening the frequently blurred borders between the legitimate and the illegitimate. This would contribute significantly to proper administration in the substantive and deep sense by fortifying the normative infrastructure upon which a more just and fair society can be built.[15]

NOTES

1. Leonardo Morlino, *Democracy Between Consolidation and Crisis*, Oxford, 1998, p.14.
2. High Court of justice (HC) 14/70, *Benjamin Shapira v. Jerusalem District Committee of the Israel BAR*, P.D. (*Piskei Din*, Judgments, official publication of judgments of the Israeli Supreme Court) 28 (1) at 325.
3. Political Appointments, *Annual Report 44 of the State Comptroller*, Jerusalem, 1994, p.932 (Hebrew).
4. High Court of Justice (HC) 5023/91, *Avraham Poraz v. Minister of Construction and Housing*, P.D. (*Piskei Din*, Judgments, official publication of judgments of the Israeli Supreme Court) 46 (2) P.D. 703, at 801–2. Emphasis added.
5. *Audit Report on Granting Support by Local Authorities*, Jerusalem, 1991, p.123 (Hebrew).

6. Ibid., p.124.
7. *Annual Report 50B' of the State Comptroller*, allocation of land to a non profit organization in the city of Ram Gan (Jerusalem, May 2000), p.607 (Hebrew).
8. High Court of Justice (HC) 4566/90 *David Dekel* v. *Minister of Finance et al.*) P.D. (*Piskei Din*, Judgments, official publication of the judgments of the Israeli Supreme Court) 45(1) at 28.
9. 'Development Towns in the South', *Annual Report 50B of the State Comptroller* (Jerusalem, May 2000), p.5 (Hebrew).
10. David Nachmias and Gila Menachem, *Public Policy in Israel*, Jerusalem, 1999, p.119 (Hebrew).
11. David Deri and Emanuel Sharon, *Economics and Politics in the State Budget*, Jerusalem, 1994, pp.28, 29 (Hebrew).
12. *Proceedings, Seventeenth International Congress of Supreme Audit Institutions* (Seoul, October 2001), p.68.
13. Ibid., p.69.
14. Ledvina V. Carino, 'Administrative Accountability: A Review of the Evolution, Meaning and Operationalization of a Key Concept in Public Administration', in A. Friedberg, B. Geist, N. Mizrahi and I. Sharkansky (eds.), *State Audit and Accountability*, Jerusalem, 1991, p.44.
15. For further discussion on the role and functions of the state comptroller see www.mevaker.gov.il.

The Press Council

RAPHAEL COHEN-ALMAGOR

The aim of this essay is to review the work of the Israel Press Council. Israel is a unitary state with its own national Press Council.[1] The Press Council deals with both print and electronic media but it lacks real ability to sanction newspapers for misconduct. The essay considers the history of the Press Council, analyzing the way it has developed, its work, and how it reached its current status. It is argued that the existing situation is far from satisfactory, and that the media should advance more elaborate mechanisms of self-control, empowering the Council with greater authority and with substantive ability to sanction.

THE ISRAEL PRESS COUNCIL

The foundations for the Israel Press Council were laid in 1956. Some prominent journalists realized that they had better do something themselves before the government began to restrict their activities. At that time there were tendencies and voices in the government in favour of a press law and restricting journalistic activities. In addition, penetrating criticism was voiced by many journalists about their own daily activity. Under this pressure, the journalists instituted a special committee, called the Ethics Committee, whose role was to legislate ethics codes and to form a body that would pre-empt 'intervention from above'.[2]

Prior to the establishment of the Ethics Committee, the activists in this initiative studied the situation in other democracies. They approached foreign journalists' organizations and finally chose the British one as the model, according to which the Israeli journalists formulated their first Code of Ethics.

Raphael Cohen-Almagor is the founder and director of the Center for Democratic Studies, University of Haifa. He was a member of the Israeli Press Council in 1997–2000

In the first five years of its activity, the Ethics Committee did not receive many complaints. The most critical rulings against newspapers were 'severe reprimand'.[3] In 1962 the National Union of Journalists was established and a year later the Press Council was formed. Many journalists supported the decision but there were also cautionary voices. Gershom Schocken, then editor of the respected *Haaretz* newspaper, said that the press should be very careful in instituting such a controlling body, and that 'we should be careful in observing the limited and well-defined authority of such a body'.[4]

The National Union of Journalists, the Press Editors' Committee and the Union of the Dailies Management decided to go ahead with the initiative and to establish the Council. The former president of the Supreme Court, Yitzhak Olshan, who in the mid-1960s became the second president of the Council (the first was Zeev Scherf who at one point became the finance minister in one of Mapai's governments), explained the rationale and the need for the Council: 'Because in the modern era there are increasing points of friction between the need for freedom of the press and the public interests, the press realized that they should take it upon themselves to bridge the gap between them.'[5]

President Olshan served two four-year terms in office before he stepped down and was succeeded by Attorney Yehoshua Rotenstreich. Olshan thought that a free press was a public right rather than a privilege of journalists. A journalist in the Press Council is first and foremost a citizen, and he or she should not subject the Council to his or her professional interests. He saw the prime aim of the Council as preventing through self-restraint abuse of the freedom journalists enjoyed. This, in turn, would avert legislative attempts designed to curb such abuse.[6] President Olshan's first motion was to propose that journalists would not publish facts or rumours before substantiating them in accordance with the best available data. His motion encountered objections from the journalists' representatives, who, Olshan said, preferred getting scoops to safeguarding the public interest. After long deliberations, the motion was accepted.[7]

Next, President Olshan strove to establish 'Clarification Committees' to consider complaints. He wanted these committees to include public figures who were not press professionals. Again, the motion encountered much opposition on the ground that journalists do not need to be subjected to external control. After a long struggle, the motion passed in the plenary.[8] The same scenario took place when President Olshan suggested including public figures in the plenary and on the Executive Committee, all with voting rights. The motion was eventually adopted.

In 1968, the Press Council decided that it also had the authority to discuss complaints against papers that were not members of the Council. In the event that a paper refused to take part in the deliberation, the Council would be permitted to publish the refusal. The Council considered itself the representative of all the media, without regard to the question of membership. However, this authority was not used systematically. On occasion the Council did deal with such complaints; on many other occasions, especially when the complaints concerned local papers, the Council refused to deal with them on the ground that the papers were non-members.[9]

Like the British and Canadian press councils, the Israel Press Council is a voluntary body whose institutions are comprised of representatives of the press (30%); representatives of publishers and editors (30%), and public representatives (40%). Sixty members sit in the plenary organ, and ten in the presidency organ that implements the decisions of the plenary. In 1998 there were discussions to expand membership in the plenary and the presidency. This is because the cable television stations as well as Galei Zahal (the military radio station) and the News Corporation of the Second Television and Radio Authority wished to join the Council, and the three major dailies – *Haaretz, Yedioth Ahronoth* and *Maariv* – demanded more representatives.[10] The functions of the Council are to protect freedom of the press and information, to crystallize ethical codes and to examine complaints regarding violations of the codes.[11]

Until 1994 the Clarification Committees considered complaints and submitted their conclusions to the Executive Committee of the Press Council. Moshe Ronen, a past member in the Executive Committee, testified that the deliberations in this body, which no longer exists, had been partisan and biased. He recalls an incident when the Executive Committee refrained from asking a newspaper to publish the Clarification Committee's ruling, which was very critical of the newspaper. After a few minutes the committee also refrained from asking the rival newspaper to publish another unpleasant ruling concerning itself. In another incident, members of the Executive Committee organized a lobby within the committee against the acceptance of the Clarification Committee's ruling concerning complaints of a journalist who became a politician. Those members opposed the politician's views and did not wish to grant him any form of support.[12]

The Israel Press Council has undergone significant changes during the past ten years or so. In 1988, Professor Yitzhak Zamir, former legal adviser to the government (attorney general), was elected president of the Council. Prior to his acceptance of the appointment, Zamir clarified that he cared very much about freedom of the press and that he objected to legal intervention to control the Council's work. At the same time, he emphasized the need for an effective mechanism of press self-regulation, with the necessary 'teeth' to maintain professional ethics.[13]

Professor Zamir testified that he had found an organization with virtually no office and no money. There were no protocols of meetings, hardly any documentation at all. In essence, he said, he found an organization under the leadership of one person: Yehoshua Rotenstreich, who served as president of the council. Rotenstreich operated the Council: he convened the meetings, decided on priorities, and ruled the body. Zamir maintains that in practice Rotenstreich ran the Council's affairs from his well-to-do law office, and with the help of the then secretary general, Yoseph Karni, who was a volunteer. The Union of Journalists gave the secretary general a desk and telephone in the Journalists' House (Beith Sokolov), and arranged for the typing of his letters. Beith Sokolov also arranged rooms for the meetings of the Council's organs. There were not many complaints because there was not much public awareness of the Council's work. The journalists and editors wanted a Press Council, but did not want to invest in it. It appears that the Council was window dressing. It was basically a fig-leaf to cover the indiscretions and breaches of ethics on the part of the journalists and their editors and publishers.

More than a year before Professor Zamir took office, Yehoshua Rotenstreich died and the Council practically ceased operations during this period. The Editor of *Haaretz* newspaper, Hanoch Marmari, later said that the Council did not operate for a year and nothing happened. He regarded this as proof that it was obsolete.[14] Zamir's first priority was to secure funds for the work of the Council. The Union of Journalists and the Editors' Committee provided a two-room office in the Journalists' House. They also undertook to pay monthly membership fees to secure a budget for the day-to-day work. Nevertheless, securing the funding was not an easy task, and the fees were hard to raise. After a few months the presidency of the Council began work on drafting Press Council bylaws and on revising the Professional Code of Ethics. Zamir proposed instituting an Ethics Tribunal to replace the existing Clarification Committees. The journalists did not like the idea of a tribunal to which they would be subordinated, and members of the Executive Committee realized that the institution of the tribunal would render them obsolete because the decisions of the tribunal would make ratification of the adjudication by the Committee unnecessary. However, the Council bylaws and the Professional Code of Ethics were slowly drafted and updated by the plenary, including the institution of the tribunal, until the discussion came to deal with the 'teeth': the powers of the tribunal.

For Zamir, the Code of Ethics and the mechanism for *effective* self-regulation were the main things. The existing most severe sanction – the publication of adjudication – was not to be ignored: journalists did not like it. At the same time, it was not a painful penalty, and, moreover, the public did not think it was a substantial sanction. Many times, the publication of adjudication was brief and the president's protests fell on deaf ears because the Council lacked real power. In such circumstances – when the journalists did not appreciate the work of the Council – no wonder it also lacked public esteem. President Zamir thought it important that the public should see the sanctions as significant, and should regard the Press Council as a shield to protect the press from legislation. He also thought that if the press did not introduce these sanctions, the legislature would find it necessary to intervene. Some press representatives calmed his worries by saying that the politicians were afraid of the press and would never resort to legislation.[15] In essence, the industry wanted a limited Council with limited powers and abilities.

The journalists and editors were willing to accept the existing sanctions: reprimand and publication of adjudication. Zamir pushed for two additional sanctions: a maximum fine of NIS 10,000 (roughly $US7,000 in 1992 terms) on newspapers, and a recommendation to suspend journalists for one month for severe breaches of the Code of Ethics.

After many hesitations and long negotiations, the journalists agreed, but the editors stood firm in their objection. Then the journalists retreated and joined the editors. Zamir explained his position and threatened to resign. When the resolution failed to pass in the plenary owing to the objection of journalists and editors, who were the majority (the public representatives supported the president's motion), he resigned from office (in 1992). Because of this episode, Zamir thinks that the majority of the Council should consist of public representatives who would truly care for the public interest.[16]

In 1993, Haim Zadok (a former minister of justice) was nominated president of the Press Council. During his first year in office, he pushed forward some of his predecessor's initiatives. The Executive Committee and the Clarification Committees were abolished. The Ethics Tribunal was established in their place. In addition, the new Press Council bylaws and the revised Professional Code of Ethics were ratified by the plenary in May 1994 and in May 1996 respectively.

The Press Council bylaws set forth the ends and functions of the Council (as described above); explicate the identity of the Council's members, in accordance with the proportion described between journalists, editors and publishers, and public representatives; set out procedures for the work of the Council, and the allocation of budget; and discuss the roles of the Ethics Tribunal. The Professional Code of Ethics covers issues like decency; fairness; truth; objectivity; privacy; coverage of specified segments of the population (victims; minors; patients etc.); racism; discrimination; 'freebies'; confidentiality of sources, etc.[17]

Complaints are dealt with according to the following procedure: the president of the Council, or person(s) appointed by him,[18] reviews the complaint upon its receipt. If the complaint is found to be lacking any substance, he/she may turn it down and inform the complainant of the reasoning. If the complaint is not rejected, it is passed to Council's legal advisor or his/her deputy (usually to the latter). The deputy legal advisor reviews the complaint and if he/she thinks it is *prima facie* valid, it is supposed to be sent within 48 hours to the media organization that is the subject of the complaint with a request to submit a response within ten days. As in Britain, the Council does not deal with complaints that are handled by judicial courts or by the police. Within ten days the complaint and the response to it are supposed to be examined by the Council's legal advisor (usually by the deputy). The examiner is required to decide within 21 days from the receipt of the complaint whether to pass it on to the chairperson of the Ethics Tribunal. The examiner will do so only if he/she thinks that there has been *prima facie* violation of the Code of Ethics. Before the complaint is passed to the chairperson of the Ethics Tribunal, the president of the Council is entitled to seek ways to settle the complaint without adjudication, provided that the complainant and the media organization concerned agree to this.[19] During the past two years, 2001-03, a student body from the Department of Communication at Tel Aviv University called 'Students for Ethics in the Media', has passed to the Press Council complaints based on a follow-up survey they conduct, and the Council addresses them. That is to say that a third party can initiate complaints. The last president of the Council to date, Professor Mordechai Kremnitzer, initiated the mediation process before passing the complaint to the Ethics Tribunal. The aim is to resolve the matter without the need for court formalities. The mediation idea is in place. It may save time and result in a much more efficient decision making process. Until March 2003 there were 4-5 cases that were resolved through mediation.[20]

Once the chairperson of the Ethics Tribunal has received the complaint, he/she appoints a tribunal comprised of three members: a public representative (chairperson of the tribunal), a journalists' representative, and a representative of the publishers and editors. The chairperson of the Ethics Tribunal makes sure that the representatives of the journalists, publishers and editors are not from the same media organ that is the subject of the complaint. The tribunal is required to submit its ruling within 21 days. The ruling is not required to be unanimous. A majority vote is binding. In the event that one of the sides wishes to appeal against the ruling, an appeal must be submitted within ten days. It will be adjudicated by a larger panel of the tribunal, comprised of five or seven members nominated by the chairperson of the Ethics Tribunal. Two of the members of the appeal panel must be public representatives. The other three are representatives of the journalists, publishers and editors.[21]

The tribunal is supposed to weigh the interests of the Press Council, and to serve as a guide and a 'watchdog'.[22] Members of the tribunal are elected for a period of three years and can be re-elected. In the event that a complaint is found justified, the tribunal can decide on one of the following measures against the journalist and/or his/her newspaper: to issue a warning; to reprimand; to ask that an apology be published; or to suspend the newspaper from the Council for a limited period of time.[23]

The punishment of suspension is not a very wise alternative given that the Council is striving to have all newspapers become members. In the words of former president, Zadok, this punishment saws off the bough one is sitting on.[24] Uri Slonim, chairperson of the Ethics Tribunal from the day of its establishment in 1994, and Bezalel Eyal, former secretary general of the Council, said that the most extreme measure taken by the tribunal was to ask the paper concerned to publish the tribunal's adjudication in a prominent place. The newspapers usually comply with the rulings of the tribunal.[25]

In 1994, the Press Council received 95 complaints; 27 complaints were submitted to the tribunal for deliberation and ruling, the others were rejected or resolved prior the tribunal. In 1995, 94 complaints were received of which 19 reached the tribunal. In 1996 the Council received 92 complaints, and 18 necessitated the attention of the tribunal. In 1997 there were 148 complaints and 17 were passed to the tribunal. In 1998 the Council received 130 complaints, most of which were pending resolution in 1999 owing to the dispute with the journalists, publishers and editors over the issues of representation and funding.[26] In 1999 there was a sharp decrease in the number of complaints, to only about 70.[27] The former secretary general, Eyal, said that on average it takes three months from the time a complaint is received until the tribunal resolves it.[28] He nevertheless admitted that the process is longer now because of the crisis that has paralyzed the work of the Council for a few months (see *infra*). My own examination of the Council's files during 1996-98, and the Council's most recent *Select Tribunal Decisions and Judgements* covering the years 1994-95, show that it takes 1 – 13 months to resolve complaints that necessitated the attention of the tribunal, and that the average time of dealing with complaints is six months. In 2003 President Kremnitzer argued that dealing with complaints lasts a few months. He could not say how many months exactly.[29]

The plenary of the Israeli Press Council, which decides on policy issues, is supposed to meet three times a year. The Ethics Tribunal of the Israel Press Council deals with complaints and meets 'in accordance to need'. The needs, it appears, are not overwhelming. The president, Kremnitzer, and his deputy, Nitza Shapira-Libai, argue that the most important body is the Council presidency and this body meets regularly, on average once every six weeks. Most of the work is done by the presidency.

In 1998, the Press Council rarely met because the journalists, who fund 40% of the Council's budget, decided to stop the funding. Former president of the Council, Zadok, tried to raise funds from independent sources but did not succeed. After long deliberations, a new arrangement is being formed according to which 80% of the budget will be funded by the publishers and editors, and only 20% by the journalists.[30] The publishers and editors offered to cover the entire budget of the Council but the Israel

Union of Journalists rejected this generous offer and agreed to provide 20%. In 2000, the three major newspapers *Yedioth Ahronoth*, *Maariv* and *Haaretz* took upon themselves to allocate most of the budget. This new arrangement will grant more power to publishers, and the Council will be more cautious in scrutinizing them. There will have to be a dramatic change to allow truly free and independent work by the Council.[31]

Zadok was, on the whole, satisfied with the Council's work. He thought that it should remain voluntary, equipped with public moral sanctions, and that the recent developments – the new Professional Code of Ethics of 1996, and the formation and work of the Ethics Tribunal – strengthened the position of the Council. One positive sign that reflects the status of the Council is the fact that its representatives are consulted whenever members of the Knesset contemplate new press laws. However, the fact that there were and are a growing number of efforts towards laws that would limit press freedom is alarming. Zadok was striving to have publishers and editors see the importance of sitting on the Council, rather than sending third-rate representatives. Only the publisher of *Haaretz* newspaper, Amos Shocken, attends the meetings from time to time. Subsequently Zadok planned to convince prominent journalists to become members. He was not very successful. At present, activists of the National Union of Journalists sit on the Council, and these are not necessarily the most prominent people in the industry. Zadok hoped that after solving the issue of representation, it would be easier to secure more funding from publishers, editors and journalists, which would foster more effective work by the Council. He did not think that funding should be secured outside the press industry, and thought that more people in the industry were more aware of the necessity of a strong Press Council, especially in the face of a growing wave of attempts to pass illiberal press laws.[32]

As a former member of the Council's plenary, I am far from satisfied with its current conduct. The Council meets irregularly, at best three times a year. It does not raise its voice with regard to important ethical concerns on the public agenda. Its budget is paltry – NIS 300,000 a year ($US74,000). This budget pays the part-time salaries of the secretary general and his secretary (the previous secretary general of the Council was a volunteer). The rest of the budget covers the office rental, organization of meetings and the infrequent publications.[33] As a body, the Council is unable to scrutinize effectively the work of the press that funds the organization. Its image among the public is one of a stagnant, ineffective body, whose work is obscure and whose existence is questionable. There needs to be a major reassessment of the work of the Press Council and a systematic reorganization of its machinery in order to make this body an effective entity that really is able to fulfil its duties of supervising and monitoring the media. The Council should be equipped with more power, and have the support of independent, non-partisan foundations that care about the media and about democracy.

One of the criticisms against the work of the Ethics Tribunal concerns its inconsistent adjudication. Different panels of the tribunal may decide similar cases differently.[34] In order to prevent this, the tribunal's decisions should be published regularly, and in any event they should be circulated among members of the tribunal. The tribunal's judgements are supposed to be published once every year. However, because of the limited budget such selections of judgements were published irregularly and infrequently, last in 1996. Kremnitzer says that during the three years 2000–2003 there were no contradictory judgements by the tribunal.[35]

Professor Amos Shapira, deputy president of the Press Council, thinks that this problem of inconsistent adjudication needs to be addressed and answered through more publication and circulation of the tribunal's decisions amongst its members.[36] Zamir thinks that one of the roles of the secretary general and the legal advisor is to review all the rulings and see that the working of the tribunal conforms to the norms and precedents.[37] This is a major issue. Members of the tribunal need to be consistent in their judgements to maintain their credibility. Inconsistency is a prescription for justified grievances. Newspapers and journalists might feel that justice would be ill served if they were found guilty of violating the Code when another paper is acquitted after committing the same questionable deed. Furthermore, it is unjust to inconsistently penalize different papers for similar ethical misconduct. One paper would be warned while the other would receive different punishment for the same misconduct. Diversity of interpretations is fine within boundaries. Each panel of judges should not decide inharmoniously without being aware of precedents.

In the current state of affairs, the Council cannot work effectively. The legal advisor and his deputy are volunteers. The legal advisor is a successful lawyer who can hardly find time to review the complaints, and the work is currently done by his deputy. The deputy has more time but his energies are also limited. There is a need to secure a budget for an independent salaried legal advisor. Maybe it was possible to resolve the problem of inconsistency at least through regular issuing of reports that cover the work of the tribunal. Former secretary general Eyal had prepared another selection of the tribunal's rulings, but because of budget constraints it could not be published by the time he left office in 2001. As for the suggestion of circulating the rulings at least among the members of the Ethics Tribunal, this too was impossible. The budget did not allow for photocopying and sending decisions to all members, and the secretary, who is part time, cannot devote time and attention to mailing more than 150 members of the tribunal.[38]

In June 2000 Mordechai Kremnitzer of the Hebrew University Law Faculty became the sixth president of the Press Council. For some six months, the Council operated without a president, as Zadok completed his term in office in December 1999. The search for an appropriate successor was conducted in a very low key and it seems that no one really cared whether or not the Council had a leader. I doubt whether the public had any idea about the six-month lack of leadership. The media industry certainly did not express much concern. During Kremnitzer's presidency, the financial situation of the Council had somewhat improved. Publishers were more willing to acknowledge the Council's importance and hence allow it to function more effectively. Unlike previous years, the transfer of money from the publishers to the Council took place on time. The annual budget of 2003 was 500,000 shekels; in addition, sums of money were allocated for journalists' advanced studies on ethics and professionalism. The financial improvement allowed a full-time general secretary to be hired and in April 2003 a former journalist of *Maariv* newspaper, Avi Weinberg, assumed office.

The advanced studies on ethics and professionalism are conducted in association with the Herzog Centre at Tel Aviv University. The funding came from someone wishing to remain anonymous. Kremnitzer assured me that the source is neither a publisher nor an editor. The intention is to conduct three to four condensed courses every year and the expectation is that the newspapers and other media organizations will share the financial load. Kremnitzer tried to raise money for the Council's activities from other sources, without success. Many organizations that were expected to show an interest and help in the Council's work are content to let the publishers sponsor it. They are quite oblivious regarding the implications on the Council's independence.

While the general secretary should be a full time employee, Kremnitzer thinks that the president should be a volunteer. There is a moral advantage in the fact that the president is not on the publishers' pay list. S/he should owe nothing to the publishers. Kremnitzer said he did not even ask for his commuting costs to be refunded.

Kremnitzer did not try to gain more powers for the Ethics Tribunals during his presidency. He does not think that the tribunal should have more sanctioning powers. The issue for him is simply of no importance.[39] In May 2003, an internet site that includes all the tribunal's adjudications was launched. There will also be an attempt to include previous adjudication on the site. In addition, the Ethics Code has been publicized. Kremnitzer completed his term in office in July 2003 and at the time of writing there is still no candidate agreed upon to replace him. Nobody seems concerned that the president's office has been vacant for such a long time.

CONCLUSION

In February 1996, the minister of justice and the minister of the interior established a public committee to check the legal arrangements relating to the work of the press in Israel. The committee, headed by the president of the Council, issued its report in September 1997. With regard to the Press Council, the Zadok Committee concluded that its voluntary status and the fact that the Council's decisions were not binding hindered its ability to enforce the Code of Ethics. The committee voiced its concern that the present situation permitted the press to ignore the professional and ethical rules, and to conduct their affairs as they saw fit. The committee therefore recommended the enactment of a new obligatory arrangement that would compel the press to abide by the Code of Ethics and, at the same time would improve the public image of the press.[40]

The arrangement, accordingly, would consist of two parts: on the one hand, the authority to write and impose the Professional Code of Ethics would remain in the independent hands of the Press Council; on the other hand, the law would determine that all journalists and all newspapers ought to conduct their affairs as prescribed by the Code of Ethics, and that they must respect the rulings of the Ethics Tribunal. At the same time, the committee decided to refrain from prescribing sanctions for the violation of the law: 'The sanctions would be public, professional and moral, determined by the Press Council's bylaws and its Code of Ethics.'[41] This arrangement of imperfect legal obligation was deemed necessary by the majority of the committee[42] in order to balance the interest of strengthening the normative status of the Code and the interest of keeping the media independent of governmental involvement in determining the contents of the Code of Ethics. The recommended law, the 'Press Council Law', would hold that 'every newspaper and every journalist will be obliged to maintain the Code of Ethics of the Press Council, and to abide by the Council's Tribunal'.[43]

The Zadok Committee expressed concern that the self-regulatory mechanisms of the media were not working as they should, and that something should be done to enforce the Code of Ethics. There is no harm in the enactment of the suggested law. This law could not undermine the independent status of the press and it might strengthen, in a positive way, the authority of the Press Council. On this issue my view is similar to that of Uri Slonim, who is also in favour of such a law, thinking that it would strengthen the status of the Council and would provide its Ethics Tribunal with 'more teeth'.[44] Former secretary general Bezalel Eyal did not think that this law would pass the Knesset in the foreseeable future.[45] Zadok hoped that it would be passed at some later stage.[46] Yitzhak Zamir is ideologically 'unhappy' with the need to resort to legislation. He would have liked the committee to specify significant sanctions for the Council.

At the same time, Zamir thinks that this might be the solution in the present state of affairs, given that the journalists and editors are unwilling to grant the Council further sanctions, and reporters continue to breach the Code of Ethics. This moderate form of legislation could prove to be the beginning of a solution.[47]

The following discussion offers some further recommendations to improve the work of the Press Council. These recommendations should be observed not only by the Israel Press Council but also by press councils in other democracies.

Many people in the media portray any limitation on free expression as the infringement of a virtue that lies at the heart of democracy. But often this portrayal is exaggerated. Often the case is not one of a zero-sum game. Quite the contrary: sometimes limitations on free speech are required to safeguard basic liberal values, like the right to privacy.[48] The freedom to print and publish does not include the freedom to unjustifiably ruin one's name, one's honour and dignity. Indeed, Israeli society (as, for instance, British and Canadian societies) has sensational tabloid journalism that does not care much for the work of the Press Council, and prints whatever story is likely to increase its sales. Financial and ethical considerations do not necessarily go hand in hand. To ensure that some standards are maintained, the press must have a strong, independent and effective Press Council, with significant powers of sanction. The Press Council should publicize itself, its powers, work and adjudication to make itself known to the public and to gain its trust. The budget to run the Press Council's affairs should be far larger than it now is. The very limited budget of the Council does not allow it to carry out its duties adequately.

The main sponsors of the Press Council are the Federation of Journalists and the publishers. The same is true for the Press Councils in Britain[49] and Canada.[50] They are said to be totally independent. But because the newspapers might cut their fees if they feel unhappy with their adjudication, the councils must be aware of their critics. They find it difficult to bite the hand that feeds them. As Charles Moore, Editor of the *Daily Telegraph*, told me in a personal interview, commenting on the British Press Complaints Committee (PCC): 'The PCC is too frightened of the proprietors ... The proprietors could bully the PCC. They can direct their papers to attack the PCC. They might threaten to leave the PCC.'[51]

The media conceive of the Press Council more or less as a lightning rod. It exists to show that the press care about ethics, that they grapple with ethical dilemmas, that they are interested in what the public thinks; therefore there is no need for restrictive legislation. Press councils are designed to receive and deal with public grievances as well as to curtail restrictive tendencies on the part of the legislature.[52]

The only power that the Israel Press Council has is the publication of adjudication against the papers. This very limited power shows that it

THE PRESS COUNCIL   183

enjoys only qualified support from the industry.[53] Consequently, the Press
Council is little known in Israel. Large segments of society are unaware of
its existence, and many of those who are aware of its presence do not
appreciate its work. The press industries want the Council to act as a
preventive body, to pre-empt measures that would interfere with press
freedom. They do not really want the Press Council to represent the public
interests. They fund the work of the Council and through this they secure
its dependence. The result is that the public conceives the Council's work as
a 'sold game', and most of it remains indifferent or uninterested in what the
Council does.[54]

Some of the papers, while upholding the idea of press freedom, abuse
that freedom. As Anthony Smith believes, it is essential that the press
councils be accorded the power to humiliate, to expose hideous and ghastly
publications and behaviour.[55] These powers should include the following:

- The publication of adjudication. Any newspaper against which a
  complaint has been upheld should publish in full the Press Council's
  adjudication on that complaint. The publication should appear in a
  prominent place. If the Council is unhappy with the placement of the
  adjudication, it should be able to ask the paper to republish the item on
  a specific page. The Council should be able to decide where, on what
  page, the adjudication should be published, so as not to allow
  newspapers to bury the adjudication-in-brief in small print on a back
  page. The publication of adjudication is the only power that press
  councils possess, and it is not enough to adequately monitor the work of
  the press. Additional powers should be granted to the councils that
  would include:
  - The ability to impose signifycant fines on newspapers for gross
    misconduct. These fines should be given to designated charities.
    Because of the inherent conflict of interests, the fines should not be
    made available to sponsor the work of the Press Council. This is in
    line with Yitzhak Zamir's suggestion.[56]
  - The ability to suspend journalists for gross misconduct for a limited
    period of time (see Zamir's initiative *supra*).
  - The ability to suspend publication of newspapers. A threat to suspend
    publication even for one day would be effective, even more so than
    fines.[57]

The Press Council should be comprised, as they are indeed now in
Israel, Britain and Canada, of public representatives and representatives of
the press industry, of the proprietors, and of the editors. A special and
independent Select (or appointed) Committee, selected by leading
publishers and prominent journalists, would decide who would serve on
the Council from those who offer their candidacy. The independent public

representatives should have a majority within the body and include the chairperson (see Zamir's experience and analysis *supra*). This would avoid a partisan majority and a leader who would care more for the interests of the industry than for those of the public.[58] The chairperson of the Council should be a public figure who enjoys a good reputation and has the respect of professionals from both the media and political spheres; someone who is able to voice his or her opinion openly and with credibility, and to serve as a mediator between journalists, proprietors, editors and politicians.

Members of the Press Council should serve for a period of five years. They could be re-elected by their colleagues for an additional five years if the majority of members felt that they could continue to carry out their duties and if the representatives felt that they were able to continue to commit themselves. After a maximum period of ten years, members should be expected to retire so as to allow the introduction of new members.[59]

Members of the Council should be paid for each meeting in which they take part. One of the inherent problems in the working of the Press Council concerns the voluntary character it assumes. The Council in Israel, as councils in Britain and Canada, are composed of relatively prominent people who do not have the time or the will to adequately meet the responsibilities involved. Volunteering is a lofty idea but it hinders the effective working of the councils. Serving on press councils should be considered a heavy responsibility that deserves some financial recognition. The exact payment should be decided in accordance with the budget of each council. In any event, the payment should not be seen in terms of a salary but as a token of appreciation for the commitment, time and effort invested by the members. Members of the Ethics Tribunal or committees dealing with complaints should convene every two or three months for a weekend during which they would hear complaints and adjudicate. Members of these organs deserve substantial payment for their involvement. Here my suggestion follows the pattern set by the British Broadcasting Standards Council, an independent body working on behalf of the audience, whose role is to consider complaints, to conduct research and monitor the broadcasting media, and to provide a forum for the discussion of wider issues. The 12 members of the Council are paid for their work (each member is paid some £14,000 a year, a sum that is more than a mere token of appreciation), and they meet several times a year for concentrated sessions of two to three days to adjudicate complaints.[60]

Complaints to the Press Council should be made in writing, by 'snail mail' or electronic mail. They should be free of charge, as is the case now. The procedure should be fast, informal and available to ordinary people. One should not need to have a lawyer in order to be represented.

Funding is an essential prerequisite for independence of any press council. The Press Council should be funded by an independent body – a charity or a foundation – that cares about the press and understands its significant role in a democratic society. This body is required to be apolitical, without any affiliation to the media. Existing bodies like the Ford or MacArthur Foundations would be suitable, or alternatively special charities ('Concerned Citizens for Accountable Media') could be founded. We must change the existing situation where proprietors fund the councils that are supposed to scrutinize their conduct. There is room to suspect that the public interests are not adequately served when the entire funding comes from the industry.[61]

The Press Council's adjudication should be made in accordance with a written Professional Code of Ethics. The Code should be written in clear language that lay people without knowledge of law could comprehend. The Code should not cover areas that are covered by the law but should set normative standards for ethical and professional reporting. The Professional Code of Ethics should be circulated among media circles and among the public at large so people will be aware of its existence. Editors should see that the Code is on the desk of every reporter.[62]

The adjudication of the Press Council should be reported regularly every few months.[63] It is assumed that if the above recommendations were accepted, there would be sufficient material to issue a report every two months or so. These reports should be sent to all people involved in the work of the Council: reporters, publishers, editors and members of the public.

NOTES

An earlier, shorter version of this article was published in *Science and Engineering Ethics*, Vol.6, No.3 (July 2000), pp.383–98.

1. The Israel Press Council was founded with the British model in mind.
2. Uri Paz, 'Inspection of the Media: The Relationship between the Press Council and the Public', MA thesis, The Hebrew University, Jerusalem, 1987, pp.43–4 (Hebrew).
3. Ibid., p.46.
4. Ibid., p.48.
5. Ibid., pp.48–9. See also Moshe Zack, 'The Press Council after Six Years', *The Journalist's Yearbook* (1969), p.336 (Hebrew).
6. Yitzhak Olshan, *Judgements and Discussions*, Jerusalem and Tel Aviv, 1978, p.383 (Hebrew).
7. Ibid., p.384.
8. Ibid., p.384.
9. Dan Caspi and Yehiel Limor, *The Mediators*, Tel Aviv, 1992, p.17 (Hebrew).
10. Israel Press Council, 'Ad Hoc Committee, Conclusion and Recommendations', 27 October 1998 (Hebrew).
11. Israel Press Council, *Israel Press Council By-Laws, Professional Ethics Code of the Press* (updated to 1 July 1996), p.5 (Hebrew).
12. Moshe Ronen, *Media Ethics*, Tel Aviv, 1998, Vol.II, pp.697–8 (Hebrew). Ronen does not elaborate what these 'unpleasant rulings' were.
13. Interview with Professor Yitzhak Zamir, then Justice of the Israel Supreme Court, 3 January 1999.
14. Hadas Manor, 'The Flickering of a Dying Candle?', *The Journalist's Yearbook* (1993), p.64 (Hebrew).
15. Interview with Yitzhak Zamir, 3 January 1999.

16. Ibid. The impotence of the Council prompted a prominent journalist, Moshe Negbi, to resign from this body. See his criticism in Manor, 'The Flickering of a Dying Candle?', p.63.
17. Israel Press Council, *By-Laws, Professional Ethics Code of the Press*, pp.15–18. Similar issues are invoked in the British and Canadian Codes of Ethics. Cf. Press Complaints Commission, *Report No. 36* (October/November/December 1996), and Ontario Press Council, *Annual Report, 1997*, Toronto.
18. The *Press Council By-Laws* says that this authority is reserved for the president of the Council or a person nominated by the president. Yitzhak Zamir and Haim Zadok, past presidents of the Council, principally refrained from interfering in the dealings with complaints (interviews on 31 December 1998; 3 January 1999).
19. Israel Press Council, *By-Laws, Professional Ethics Code of the Press*, pp.11–12.
20. Phone conversation with Mordechai Kremnitzer, 19 March 2003.
21. Israel Press Council, *By-Laws, Professional Ethics Code of the Press*, pp.11–12.
22. Israel Press Council, *Ethics Tribunal, Select Decisions and Judgements*, 16 September 1996, p.5 (Hebrew).
23. Israel Press Council, *By-Laws, Professional Ethics Code of the Press*, p.12.
24. Interview with president of the Press Council Haim Zadok, 31 December 1998.
25. Interviews with Uri Slonim, 20 December 1998, and Haim Zadok, 31 December 1998.
26. Statistics compiled by the Press Council. I thank Bezalel Eyal for the information.
27. Yehiel Limor, 'The Israel Press Council as a Mechanism of Self-Regulation', Ph.D. thesis, Bar-Ilan University, 2000, p.284.
28. Interview with Bezalel Eyal, secretary general of the Press Council, 27 December 1998.
29. Phone conversation with Mordechai Kremnitzer, 19 March 2003.
30. Discussion with Bezalel Eyal, 25 November 1998.
31. For further criticism of the Israel Press Council, see Dan Caspi and Yehiel Limor, *The Mediators*, Tel Aviv, 1992, pp.185–6, 207–12 (Hebrew).
32. Interview with Haim Zadok, 31 December 1998.
33. Discussions with Bezalel Eyal, 25 November 1998, 27 December 1998, and Professor Amos Shapira, deputy president of the Council, 13 December 1998.
34. The British Press Council and the Canadian Press Council suffered from the similar problem of inconsistency of their adjudication. This inconsistency damaged their reputation. Interviews with Professor Hugh Stephenson, Department of Journalism, City University, London, 1 October 1997; Charles Moore, Editor, *Daily Telegraph*, 21 October 1997; Professor Enn Raudsepp, Concordia University, 22 September 1998. See also David Pritchard, 'The Role of News Councils in a System of Media Accountability: Le Conseil de Quebec at Age 16', paper prepared for presentation to the annual meeting of the Canadian Communication Association, Victoria, BC, 1 June 1990, pp.18–19.
35. Phone conversation with Mordechai Kremnitzer, 19 March 2003.
36. Interview with Amos Shapira, 13 December 1998.
37. Interview with Yitzhak Zamir, 3 January 1999.
38. Interview with Bezalel Eyal, 27 December 1998.
39. Phone conversation with Mordechai Kremnitzer, 26 March 2003.
40. *Report of the Public Committee on Press Laws*, presented to the minister of justice and minister of the interior, September 1997, p.62 (Hebrew).
41. Ibid., pp.62–3.
42. Four members of the Committee backed the decision. One member, Professor Zeev Segal, thought that the recommended legislation might hinder the work of the Press Council and its independent discretion to formulate ethical norms as it sees fit. Ibid., p.63.
43. Ibid., p.63.
44. Interview with Uri Slonim, 20 December 1998.
45. Interview with Bezalel Eyal, 27 December 1998.
46. Interview with Haim Zadok, 31 December 1998.
47. Interview with Yitzhak Zamir, 3 January 1999.
48. See, for instance, the story of Oliver Sipple in R. Cohen-Almagor, *The Boundaries of Liberty and Tolerance*, Gainesville, FL, 1994, chapter 6. I have changed my mind regarding the Sipple story. See 'The Right to Privacy: Part I', in my forthcoming book *The Scope of Tolerance*, London, 2005. See also Richard L. Abel, *Speaking Respect, Respecting Speech*, Chicago and London, 1998.

49. Cf. George Murray, *The Press and the Public*, Carbondale and Edwardsville, IL, 1972; Geoffrey Robertson, *People Against the Press*, London, 1983; Home Office, *Report of the Committee on Privacy and Related Matters*, London, June 1990, Cm 1102; Sir David Calcutt, *Review of Press Self-Regulation*, London, January 1993, Cm 2135; Thomas Gibbons, *Regulating the Media*, 2nd edn., London, 1998.
50. Special Senate Committee on Mass Media, *The Uncertain Mirror*, Ottawa, 1970, Vol.I (Davey Committee); David Taras (ed.), *Media, Power and Policy in Canada*, Toronto, 1992; Arthur Siegel, *Politics and the Media in Canada*, 2nd edn., Toronto, 1996.
51. Interview with Charles Moore, Editor of the *Daily Telegraph*, 21 October 1997.
52. In another study I analyze the work of the press councils in Israel, Canada and Britain. This statement is true for all these councils. Cf. R. Cohen-Almagor, *Speech, Media and Ethics*, Houndmills and New York, 2001.
53. The same is true also for the press councils in Britain and Canada. In the three democracies, papers that do publish adjudication of justified complaints against them do not necessarily grant the adjudication a prominent place in the newspaper.
54. The same can be said with regard to the British and Canadian publics and their attitude towards their respective press councils. Interview with Kenneth Morgan, former director of the Press Council and for one year, 1991–92 (the first year of establishment), director of the Press Complaints Commission, 3 September 1997; discussions with Geoffrey Marshall, Provost of Queen's College, Oxford, 29 August, 25 September, 31 October 1997; interviews with Mel Sufrin, executive secretary of the Ontario Press Council, 6 October 1998; Professor Enn Raudsepp, Department of Journalism, Concordia University, 22 September 1998, and Professor G. Stuart Adam, vice-president (academic) of Carleton University, and formerly director of the School of Journalism and Communication at Carleton, Ottawa, 29 September 1998.
55. Interview with Anthony Smith, President of Magdalen College, Oxford, 16 October 1997. Mr. Smith was also the director of the British Film Institute for ten years.
56. After the tragic death of Princess Diana in 1997, the British PCC contemplated this idea but in the end it was decided not to expand the powers of control. Charles Moore and Anthony Smith, like Yitzhak Zamir, think that the ability to impose fines is a good idea that would enhance the effective working of the PCC. Interviews with Yitzhak Zamir, 3 January 1999, Anthony Smith, 16 October 1997, and Charles Moore, 21 October 1997.
57. This is the suggestion of Martin Bell, MP. Interview in the House of Commons, 21 October 1997. In Britain, where competition between the tabloids is particularly fierce, readers looking for their usual paper would not find it, and would buy another paper, and might switch their allegiance.
58. In one of my interviews, an authority on one of the press councils told me that on occasion the journalists exerted pressure on him to represent their interests better. He said that he needed to remind them that he also represents the editors and publishers. I reminded him, in turn, that the Council is comprised also of a third, no less important, component: the public. Indeed, I often felt that decision makers on the press councils are preoccupied with the needs and interests of the press industry and less so with those of the public.
59. The Israel Press Council decided (on 13 December 1998) that members of the plenary could serve a maximum of three consecutive terms of three years each and then retire so as to allow the introduction of new members. Professor Asa Kasher strongly disagreed with this motion, saying that the Press Council should be viewed as a professional body on which ethics professionals should sit as long as they express willingness to continue their voluntary work.
60. Interview with Stephen Whittle, director of the Broadcasting Standards Commission, 9 October 1997. For further deliberation, see Broadcasting Standards Council, *A Code of Practice*, 2nd edn., London, February 1994; Broadcasting Standards Council, *Complaints Bulletin*, No.54, 25 July 1995.
61. The Quebec Press Council was donated $1 million by a private foundation. Interview with Michel Roy, president of the Quebec Press Council, 18 September 1998.
62. This is not the case now in most media organizations in Israel, Britain and Canada.
63. In Britain, the Press Complaints Commission (PCC) issues a report every several months. This, of course, requires an adequate budget. Interview with Janet Anderson, press officer of the PCC, 23 September 1997.

Israeli Institutions
at the Crossroads

RAPHAEL COHEN-ALMAGOR

THE ROLE OF THE PRESIDENT

Yitzhak Navon discusses in his article the SHABAC (line 300 episode) of 12 April 1984, specifically the decision of President Haim Herzog to grant clemency to the SHABAC agents involved in the killing – and its cover-up – of the two Arabs who kidnapped a bus and were subsequently caught. Israeli democracy has known many tragic affairs and scandals but I think the SHABAC affair is arguably the most serious of all. Almost all the key figures involved in this episode acted, in my opinion, wrongly. The affair started with the decision of the head of the SHABAC, Avraham Shalom, to execute the two kidnappers after they surrendered; continued with the SHABAC attempts to sabotage the work of two investigation committees – the Zorea Committee established in April 1984 and the Blatman Committee established in April 1985. The SHABAC insisted on having a representative in the Zorea Committee and here SHABAC top agent, Yossi Genosar, excelled himself in his attempts to clear his colleagues and in incriminating Brigadier General Yitzhak Mordechay, who interrogated the two Arabs in the field outside the bus but did not kill them. Mordechay had to face a trial,

Raphael Cohen-Almagor is the founder and director of the Center for Democratic Studies, University of Haifa.

which exonerated him. Then, in October 1985, three top SHABAC officers, Reuven Hazak, Peleg Raday and Rafi Malka, who could not continue living with the deceit, approached Prime Minister Shimon Peres and told him what they knew about the affair. However, Peres preferred to back Avraham Shalom. Consequently, the three officers were forced to resign from the service. The two other members of the 'Prime Ministers' Forum', Yitzhak Shamir and Yitzhak Rabin, backed Peres' erroneous decision.

The government, wishing to put an end to this affair, in effect terminated the attorney general's term in office, although Yitzhak Zamir made it clear that he wished to serve in office until the affair was concluded. The main figure who stood for law, order and furthering truth and justice had to step down from office because of his determination to pursue the matter by ordering a police investigation. However, the scheme did not help as Zamir's replacement, Yoseph Harish, who entered office in June 1986, reached the same conclusion and ordered the opening of a police investigation.

Then came President Herzog's shameless decision to to grant clemency to the SHABAC agents before they were convicted. The decision was backed by Yoseph Harish, the minister of justice Yitzhak Modai, the minister of defence Arens and most of the government ministers (the only objection came from Ezer Weitzman, who later became president). This act mocks the procedures of justice. And finally the Supreme Court refrained from overturning the amnesty, preferring security considerations over the principle of equality before the law. The Supreme Court, in a 2:1 decision (Meir Shamgar and Miriam Ben-Porat *v.* Aharon Barak) held that were the SHABAC agents to stand trial, severe damage was to be expected to the public interest, and that under the circumstances no other reasonable solution could be reached. I beg to differ. To my mind, severe damage was inflicted on the public interest as a result of the decision to grant clemency, and the reasonable solution should have been to unveil the deceit and corrupt behaviour of the SHABAC in this affair, introducing law and order norms into a service that was acting secretely, away from the public eye, and consequently allowing itself to condone unacceptable norms of murdering people after they surrender, lying to law and order authorities, blaming others for their own misdeeds, and then getting away with this misconduct by approaching the state president, pleading the altar of security. Never in our history there was such a lunar eclipse, where key figures cooperated to defend a corrupt secret service, holding false security considerations as a supreme value.[1]

THE GOVERNMENT

In the near future it seems that the Likud Party will continue to lead the country. The Labour Party should resist the temptation to join another coalition government with the Likud. Stable democracy needs a strong government and no less importantly a strong coalition. Labour, and Israel, paid a high prize for sitting with the Likud in the previous governments. Labour lost its identity. You cannot be part of a government and then go out and criticize it for misconduct. The public is not stupid. The public realizes that Labour was part of this same government until recently and all it has to offer is different people, not a different direction. If the choice is between the original and the copy, the original is preferable.

Israel also paid a high price. I see a direct link between the lack of strong opposition and the rising corruption. Without sufficient safeguards and restraints, both parties are celebrating their powers and some are tempted to cross not only ethical but also legal boundaries. I think that the only exception to this anti-Likud/Labour coalition is a time of war. Such a coalition was justified in 1967, on the eve of the Six Day War for a limited period of time. I did not imagine that Labour and the Likud would stick to this coalition for years after the 1980s. I hope the leaders of the second largest party will be wise enough to understand the political price they will have to pay if they do this. The Labour leaders were not very prudent in entering into coalition government under Ariel Sharon's leadership. Now they are paying the price.

In the long run patience will have its reward. To be credible, the second major party should offer an opposition to the government, otherwise it would lose its identity.

THE KNESSET

The Knesset, as Naomi Chazan rightly notes, has far too many parties. Consequently, its legislative effectiveness is relatively low, and the government's ability to sustain power is lessened. The multi-fraction composition opens the way to manipulation, gives rise to blackmail and undermines the coalition. The threshold to enter parliament, 1.5% of the electoral vote, gives a lot of leeway to representation and exploitation at the expense of stability, working to further the ends of partisan groups. I would suggest raising the threshold to 5%, as in Germany. Effectively, this law restricts the number of splinter parties in the Bundestag and the regional parliaments and promotes political stability.[2] The 5% clause has been a factor in every federal election since 1957.

Germany has certainly learnt the lessons of its history and can serve as a model also with regard to the voting system. Germany uses a mixed electoral system[3] in which part of the Bundestag is elected in single majority districts in which a candidate must gain the greatest number of votes to win, and part is elected through proportional representation, which gives all parties a fair opportunity to gain some representation in the legislature based on their electoral strength. Germany's policy makers after World War II wanted to avoid a repetition of the Weimar proportional representation system, which encouraged multiplicity of parties to run candidates for the Reichstag, thereby contributing to political instability and to the rise of National Socialism.[4] In the early 1990s, Russia, Mexico and Japan adopted a similar mixed electoral system. I suggest the same for Israel: 60% of the Knesset to be elected directly via a party list as is now the case in the proportional system, and 40% to be elected in the provinces.[5] The idea is to split Israel into several provinces in a way that would reflect the various groups in society and their relative prominence.[6] Each voter would cast two ballots: the first for one of the competing party candidates in the province; the second for one of the lists of candidates drawn up by each party. The number of mandates received by the party is based on its percentage of votes in the entire country. The seats are then distributed to the parties according to their strength in each province.[7] The combination of a relatively high threshold and a mixed electoral system would reduce the ability of small interest group parties to be elected, make the Knesset less diversified, with five or six parties at most, and reduce the influence of the small parties, some of which would disappear altogether. The Knesset's power would increase and its effectiveness as a legislative body would grow.

I am not the first to suggest these reforms. They have been put on the public agenda time and again, and every time have been turned down due to pressure exerted by the small parties fighting for their survival. Most notably, the religious parties have resisted such attempts. Israel needs strong and bold leaders who are able to rise above and beyond their immediate interest to sustain power in order to carry out these reforms to better legislative ability.

THE SUPREME COURT

The Supreme Court has attracted quite a lot of criticism in recent years. It was attacked by conservative and religious circles for its liberal adjudications on civil matters. In turn, the court was attacked by the political left for its often hard-line approach on security matters. I would like to take issue with two general lines of criticism: the court's activist approach, and its lack of representation of significant segments of society.

As for the first issue, Israel has no constitution, no bill of rights, not even a Basic Law to defend fundamental civil liberties, thus the Supreme Court is the main bastion of safeguarding democracy and human rights. For this reason justices of the Supreme Court are often required to adopt the creative approach in adjudication. The court cannot hide behind the lack of explicit written provision when crucial questions of a constitutional nature are at issue, leaving their resolution in the hands of partisan politicians. Since political parties had failed to reach a compromise over the enactment of a law to safeguard civil rights, requiring individuals and bodies to approach the court to find assistance, it should not refrain from taking a stand on constitutional matters. Having said that, the court derives its authority from the law, and it has to adjudicate in accordance with the law. In addition, it cannot ignore the social and political environment in which its decisions are made and their likely implications.

This collection describes in detail the tensions and schisms that are part and parcel of Israeli life. In such an atmosphere, the role of the judge is to set standards of action for both politicians and the courts when they are faced with constitutional matters, especially where attacks on the very foundations of democracy are concerned. Hence scope exists for taking normative constitutional principles into account. These principles may in some 'hard cases' convince the Supreme Court to take a creative approach.[8] Here are two set of considerations that inevitably play their part when judges come to formulate a judgment. One set is related to the moral convictions held by the judges, influenced by their own upbringing and educational background, as well as by the tradition and values of the society in which they live. The other is concerned with the specific legal history. Precedents and other legal facts are bound to limit the moral considerations of judges but they should not exclude moral considerations altogether. When faced with an unprecedented situation, in which they are required to use their discretion to find a judicial solution to a 'hard case', judges should decide the case by interpreting the political structure of their community so as to find the best possible justification, in principles of political morality, for the structure as a whole. Accordingly, if the right of people to be treated as equals and not to be harmed by others can be defended only by creative adjudication, then creativity is not only in order but necessary. This is the case so long as the judge tries to make the creative decisions in line with previous ones rather than starting in a new direction.[9]

At the same time, a difference exists between *creative interpretation* and *judicial legislation*. It is not the role of the court to legislate. Instead, one of its roles is to scrutinize the legislature. One may argue that the difference between the two concepts is merely semantic. I, on the other hand, think that the tone often makes the music. Even only for tactical reasons, the court should be aware of its place and of its role in the democratic system and exhibit its awareness to the public. It should not attempt to replace the work of the Knesset.

The second major critique that is often voiced against the court relates to its lack of representation. It has been attacked for its social homogeneity. There has never been an Arab justice in permanent appointment. The court consists of mainly Ashkenazi, secular Jews and it is argued that they tend to have much in common. Consequently their adjudications do not reflect ideas and opinions that are prevalent among the Sephardi and the more traditional circles.

The ethnic/religious/national origins of a candidate should not be the major consideration in appointing him or her to the court. Merit, of course, should be the first and foremost consideration. But sometimes there may be two or three candidates with similar credentials and experience. Then the candidate's social background may play a role. The court should strive to represent major spheres of society, and not hold itself aloof from the social environment and the citizens whom it serves. It is to its advantage to try to represent large segments of society and to have plurality of worldviews stemming from different religious, national and cultural backgrounds.

NOTES

1. For further discussion, see 'Maariv Report: The Shabac Affair', *Maariv*, 18 July 1986, pp.6–8 (Hebrew); M. Kremnitzer, 'The Case of the Security Services Pardon', *Tel-Aviv Univ. L. Rev.*, Vol.12 (1986), p.595; Ilan Rachum, *The Shabac Affair*, Jerusalem, 1990 (Hebrew).
2. In Germany, parties that achieve less than 5% of the votes or do not receive at least three direct mandates for the constituency candidates cannot participate in the allocation of seats. See Eckhard Jesse, *Elections: The Federal Republic of Germany in Comparison*, New York, 1990, p.71.
3. But see Eckhard Jesse, 'The Electoral System: More Continuity than Change', in Ludger Helms (ed.), *Institutions and Institutional Change in the Federal Republic of Germany*, Houndmills, 2000, pp.124–42, esp. p.127.
4. Gerhard Braunthal, *Parties and Politics in Modern Germany*, Boulder, CO, 1996, p.46. See also Susan E. Scarrow, 'Political Parties and the Changing Framework of German Electoral Competition', in Christopher J. Anderson and Carsten Zelle (eds.), *Stability and Change in German Elections*, Westport, CT, 1998, pp.301–22.
5. In Germany, each of the two systems carries 50% of the voting power. I suggest breaking the balance and giving more weight to the proportional system because experience of primaries held in the two major parties, Labour and Likud, showed that candidates competing on the national level were better equipped to serve as legislators than representatives elected in the provinces. The Likud does not hold primaries any more and shifted the locus of power to its central committee. Labour still resorts to primaries that combine the mixed electoral system: some are elected nationally; others in the provinces.
6. Until German unification in 1990, each Bundestag had at least 496 deputies, half of them elected directly by plurality in the 248 single member provinces and the other half elected on a system of proportional representation by party lists in the country. Since unification, the deputies number at least 656, and the provinces 328 to provide sufficient representation to eastern German voters. The size of each province must not deviate by more than one-quarter from the national average. See David P. Conradt, 'The 1994 Campaign and Election', in David P. Conradt, Gerald R. Kleinfeld, George K. Romoser and Christian Soe (eds.), *Germany's New Politics*, Providence, RI, 1995, p 2; Braunthal, *Parties and Politics in Modern Germany*, p.47. See also Peter James, *The German Electoral System*, London, 2003.
7. Of the two ballots, the second is the more important because it will determine the number of parliamentary seats that each party gains. If a party receives more direct seats than it would be entitled to under proportional representation, then it receives additional seats. In the 1994 Bundestag elections, two of the parties (CDU and SPD) received 16 additional mandates. For further discussion, see Gert-Joachim Glaessner, *The Unification Process in Germany*, London, 1992.
8. Ronald M. Dworkin, 'Hard Cases', *Harvard Law Review*, Vol.88, No.6 (1975), pp.1057–109; idem, *Law's Empire*, Cambridge, MA, 1986.
9. R. Cohen-Almagor, *The Boundaries of Liberty and Tolerance*, Gainesville, FL, 1994, chapter 11.

NOTES ON CONTRIBUTORS

Ori Arbel-Gantz is a Ph.D student at Tel Aviv University, and Research Associate in the Israel Democracy Institute. His dissertation is on Regulation and Regulators in Israel. His research interests are also in public responsibility and administrational ethics, policy design and policy implementation.

Naomi Chazan, former Deputy Speaker of the Knesset, served as a member of the Knesset on behalf of the Meretz party for three terms (1992–2003). She is professor of political science and African Studies at the Hebrew University of Jerusalem, and has published eight books and dozens of articles on comparative politics, the Arab-Israel conflict, and Israeli politics.

Raphael Cohen-Almagor, D. Phil. (Oxon., 1991) was a Senior Fellow at the center for Policy Studies and lecturer at Johns Hopkins University (2003–2004); Associate Professor, Department of Communication, University of Haifa, where he directs the Center for Democratic Studies; Member, Israel Press Council (1997–2000); Visiting Professor and the Fulbright-Yitzhak Rabin scholar for this year, UCLA School of Law and Department of Communication (1999–2000); Chairperson, Library and Information Studies (2000–2003); author of *Middle Eastern Shores* (1993, Hebrew, poetry), *The Boundaries of Liberty and Tolerance* (Gainesville FL.: University Press of Florida, 1994), *Speech, Media and Ethics* (Houndmills and New York: Palgrave, 2001, 2005), *The Right to Die with Dignity: An Argument in Ethics, Medicine, and Law* (Piscataway, NJ.: Rutgers University Press, 2001), *Euthanasia in the Netherlands* (Dordrecht: Kluwer-Springer, 2004), *The Scope of Tolerance* (London: Routledge, forthcoming), and editor of *Basic Issues in Israeli Democracy* (1999, Hebrew), *Liberal Democracy and the Limits of Tolerance: Essays in Honor and Memory of Yitzhak Rabin* (Ann Arbor, MI.: University of Michigan Press, 2000), *Challenges to Democracy: Essays in Honour and Memory of Isaiah Berlin* (London: Ashgate, 2000), *Medical Ethics at the Dawn of the 21st Century* (New York: New York Academy of Sciences, 2000), and *Moral Dilemmas in Medicine* (2002, Hebrew). Professor Cohen-Almagor is now completing a poetry book titled *Travels.*

Eliezer Goldberg was elected by the Knesset as State Comptroller and Ombudsman of the State of Israel on 26 May 1998. He served as a justice of the Supreme Court of Israel from 1984 until the time of his present appointment. From 1974 to 1982 he served as a judge of the District Court in Jerusalem and from 1965 to 1974 as a judge of the Magistrate Court in Jerusalem. He studied law at the Hebrew University School of Law and was awarded the Israel Bar Association licence to practice law in 1957. Justice Goldberg served as the Chairman of the Central Election Committee for the 12th Knesset and was first a member and then chairmod of the Criminal Procedure Committee.

Orit Ichilov chaired the Department of Educational Sciences at the School of Education, Tel-Aviv University, and was Vice-President of the International Society of Political Psychology. She is an educational sociologist whose research has focused on political socialization and citizenship education. Ichilov was the principal investigator in Israel of the IEA International Civic Education Study. As fellow at the Woodrow Wilson International Center for Scholars in Washington D.C., Ichilov recently completed a book on *Political Learning and Citizenship Education Under Conflict*.

Dan Inbar is a professor and the former Dean of the school of Education at the Hebrew University of Jerusalem. His current main interests are in educational policy, leadership and organizational behavior. He has published a number of books (*Responsibility in Education, Second Chance in Education, Planning for Innovation in Education*) and numerous articles in the area of politics, ethics and educational planning. He is currently the editor of the *Journal of Educational Studies and Teacher Training (Dapim)*.

David Nachmias is Professor of Public Policy at the Inter Disciplinary Center, Herzliya. He is the author of numerous books and articles on public policy, public administration and methodology. His most recent book (co-authored) is *Executive Governance in Israel* (New York: Palgrave, 2002).

Yitzhak Navon was born in Jerusalem on 9 April 1921. In 1951 he was appointed political secretary to Foreign Minister Moshe Sharett. In 1952, he became political secretary to the Prime Minister David Ben Gurion. He served in this capacity until 1963, when Ben Gurion resigned from premiership. For the next two years, Mr. Navon was the Director of the Culture Department of the Ministry of Education and Culture.

Resigning from the civil service, he was elected to the Knesset as a member of "Rafi" – Ben-Gurion's newly formed party. During his Knesset years, Yitzhak Navon served as Deputy Speaker and Chairman of the Defence and Foreign Affairs Committee. Navon was elected by the Knesset as the Fifth President of the State of Israel from 1978 through 1983. Upon completion of his term of office, he was appointed Deputy Prime Minister and Minister of Education and Culture until 1990. Mr. Navon has served as the Chairman of the World Zionist Council. Currently he serves as Chairman of the Jerusalem Academy for Music and Dance and as Chairman of the "Neot Kdumim" Society – a biblical and Talmudic nature reserve. He is also Honorary Chairman of the "Abraham Fund" for projects intended to promote fruitful co-existence between Jews and Arabs in Israel and the Chairman of the National Authority for the Ladino Language and Culture. Navon wrote several literary works which gained much success.

Yoram Peri is a professor of political sociology and communication in the Department of Communication at Tel-Aviv University, and the Head of the Haim Herzog Institute for Media, Politics and Society. A former political advisor to Prime Minister Rabin and Editor in Chief of the daily *Davar*, he is an expert on civil-military relations. Among his various publications is *Between Battles and Ballots: Israel Military in Politics* (Cambridge University Press, 1983), *The Rabin Assassination* (Stanford University Press, 2000) and *Telepopulism: Media and Politics in Israel* (Stanford University Press, 2003).

Elyakim Rubinstein (born 1947) was the Attorney General of Israel (1997–2003). He served before as Legal Adviser of the Foreign and Defence Ministries, Minister, deputy chief of mission at the Israeli Embassy in Washington, Government Secretary and a Judge at the Jerusalem District Court. He participated in peace talks with Egypt, Lebanon, Jordan, the Palestinians and Syria, and headed the Israeli Delegation that negotiated the Treaty of Peace with Jordan. He taught in Israeli Universities and authored books and articles on Israeli public law and legal history as well as on the peace process.

Gavriel Salomon, past dean of the Faculty of Education, at the University of Haifa, is currently the founder and director of the Center for Research on Peace Education. He has published six books on mind and technology, computers in education and peace education, and more than one hundred research and theory articles in international journals. He served as editor of the journal *Educational Psychology* and is the recipient of an honorary doctorate from the Catholic University of Leuven, Belgium, and of the Israel National Award for scientific achievements in educational research.

Meir Shamgar served as Military Advocate General (1961–1968; final rank Brig. General). In 1968 he became Attorney General and served in this office for seven years until his appointment to the Supreme Court. In 1983 he became President of the Israel Supreme Court. He retired from the presidency in 1995. President Shamgar has received many prizes, among them the Israel Prize (1996), the Ben Gurion Prize (1998), and the Israeli Bar Prize (2001). He taught law at the Hebrew University and Tel Aviv University. Among his writings *Military Government in the Territories Administered by Israel, 1967–1968* (Jerusalem, 1982).

Gad Yaacobi has been a Minister in several Israeli Cabinets, a Member of Knesset and Israel's Ambassador to the United Nations. He lectures at Tel Aviv University and serves as the Chairman of the Israel Ports and Railways Authority. Some of the books he has written include: (in Hebrew) *The Power of Quality* (1972), *The Freedom to Choose* (1975), *The Government* (1980), *On a Razor's Edge* (1990), *The Future Starts Now* (1992), *New York Diaries* (1997) and *Grace of Time – an Autobiography* (2002). He has also published several books in English including *Breakthrough: Israel and the International Community* (1996) as well as two books of poetry and a novel.

INDEX

For Product Safety Concerns and Information please contact our EU
representative GPSR@taylorandfrancis.com
Taylor & Francis Verlag GmbH, Kaufingerstraße 24, 80331 München, Germany

www.ingramcontent.com/pod-product-compliance
Lightning Source LLC
Chambersburg PA
CBHW050707280326
41926CB00088B/2865

9 781138 973442